Second Edition

Statistical Analysis in Criminal Justice and Criminology

Second Edition

Statistical Analysis in Criminal Justice and Criminology

A User's Guide

Gennaro F. Vito
University of Louisville

Michael B. Blankenship
Boise State University

Julie C. Kunselman
Northern Kentucky University

WAVELAND

PRESS, INC.
Long Grove, Illinois

For information about this book, contact:
Waveland Press, Inc.
4180 IL Route 83, Suite 101
Long Grove, IL 60047-9580
(847) 634-0081
info@waveland.com
www.waveland.com

10 digit ISBN 1-57766-524-4
13 digit ISBN 978-1-57766-524-3

Printed in the United States of America

7   6   5   4   3   2

To the Vito Family:
Mary, Anthony, and Gina
For their patience and support
G.F.V.

To Frank P. Williams,
who taught me how to be a social scientist and
has remained a true mentor throughout the years
M.B.B.

To my mentor, family, and friends:
Thank you for your continued generosity
J.C.K

Contents

Preface   xi

To the Student   xiii

1   The Purpose of Statistical Analysis   1

The Validity and Reliability of Crime Statistics   2
   The Uniform Crime Report   3
   The National Incident-Based Reporting System   6
   The National Crime Victimization Survey   9
   Calls for Service Data   13
   Routine Activities Theory and Crime "Hot Spots"   15
   The Compstat Program   15

Percentage Change Analysis   17

Lying with Statistics   19

Summary   20

Key Terms 20 / Exercises 21 / Notes 26

2   Basic Elements of Criminal Justice Research   29

Elements of the Research Process   29
   Problem Identification   30
   A Note on the Language of Science   31
   Research Design   32
   A Note on Human Subjects   35
   Data Collection   36
   Data Analysis   36
   Interpretation and Presentation of the Research Results   36

Program Evaluation   36

Levels of Measurement   38
   The Nominal Level of Measurement   38
   The Ordinal Level of Measurement   39
   The Interval Level of Measurement   39
   The Ratio Level of Measurement   40

Measurement and Types of Variables   41
Using SPSS: An Introduction   42
Summary   46
Key Terms 46 / Exercises 48 / Notes 49

3   Summarizing Data and Presenting the Results   **51**

Frequency Distributions   51
Displaying Frequency Distributions Graphically   53
   Creating Bar Charts with SPSS   54
   Creating Pie Charts with SPSS   56
   Creating Histograms with SPSS   56
   Creating Line Graphs with SPSS   57
Presenting Your Results   58
Summary   60
Key Terms 61 / Data Analysis 61

4   Measures of Central Tendency   **63**

Measures of Central Tendency   63
   Constructing a Frequency Distribution   63
   The Mode   64
   The Median   65
   The Mean   66
   A Measure of Shape   67
Using SPSS to Analyze Data   69
Summary   75
Key Terms 75 / Exercises 76 / Data Analysis 77

5   Measures of Dispersion   **79**

Measures of Dispersion Defined   79
   The Index of Dispersion   80
   The Range   80
   The Variance and Standard Deviation   81
Calculating Measures of Dispersion with SPSS   84
Summary   88
Key Terms 89 / Exercises 89 / Data Analysis 90

6   Contingency Table Analysis   **91**

Nonparametric Statistics   91
Constructing Contingency Tables   92
   Summary: Rules for the Construction and Interpretation of Tables   94
Chi-Square Test for Independent Samples   94

Calculating Chi-Square   96
   Chi-Square Calculations by Hand   96
   Calculating Chi-Square Using SPSS   97
Measures of Association with Chi-Square   102
   Cramer's V and SPSS   102
Introducing a Third Variable   104
Summary   108
Key Terms 109 / Data Analysis 110 / Notes 115

7   Probability and the Normal Curve   **117**

Introduction to Probability   117
   Mathematical Rules of Probability   118
   Other Rules of Probability   119
   Shooting Craps   120
   Reading Tables to Determine Empirical Probability   121
   Probability Distributions   125
Probability and the Normal Curve   126
The Binomial Distribution   129
The Central Limit Theorem   130
Establishing Confidence Intervals   131
Summary   134
Key Terms 135 / Exercises 136 / Notes 136

8   Difference between Means: The *t*-Test   **139**

The *t* Distribution   139
Hypothesis Testing   140
   Stating Hypotheses   141
   Decisions under the Null Hypothesis   144
   t-Test for Related Samples   145
   t-Test for Independent Samples   147
   SPSS: *t*-Test for Independent Samples   147
Summary   152
Key Terms 154 / Data Analysis 155 / Notes 157

9   Analysis of Variance (One Way)   **159**

Source of ANOVA   159
The *F* Test (*F* Ratio)   161
Calculating ANOVA by Hand   161
One-Way ANOVA Using SPSS   165
Summary   172
Key Terms 172 / Data Analysis 172 / Notes 175

10 Correlation   177

Defining Correlation 177

Interpreting Correlation 178
  Direction of the Correlation Coefficient 179
  Magnitude of the Correlation Coefficient 181
  Percentage of Variance Explained 181

Considering Causation 182
  Five Criteria for a Causal Relationship 182
  Calculating Pearson's r 183

Bivariate Correlation Using SPSS 185

Summary 192

Key Terms 192 / Data Analysis 193 / Notes 195

11 Regression   197

Defining Regression 197
  Using Regression to Predict Prison Population Size 198
  Calculating Regression Coefficients by Hand 199
  Linear Regression Using SPSS 203

Summary 209

Key Terms 209 / Data Analysis 210 / Notes 214

12 The Use of Statistics in Policy Analysis   215

The Purpose of Research 215

Examples of Successes and Failures 217
  Kansas City Preventive Patrol Experiment 217
  Kansas City Gun Experiment 217
  Capital Punishment 218

Closing Comments 219

Notes 219

Appendix 221
Index 245

Preface

When are you ever going to use statistical analysis? The answer is every day! Knowledge of statistical analysis and interpretation of statistical results means doors will open to understanding why crime rates increase; why more law enforcement officers should be on duty around schools at 3:30 PM; and whether a particular geographic location is safe with regard to the likelihood of car theft, robberies, or burglaries. All this and more is learned through statistical analysis.

As a criminal justice professional you need to be an informed consumer and a diligent producer of research. Not only will you need to understand research methods to make sure that researchers are applying the correct research methodology, but you will also need to be able to interpret research findings. Your ability to be an informed consumer and experienced producer of research will help policy makers critically evaluate program and policy proposals for decision making.

The key to understanding research methodology and statistical analysis is applying the concepts. Our goal in this book is to make sure that you (the student) can apply the concepts, methodology, and statistical procedures that you learn in the classroom. Exercises in the text are set up from an initial step, and your application of concepts involves integrating and following the scientific method, through interpreting statistical tests in a meaningful way. We challenge you to provide meaningful interpretation of hypotheses testing as a means of showing your knowledge and understanding of the research process.

As a criminal justice professional you will have the opportunity to present crime trends, arrest data, and other descriptive criminal justice statistics to both policy makers and citizens. Your ability to interpret statistical tests in a meaningful way are important in guiding decision making, focusing crime prevention efforts, and promoting efficient utilization of resources. Research results obtained from following the scientific method can also help in developing and evaluating criminal justice policies and programs. As a criminal justice professional you will need to determine if variation exists in data distributions, in addition to understanding how and why the variation is occurring. For example, you might be interested in the variation of crime statistics among cities or states that are similar to the one in which you work or live, or you might simply look for variation in the time at which certain crimes are being committed in your jurisdiction. As a criminal justice administrator, probabilities are helpful in determining allocation of crime prevention resources. As a citizen, probabilities are useful in determining whether a particular geographic location is safe with regard to the likelihood of assaults, robberies, or homicides.

This text is written at a level that focuses on students' understanding of fundamental statistical *analysis*, and not comprehensive statistical *tests* that are superfluous. In other words, our approach is not to provide an encyclopedia of statistical tests, but to guide you through the process of statistical analyses that are commonly encountered in the social sciences. The text is premised on active learning, utilizing common statistical tools to analyze criminal justice data sets. There are five data sets included in this *Second Edition* and the expanded number and types of exercises are based on these data sets. We believe that the best way to learn statistical analysis is by doing it—and the comprehensive SPSS screen shots within the chapter and other ancillary materials will help guide you as you learn a new language, as well as a new way of thinking and problem solving. Consider, for example, as a student you might want to predict the grade you will earn on an exam based on the length of time you studied for the exam. To obtain several observations for both the dependent variable (grade earned on the exam) and the independent variable (length of time studied) you might ask your classmates after each exam of the semester the length of time they studied and what they earned on the exam. At the end of the semester you could use *regression analysis* to predict the grade a student would earn on an exam given the amount of time that student studied for the exam. By conducting this research, you are learning the language and application of statistics!

The exercises and discussions in the textbook are grounded in the notion that criminal justice research is a vital component of policy making. As you will see throughout this text, research can be generated by policy concerns just as policy can be created through proper research. As practitioners of criminal justice it is our responsibility to be able to understand the importance of research in the policy analysis process. Absent sound research, policy initiatives can be disastrous. Thus, it is critical that we understand the statistical analyses that are being used in policy discussions. It is even more important that we put them in proper perspective so we can become informed decision makers. This is the strength of this text; it introduces students to analyzing data and interpreting results and the way social scientists actually do research.

We express our gratitude to our reviewers Tom Lucadamo at the University of Baltimore, Steve Holmes at the University of Central Florida, and Leon Pettiway of Indiana University. We also thank our editor, Jeni Ogilvie, and our publisher, Neil Rowe, for their patience and understanding.

Please feel free to contact us directly with questions or comments about this text at: gf.vito@louisville.edu or mblanken@boisestate.edu or kunselmanj1@nku.edu.

Gennaro Vito
Michael Blankenship
Julie Kunselman

To the Student
Suggestions for Success in this Course

Based on our experience as professors, we suggest that you consider the following as you prepare for this class:

1. **There are no shortcuts to learning statistical analysis**. Like physical training, no pain, no gain! We believe that success requires diligence, dedication, and attention to detail.

2. **Attend class every day.** This advice holds true for every class, but is especially true for statistics courses. We encourage you to make the most of your class time by taking notes, by participating in discussions, and by asking questions. Unlike other topics, mathematics involves a fairly linear learning process. It is a building process—it is difficult to move to the next topic without having mastered the preceding material. For example, early on, we will introduce you to the concept of levels of measurement. Failure to truly understand this concept will seriously impede progress in subsequent chapters.

3. **Prepare for class prior to attending**. The rule of thumb for college-level classes is three hours of preparation for each contact hour in class. We understand that students have a multitude of things to balance in their daily lives, but we encourage making college a priority. We have observed a tendency to try to "rush through" college as quickly as possible. Research has shown that the average time to graduate is now around six years at many four-year institutions. So, don't become bogged down in the "four-year" myth—take your time and make the most of your investment in your future.

4. **Keep pace with the material**. Sometimes students fail to adequately plan their academic term and/or don't maintain a balance between college, employment, and some semblance of a social life. The result is falling behind in assignments or waiting until the last possible moment to initiate assignments. Not only is this strategy conducive to poor academic performance, but it adds significantly to the stress levels of academic life. Set aside a specific time on a regular schedule for study and

completion of assignments. Find a quiet place that is your own space and that has everything you need to conduct your work.

5. **Take advantage of resources**. Your college or university probably has some fantastic resources to assist in your quest for academic success. We suggest that one of the biggest steps you can take in maximizing your learning experience is asking for help. Most universities offer writing and math help centers. Don't forget the Internet—a Google search of the phrase "help with statistics" yielded a multitude of hits! The most valuable resource you will encounter is your professor. We have discovered that too many students are reluctant to ask questions during class and fail to make time to approach their professor outside of the classroom. We encourage you to avoid falling into this trap—never leave without an answer!

chapter 1

The Purpose of Statistical Analysis

Here you are in your first course in statistics. You are probably wondering why you are forced to endure this subject matter. After all, what does criminal justice have to do with statistical analysis and math? As a criminal justice professional we strongly believe that you need to be both an informed consumer and a diligent producer of research. Not only will you need to understand research methods to make sure that researchers are applying the correct research methodology, but you will also need to be able to interpret research findings. If you do not approach the task correctly, reading and applying statistics can be a tedious chore and, therefore, we understand your reluctance. Our objective is to help you gain an appreciation for and an understanding of why statistical analysis is critical in criminal justice.

One of the most important skills you can develop while studying this text is the ability to interpret statistical analysis. In fact, this skill is a major goal of both this text and, we hope, your professional career. We use statistics to convey information. We take a group of data, organize it, and put it in a format (tables, graphs) that makes it possible to interpret, understand, and reach conclusions on the basis of the data. Statistics are the keys that unlock the information contained in a data set. A **data set** contains information that has been collected and organized by the researcher. In this text, you will see data sets that contain information about crime and attitudes toward crime and the criminal justice system. Like other forms of statistics, crime figures are a source of information. The purpose of generating information is to communicate. Thus, you are learning how to use a new language that is universal, efficient, and has the potential to be effective.

In this chapter, we consider several of the major sources of crime statistics. As you approach the official sources of statistics, examine the data presented for patterns. For example, one perennial perception, even among criminal justice students, is that crime is increasing.[1] What is the reality? Is crime increasing, decreasing, or remaining at the same level over time? Which crimes are most prevalent? Who is likely to be the victim of a certain type of crime? When and where are crimes most likely to occur? This type of information can help us to minimize the damage caused by crime.

This text presumes that you have no statistical background and begins with the most fundamental methods for drawing statistical inferences to a variety of criminal justice applications. In fact, you might consider analysis and interpretation of statistics as simply "looking at data in different ways," instead of focusing on the numbers, formulas, and calculations. In other words, don't get bogged down with the "trees" and forget that you are looking at a "forest." Consider, for example, a correctional reading program that boasts an average reading level of 10.5/12.0 among participants completing its program. Should you take such "boasting" at face value and simply agree that the program is a success? Or, is it important to ask whether participants volunteered for the program, were selected based on some criteria, or were court ordered, or, whether the difference in the average reading level after program completion was significantly different than the average reading level prior to participating in the program. Understanding that you should not take at face value everything you read, especially on the Web, is an important lesson in beginning your development as both an astute consumer and an analyst of data.

The Validity and Reliability of Crime Statistics

How do we know crime measures are accurate and consistent in gauging the amount of crime in society? Here, the issues are the validity and reliability of the data. **Validity** is the degree to which an instrument measures what it intends to measure. Does the measure of crime accurately gauge the amount of crime in society or does it tally something else? **Reliability** refers to the extent to which the measure is a consistent and dependable indicator of the level of crime. Are the crime measures consistent over time and do they yield consistent results? If the crime statistics are invalid and unreliable, they cannot serve as a basis for information for prevention and planning. In this section, we focus on traditional crime measures and examine their ability to provide accurate data.

Some debate arises over what official crime statistics actually measure. Often, official crime data reveal more about how the criminal justice system reacts to crime than the frequency of crime.[2] If reported crime increases, does this mean the police are doing a better or worse job at preventing crime? Criminologists interested in the incidence of crime—how much of it occurs in society—are faced with the problem of whether or not the different measures are valid indicators of crime. They typically consider data from the Uniform Crime Report (UCR) (crimes reported to the police). We later examine data from the newly implemented National Incident-Based Reporting System (NIBRS). Incident-based reporting generates detailed data about the nature of the crime and the law enforcement response. Data are collected on each single crime incident. It may sound awkward, but keep in mind that the term *data* is plural. Thus, "data are" is the correct form to use. Never use "data is," unless you're referring to the Star Trek character!

The problem with official police-based statistics is that they do not contain information on unreported or undiscovered crime. For this information, criminologists consult data from the National Crime Victimization Survey (NCVS). The NCVS contains both reported and unreported crime, but has its own set of limitations. We examine data from this source.

Together, these sources (UCR, NIBRS, and NCVS) present data on the level of crime in society. In addition to providing descriptive information, statistics can generate information to guide program operations. Two other data sources are valuable: calls for service (CFS) data are used to identify the frequency and locations of crimes and Compstat is a compilation of statistics that the New York City Police Department uses to manage police activity and guide policy.

It is important for you to understand and use official sources of crime statistics for interpreting crime trends, examining prevention and treatment strategies, or minimizing the damage caused by crime. The following sections focus on sources of crime statistics, identification and analysis of patterns, interpreting statistical data, and communicating statistical results.

The Uniform Crime Report

Since 1930, the Federal Bureau of Investigation (FBI) has compiled nationwide data on the number of crimes reported to the police. These figures are then published yearly as *Crime in the United States*, also known as the Uniform Crime Report (UCR). The UCR program is completely voluntary. Typically, police agencies report the number of crimes uncovered within their jurisdiction over the past year. These agencies report to a centralized state clearinghouse (e.g., the State Police). The statistics are then reported to the FBI. Thus, *Crime in the United States* consists of crimes reported to or uncovered by the police.

The UCR is the major source of nationwide crime data. It contains information from most jurisdictions. This relative comprehensiveness makes it possible to examine the number of reported crimes for a particular area. However, because so many law enforcement agencies are collecting crime information and reporting to the UCR, definitions of crime must follow the same format. Thus, one crucial measurement issue is reliability or the consistency of definitions of crime.

The UCR features standardized definitions of crime, so the measures are "uniform." *Crime in the United States* highlights what are called **Part I** or **Index offenses.** These crimes (murder, rape, robbery, assault, burglary, larceny-theft, motor vehicle theft, and arson) are the most serious. Thus, the **crime index** is an indicator of the level of serious crime in America.

The FBI crime report presents crime rates, such as the incidence of crime per 100,000 population. A rate performs a valuable function in statistics. Unlike a raw number, a rate gives you a built-in point of comparison. The use of a rate makes it possible to compare the number of crimes reported in cities, towns, and states of different sizes. (You can access current information from the Uniform Crime Report at the Web site of the Federal Bureau of Investigation: www.fbi.gov/ucr/ucr.htm.)

Figure 1.1 presents the UCR violent crime rates for 2005. Figure 1.2 contains the UCR property crime rates for 2005. Property crimes (larceny-theft, burglary, and motor vehicle theft) are the most common. Violent crimes such as assault, robbery, and rape do not occur as often. Rape, however, presents a particular problem because the low rate may reflect a reluctance to report the crime. This single example suggests, naturally, some question concerning the validity and reliability of these data.

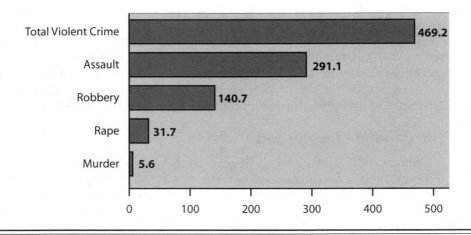

Figure 1.1   UCR Violent Crime Rates per 100,000 Population, 2005

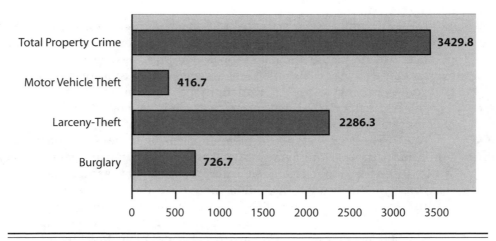

Figure 1.2   UCR Property Crime Rates per 100,000 Population, 2005

Limitations of the Uniform Crime Report

Typically, the following factors affect the accuracy of UCR figures and the extent to which they measure the actual volume of crime.[3]

1. *The figures reflect only the crimes that have been reported to the police.* Several reasons explain why victims do not report crimes to the police. For example, the victim may believe the crime is not serious. They may also be embarrassed by their victimization (e.g., cheated when buying drugs). Rape victims may not report the crime because they know the offender (e.g., incest or date rape) or because they fear the consequences of reporting (e.g., testifying in court and facing their assailant), or they may be offenders themselves.

2. *The figures are affected by the recording practices of the police.* The police may report crimes in a way that presents them and their community in the best light. One of the authors, a former police officer, remembers a "breaking and entering" at a medical practice. Because nothing was taken, the incident was recorded as a "damage to property," although there was clear evidence that entry and theft was in progress. No city wants to be the "murder capital" of the United States.

3. *The UCR emphasizes street crime and presents little or no data on white-collar crime.* These crime figures represent only part of the crime problem. The focus upon street crime obscures the impact of white-collar crime. Crimes such as price-fixing, bank fraud, health and safety violations, and environmental and political offenses are ignored.[4]

4. *Crimes reported to the police reflect the results of their style of work more than anything else does.* Of course, these statistics reflect the actions of the police. In fact, police departments routinely "unfound" crimes before they record them. Crimes are unfounded when there is no evidence that a crime was committed. Crime is more likely to be recorded when an arrest is possible.[5] Consequently, the UCR data have been viewed as "society's production figures." They indicate how the police operate rather than how much crime exists at a given time.[6] If the police concentrate on a certain type of crime (such as prostitution), the rate of this crime is likely to appear to go up because of their enforcement efforts.

5. *Not every department participates.* Some small cities and rural counties do not participate in reporting. If a single offender commits a string of offenses, only the one most serious crime is reported.

For these reasons, these figures are not fully representative of the actual level of crime in society. To be "educated consumers" of official statistics, students must recognize such limitations.[7]

Strengths of the Uniform Crime Report

UCR data also have some obvious strengths. The UCR is the major source of crime statistics in this country. It presents data from every region of the country. Walter Gove, Michael Hughes, and Michael Geerken have argued that the UCR is a valid indicator of serious crime in America. The main reason for this conclusion is that both citizens and the police agree on what constitutes a serious crime. If they agree on the seriousness of a crime incident, it is more likely to be reported and recorded.[8] For citizens, the seriousness of the offense is the most powerful predictor of crime reporting. Police are most likely to be called when (1) a weapon is used (especially a gun), (2) there is injury to a victim (particularly serious injury), and (3) there is great financial loss.[9] Therefore, official crime rates are in part a measure of the extent to which citizens feel injured, frightened, and financially hurt by a criminal act.[10] Typically, citizens are more likely to report offenses by strangers than offenses between members of the same family. The "key determinant" in crime reporting is the decision of the victim to notify the police.[11] The measures of crime are consistent over time and across jurisdictions.

Factors That Influence Crime Reporting

Four factors determine whether the police record an incident as a crime. These factors also influence the validity of reported crime because unreported crimes will not be counted, even though they did occur. First, a crime is more likely to be recorded when the evidence shows that a crime has actually been committed. This "unfounding" of crimes is the strength of the program: "In the UCR, the police must decide to their satisfaction that an assault or rape occurred. To do so they must conduct an investigation to learn if the incident fits the criteria for that particular crime." They make a determination of lawfulness or intent.[12]

Wishes of victim. Second, the police routinely follow the wishes of the victim. The crime will not be reported if the victim wishes to treat the matter informally. Third, the more serious the crime, the more likely it is to be reported. Finally, the more "professional" the department, the more likely the officer is to report the incident. If the department takes its law enforcement role seriously, the crime is more likely to be reported. Together, victims and the police decide whether a crime is recorded and reported.

The National Incident-Based Reporting System

Beginning in 1991, the UCR program began moving toward a system of crime data collection that increases the ability to conduct crime analysis. This system, the **National Incident-Based Reporting System (NIBRS)**, is designed to collect more detailed information on crimes. NIBRS reports both crimes and arrests. It will eventually replace the UCR as the source of official FBI counts of crimes reported to law enforcement agencies.

One major difference between NIBRS and the UCR is the number of crime categories. Rather than concentrate on the eight Index Crimes, NIBRS provides detailed information on 46 "Group A" offenses representing 22 categories of crime (see Table 1.1). Unlike the UCR, NIBRS also

- Makes a distinction between attempted and completed crimes
- Provides more inclusive definitions of crime (e.g., the definition of rape has been expanded to include male victims)

Table 1.1   The NIBRS Group A Offenses

Arson	Homicide Offenses:
Assault Offenses:	Murder/nonnegligent manslaughter
Aggravated assault	Negligent manslaughter
Simple assault	Justifiable homicide
Intimidation	Kidnapping/abduction
Bribery	Larceny-theft Offenses:
Burglary/breaking and entering	Pocketpicking
Counterfeiting/forgery	Purse snatching
Destruction/damage/vandalism of property	Shoplifting
Drug/narcotic Offenses:	Theft of motor vehicle parts and accessories
Drug/narcotic violations	All other larceny
Drug equipment violations	Theft from coin-operated machines
Embezzlement	Motor Vehicle Theft:
Extortion/blackmail	Theft from motor vehicle
Fraud Offenses:	Pornography/Obscene Material
False pretenses/swindle/confidence games	Prostitution Offenses:
Credit card/ATM fraud	Prostitution
Impersonation	Assisting or promoting prostitution
Welfare fraud	Sex Offenses, Forcible:
Wire fraud	Forcible rape
Gambling Offenses:	Forcible sodomy
Betting/wagering	Sexual assault with an object
Operating/promoting/assisting gambling	Forcible fondling
Gambling equipment violations	Sex Offenses, Nonforcible
Sports tampering	Stolen Property Offenses
	Weapons Law Violation

Source: Brian A. Reaves, *Using NIBRS Data to Analyze Violent Crime* (Washington, DC: U.S. Department of Justice, Office of Justice Programs, Bureau of Justice Statistics, 1993), 1.

- Counts all offenses that occur during an incident rather than concentrating upon only the most serious crime

The major distinction between the two is that NIBRS can link information about many aspects of a crime to each incident. Specifically, it includes "segments" detailed in Table 1.2. This detailed information will greatly enhance the capabilities of crime analysis.

The potential uses of NIBRS data are displayed in the murder section of the Uniform Crime Report. Here, incident-based data from the Supplemental Homicide Reports are presented. Specific information is given regarding the murder victims, offenders, and circumstances of the offense. The following section presents homicide patterns for 1976–2004 to highlight the purpose and practical uses of statistics.

Table 1.2 NIBRS Data Elements

Administrative Segment:	27 Age of victim
1 ORI number	28 Sex of victim
2 Incident number	29 Race of victim
3 Incident date/hour	30 Ethnicity of victim
4 Exceptional clearance indicator	31 Resident status of victim
5 Exceptional clearance date	32 Homicide/assault circumstances
Offense Segment:	33 Justifiable homicide circumstances
6 UCR offense code	34 Type of injury
7 Attempted/completed code	35 Related offender number
8 Alcohol/drug use by offender	36 Related to victim or offender
9 Type of location	*Offender Segment:*
10 Number of premises entered	37 Offender number
11 Method of entry	38 Age of offender
12 Type of criminal activity	39 Sex of offender
13 Type of weapon/force used	40 Race of offender
14 Bias crime code	*Arrestee Segment:*
Property Segment:	41 Arrestee number
15 Type of Property Loss	42 Transaction number
16 Property description	43 Arrest date
17 Property value	44 Type of arrest
18 Recovery date	45 Multiple clearance indicator
19 Number of stolen motor vehicles	46 UCR arrest offense code
20 Number of recovered motor vehicles	47 Arrestee armed indicator
21 Suspected drug type	48 Age of arrestee
22 Estimated drug quantity	49 Sex of arrestee
23 Drug measurement unit	50 Race of arrestee
Victim Segment:	51 Ethnicity of arrestee
24 Victim number	52 Resident status of arrestee
25 Victim UCR offense code	53 Disposition of arrestee under 18
26 Type of victim	

Source: Brian A. Reaves, *Using NIBRS Data to Analyze Violent Crime* (Washington, DC: U.S. Department of Justice, Office of Justice Programs, Bureau of Justice Statistics, 1993), 2.

Homicide Patterns, 1976–2004

In their review of homicide statistics collected by the FBI, Fox and Zawitz discern the following patterns from these data:[13]

- Blacks are featured predominantly in the number of homicide offenders and victims. Blacks were six times more likely to be murdered than whites. Blacks were seven times more likely to be homicide offenders than whites.

- The majority of murder victims (77%) and homicide offenders (almost 90%) were male. Males were three times more likely to be murdered than females. Males were eight times more likely to be homicide offenders than females.

- About one-third of the murder victims and about one-half of the victims of homicide were under the age of 25.
- Overall, black males 18–24 years old had the highest homicide offense rates.
  — Most murder victims were familiar with their assailants.
  — Spouses and family members made up 15 percent of all homicide victims.
  — About one-third of the victims were acquaintances of the assailant.
  — About one-third of the female murder victims were killed by an intimate (spouse, ex-spouse, boyfriend).
  — Over two-thirds of the spouse and ex-spouse victims were killed by guns.
  — In about 14 percent of homicides, the victim and offender were strangers.
- Homicides are more likely to feature multiple offenders than multiple victims.
- Homicides are most likely to be committed with handguns.

Purpose: These statistics reveal long-term patterns in homicides in the U.S. The results can be viewed as probabilities. For example, it appears that female homicides occur within relationships. When this type of homicide is investigated, the police can thus question persons close to the victim concerning their involvement. Of course, this is a commonsense conclusion. The data confirm it, however, and make it stronger than a hunch.

Practical Use: Statistics have a place in criminal investigation. In certain cases, they provide some indication of the probability that the offender might have specific characteristics. Again, these results can serve as a guide or "profile" to help in crime investigation. For example, the high close rate for homicides is a result of analysis of the data. Most murder investigations begin with people known to the victim as potential suspects. The down side is that police may fix on a particular suspect because of patterns and fail to remain open to other suspects. The data can also be analyzed to provide information about the nature of a crime problem and exactly what factors should be addressed to attempt to prevent it (e.g., neighborhood crime watch, community oriented policing). (You can obtain current information about the National Incident-Based Reporting System (NIBRS) at www.fbi.gov/ucr/ucr.htm

The National Crime Victimization Survey

Another source of crime information is the **National Crime Victimization Survey**. The Bureau of Justice Statistics has conducted this survey since 1972. Its aim is to uncover unreported crime and thus learn the actual level of crime in the country. It attempts to eliminate the "go-between" (the police) by going directly to the victim. The NCVS is a randomly designed survey of U.S. households. It is designed to represent the nation. Approximately 60,000 households respond to the survey each year. Information in this report is also presented as a population rate: the number of victims per 1,000 households.

Unlike the UCR, whose data may lead us to assume incorrectly that every individual has an equal chance of becoming a crime victim, the NCVS is an estimate of the risk of crime victimization. The NCVS is an improvement over the UCR for two reasons. First, the survey presents information taken directly from victims whether they report the crime to the police or not. Second, it collects background information on victims, making it possible to decide which groups have the highest rates of victimization for particular types of crime.

Table 1.3 shows that the NCVS does uncover more crime than is reported in the UCR. In 2005, approximately eight million more crimes were uncovered by the NCVS. The difference, however, was not apparent for every crime classification. The NCVS recorded fewer motor vehicle thefts than the UCR. The greatest difference for "uncovering" crime was for larceny-theft; the NCVS reported almost seven million more thefts than the UCR.

Table 1.3   UCR and NCVS Crime Totals, 2005

Type of Crime	UCR	NCVS
Rape	93,934	69,370
Robbery	417,122	624,850
Assault	862,947	1,052,260
Burglary	2,154,126	3,456,220
Larceny-Theft	6,776,807	13,605,590
Motor Vehicle Theft	1,236,226	978,120
Total	11,541,162	19,786,410

Although the volume of crime revealed by the two sources differs, the pattern of crime is consistent. Figure 1.3 presents the NCVS personal crime victimization rates per 1,000 households for 2005. Assault was by far the most common NCVS violent crime and rape was the least reported. In Figure 1.4, we see that theft has the highest property crime victimization rate followed by burglary and motor vehicle theft. (You can obtain current information on the National Crime Victimization Survey at the Web site of the Bureau of Justice Statistics: www.ojp.usdoj.gov/bjs/cvict.htm.

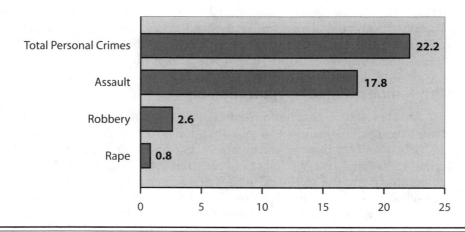

Figure 1.3   NCVS Personal Crime Victimization Rates per 1,000 Households, 2005

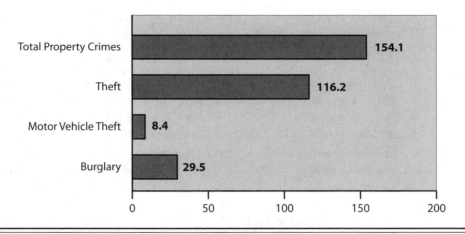

Figure 1.4 NCVS Property Crime Victimization Rates per 1,000 Households, 2005

Limitations of the National Crime Victimization Survey

Although data for the NCVS are obtained directly from victims, several problems affect their validity:[14]

1. *Accuracy.* Since it asks respondents to recall events over a specific period, forgetting and telescoping (moving a crime event from the past forward or pushing victimization backward to be included) are problems. The survey may tend to undercount "series offenses"—incidents that are so frequent, similar in character, or otherwise difficult to separate that the victim cannot disentangle them during the interview into concrete events occurring at specific times.[15] Most often, these are violent crimes.

2. *Lying.* People may conceal victimization because of embarrassment or report crimes to please the interviewer.

3. *The NCVS asks questions about rape in an indirect fashion.* Respondents are never asked whether they have been the victims of an attempted or completed rape. After the other crime victimizations are addressed, they are asked whether they have been attacked "in some other way." Assaults and rapes committed by acquaintances tend not to be reported in subsequent interviews.[16]

4. *There could be problems administering the survey or coding the data.* The accuracy of any survey is dependent upon the way it is conducted. If the questions are unclear or if sample members are not reached, the validity of the results is compromised. If responses are not recorded accurately, the results are imprecise.

5. *The survey represents the nation as a whole but does not contain specific information on any local area.* The NCVS provides breakdowns by geographic area of the country, but the UCR remains the sole source of

detailed regional crime information. In addition, the survey concentrates upon large cities and may not adequately represent the victimization pattern in other areas.

6. *The NCVS depends on identifiable victims.* For example, the NCVS does not measure the victimization of nonresidents (e.g., transients, commuters, and visitors) that may appear in police crime statistics. Nonresidents are more likely to be victimized by strangers, and crimes are more likely to be reported when the offender is a stranger.

7. *The survey tends to overrepresent nonserious crime.* Crimes that are not reported to the police may be more likely to be mentioned to surveyors.[17]

In addition, police classify crimes differently than victims. That is, a victim's version of a crime could indicate it to be very serious (because the crime was personal), while the police reporting of the crime could show it to less serious (unless it is a crime of violence). Furthermore, minor variations in the wording of questions and when they are asked have substantial effects on responses (e.g., meaning of the word "incident").[18] Despite these weaknesses, the NCVS provides vital, detailed information about crime victimization. It can be used to direct crime prevention efforts because it collects information from the victim.

Factors Influencing the Reporting of Crimes to the Police

The NCVS also provides information on when and why citizens report crimes to the police. In 1996, 35 percent of the crimes included in the NCVS were reported to the police. Victims were most likely to report car thefts (89 percent). They were unlikely to report personal thefts without contact that involved losses of less than $50. In general, crimes involving injury (e.g., a completed robbery) were reported more often (72 percent). The larger the loss, the more probable it is that the victim will report a property crime.[19]

Marianne Zawitz found that over a 20-year period, the relationship between the victim and the offender did not affect crime reporting in violent crimes (about 50 percent) or thefts involving contact (31 percent). In terms of age, violent crime victims ages 12 to 19 are less likely than other groups to report the crime to the police. Few measurable differences existed in reporting rates among persons age 20 or older. Females were more likely to report violent victimizations to the police (56 percent) than were males (45 percent). No difference between the sexes existed in terms of reporting property crimes. The proportion of crime reported to the police was similar for blacks, whites, and Hispanics.[20]

Economic status affected crime reporting. Homeowners (44 percent) were more likely to call the police than were renters (38 percent). This pattern held for whites, but black homeowners were no more likely to report crimes than were black renters. High-income families (over $50,000—43 percent) had a higher rate of crime reporting than low-income families (less than $7,500—38 percent).

Several common reasons were given for not reporting crimes to the police:

- ***Violent Crimes:*** the crime was a personal or private matter, or the offender was not successful

- **Theft:** the stolen object was recovered, the offender was unsuccessful, it was reported to another official, or there was no proof
- **Household Crimes:** the stolen object was recovered, the offender was unsuccessful, the police would not want to be bothered, or there was no proof[21]

Conversely, victims gave the following reasons for reporting crimes to the police:

- **Violent Crimes:** to prevent future crimes by the offender, to stop or prevent the incident, or because it was a crime
- **Theft:** to recover stolen property, because it was a crime, to collect insurance, or to stop or prevent the incident
- **Household Crimes:** to recover property, because it was a crime, or to prevent further crimes by the offender[22]

The police responded to the victim in 75 percent of the violent crimes, 67 percent of the household crimes, and 50 percent of the thefts.[23]

Overall, these reporting patterns are remarkably consistent over time. In 1976, criminologist Wesley Skogan reported the same results in a review of the early years of the victimization survey program.[24] Indeed, police departments wishing to increase reporting of certain crimes can use these data to guide their initiatives.

Calls for Service Data

Another source of crime data is the number of calls for service (CFS) received by the police. Typically, CFS data are based upon calls to the 911 operator or a Computer Aided Dispatching (CAD) system: "The CAD system collects and stores on magnetic tape several pieces of information on each call received—including the location and original categorization of the request for service as entered by the 911 operators." As a result, this measure of crime is based upon the descriptions of the event provided by the complainant.[25]

Strengths of CFS Data

CFS data have several advantages over the UCR:

1. "Gatekeeping" procedures used by the police are bypassed because computers maintain running records of all calls, whatever their seriousness.
2. The interviewer and memory bias effects that plague the NCVS are absent. Because all calls are recorded, sampling effects are nonexistent.
3. Because they are virtually unscreened, they are not susceptible to police biases.[26] They avoid any discretionary bias due to police decisions on whether to file a report.

Weaknesses of CFS Data

Even CFS, however, may not be valid indicators of crime. Several potential problems exist, including the following:

1. A complaint must be made before it is recorded by the system.

2. Overreporting can occur if several citizens report the same incident.

3. CFS data do not necessarily include the location of the offense—only the caller's location, or the location to which a police car has been dispatched.

CFS Data vs. Number of Arrests

If the number of arrests is used as a crime measure, the accuracy of the information is questionable for several reasons:

1. The size of police forces and municipal expenditures for police varies with the percentage of nonwhite population in an area.[27] Of course, expenditures affect the size of the police department and its ability to do its work. Police departments that have limited resources are less likely to make arrests than police departments that have adequate resources (e.g., personnel, vehicles, computers, etc.).

2. Even when such factors as the type of crime and the characteristics of the offender are considered, the police are more likely to make an arrest in a poor neighborhood.[28] Remember that the police are likely to follow the wishes of the crime victim. In poorer neighborhoods, individuals are more likely to want the offender arrested.

3. A study by the Police Foundation found that police arrest statistics were inaccurate.[29]

4. Policing styles may impact arrest rates. James Q. Wilson suggests that the "legalistic style" of policing may result in more arrests than either "service" or "watchman" style policing.[30]

The behavior of the offender and the willingness of the citizen to report the crime do not affect the calls for service data because the offense has been reported.[31]

Using both CFS and UCR Data

CFS and the UCR data can be used to supplement each other and serve as multiple indicators of the crime problem. For example, Robert Bursik and Harold Grasmick examined crime trends in Oklahoma City using both data sources for 1986–1988. They found that each source led to different conclusions about the crime rate. Overall, the CFS data supported a declining trend in the rate of motor vehicle theft, robbery, and burglary offenses. In the summer months, however, aggravated assault, burglary, and motor vehicle theft increased.[32] When both sources were combined, significant declines were reported in burglary, motor vehicle theft, and robbery. Aggravated assault still tended to increase during the summer months. Combining these crime measures resulted in a more accurate determination of crime rates. This information can then serve as a basis to plan crime prevention efforts.

The following section discusses the use of theory to guide research methods. There are several criminological theories that explain why crime occurs in certain places. Here, routine activities theory is used to explain crime "hot spots."

Routine Activities Theory and Crime "Hot Spots"

Criminological theory offers some support for the use of calls for service data to examine crime patterns. Routine activities theory states that for any crime to occur, three elements must converge:

1. A motivated offender
2. A suitable target
3. The absence of a capable guardian to prevent crime

The basic premise of this theory is that the daily routine movements of people explain victimization patterns. Thus, the most effective way to control crime is to try to understand the ebb and flow of human traffic so that offenders and targets seldom converge without guardians.[33]

Routine activities are "recurrent and prevalent" movements (e.g., work and leisure activities) that are motivated by basic needs.[34] The bulk of criminal activity occurs outside the home—where the potential for interaction with offenders increases. A study of calls to the police supports routine activities theory. Lawrence Sherman, Patrick Gartin, and Michael Buerger examined data on 323,979 calls to the police over all 115,000 addresses and intersections in Minneapolis over a year. A few hot spots accounted for all calls to the police, especially for predatory crime (robbery, rape, and auto theft).[35]

Similarly, D. W. Roncek and P. A. Maier examined the effect of taverns and cocktail lounges upon neighborhood crime rates in Cleveland from 1979 to 1981. Several reasons explain why certain crimes are likely to occur near a bar. First, bar patrons make attractive targets. They may become intoxicated, impeding their physical and mental dexterity and their ability to defend themselves. They are likely to have cash. Second, the taverns themselves have cash on hand and have goods that can be easily sold. Third, intoxicated patrons may also commit crimes that they would not attempt when sober. In addition, the bar is a setting in which disputes, fueled by alcohol, may lead to violence. The authors found that, on average, the presence of a tavern on a block increased the probability of violent crime by 17.6 percent and of property crime by about 13 percent.[36]

These findings show that certain crimes are more likely to occur in particular areas of a city. Close examination of these areas can provide some tips on how to prevent offenses from occurring. For example, if a neighborhood is particularly prone to a type of crime (e.g., burglary), the police can decide how to prevent it. Consider this question from a routine-activities perspective—why would residential burglaries tend to increase between Thanksgiving and New Year's Day?

The Compstat Program

The major value of statistical analysis is the creation and presentation of information that can be used to inform policy making. Statistical information is a key element in the planning of operations across the criminal justice system. Here, we present a current example of how statistics provide information to plan and evaluate police operations: the Compstat Program in the New York Police Department (NYPD).

The abbreviation **Compstat** stands for computer statistics. Statistics are compiled at the precinct level and sent to headquarters for analysis. These data are used as information to provide operational guidance. The timely flow of information allows precinct commanders to make effective use of their resources. Compstat is a four-step process, involving

1. Accurate and timely intelligence: To reduce crime, you must know about it.

   • What type of crime is it (e.g., drug sales, robbery, and burglary)?

   • Where is crime occurring (areas, types of location)?

   • When is crime happening (day of week, hour of day)?

   • Why is crime happening (motive, e.g., drug-related shootings)?

2. Rapid deployment: By providing weekly crime statistics, the Compstat process allows administrators to assess this intelligence. Commanders can then deploy their resources as rapidly as possible to address crime conditions.

3. Effective tactics: Specific resources are focused on specific problems.

4. Relentless follow-up and assessment: The first three steps are effective only if commanders constantly follow up on what is being done and assess their results.[37]

The Compstat system stresses accountability. Every component of the police department is examined and held accountable for the overall goal of reducing crime in New York City. Statistics are the starting point to give managers the information they need to evaluate the effectiveness of their crime control strategies. Precinct commanders are given increased power and resources to focus on departmental goals, rather than maintaining their own commands. As former NYPD Commissioner William Bratton states:

> There are four levels of Compstat. We created a system in which the police commissioner, with his executive core, first empowers and then interrogates the precinct commander, forcing him or her to come up with a plan to attack crime. But it should not stop there. At the next level down, it should be the precinct commander, taking the same role as the commissioner, empowering and interrogating the platoon commander. Then, at the third level, the platoon commander should be asking his sergeants, "What are we going to deploy on this tour to address these conditions?" And finally, you have the sergeant at roll call doing the same thing. All the way down until everyone in the department is empowered and motivated, active and assessed and successful. "It works in all organizations, whether it's 38,000 New York cops or Mayberry, R.F.D."[38]

In addition to generating information and clarifying organizational goals and their attainment, the Compstat process encourages the exchange of information at all levels: commanders, patrol, and the community. All levels of the department see that the information generated by statistical analysis is important. The reports that officers routinely fill out are given merit. They are responsible for obtaining and recording information that is thoroughly used.

In sum, the Compstat process leads to:

- Enforcement strategies to target specific crimes or conditions
- Refocusing its strategy of community policing by giving the main responsibility for problem solving and for getting concrete results to the precinct commanders
- Giving precinct commanders the authority to address crime and disorder in their precincts and more freedom to manage their own commands
- Holding precinct commanders accountable for their results in reducing crime in their commands

The NYPD has measured the effectiveness of Compstat through statistical analysis of reported crime in New York City. This method of percentage trend analysis is a standard part of statistical analysis in criminal justice.

Percentage Change Analysis

One of the most basic, but solid and traditional, methods of statistical analysis in criminal justice is the examination of percentage changes in the crime rate. This section focuses on reading tables and graphs, identifying and analyzing trends, calculating average and percent change, and displaying and interpreting statistics. Again, Compstat provides an example of this method.

Table 1.4 presents crime reported to the NYPD in the period 2002–2003. Tables are a staple of statistics. They present a great deal of information, organized in a logical format. The construction and interpretation of tables are significant skills that must be mastered.

Examine Table 1.4 carefully. It begins with a label that identifies the table contents. The first column lists the major index crimes in order of their severity, from murder to auto theft. The second column lists the number of these crimes reported in 2002. The third column lists the number of these crimes reported in 2003. The fourth column lists the percentage change for each type of crime between 2002 and 2003.

How was this crime change percentage calculated? To calculate a percentage change, take the following steps:

Table 1.4 Crime Reported to the New York City Police Department, 2002–2003

Type of Crime	2002	2003	Change
Murder	587	597	1.7%
Rape	1,689	1,609	24.7%
Robbery	27,229	25,989	24.6%
Felony Assault	34,334	31,253	29.0%
Burglary	30,102	28,293	26.0%
Grand Larceny	129,655	124,846	23.7%
Auto Theft	27,034	23,628	212.6%
Total	250,630	236,215	25.8%

1. Determine the earliest point in time. In this case, the "base year" is 2002. The number of murders reported to the NYPD in 2002 was 587.

2. Find the number of murders reported in 2003—597.

3. Subtract the number from step 1 from that in step 2 and determine what happened to the number of murders reported to the NYPD between 2002 and 2003. Here, we see that the number of murders *increased* by 10 (597 minus 587).

4. Now, determine the percentage change between 2002 and 2003. Take the difference between the two years and divide it by the number of murders in the base year: divide 10 by 587 and multiply the answer by 100. The percentage change is 1.7 percent. In this case, the percentage change is labeled positive because the number of murders reported to the NYPD went up between 2002 and 2003.

5. Therefore, the percentage change in the number of murders reported to the NYPD between 2002 and 2003 is 1.7 percent.

Or these steps can be reduced to a formula:

Base Year Number – Current Year Number / Base Year Number × 100

Calculation Formula: Averages and Percentages

One element of basic mathematics is the calculation of averages and percentages. We deal with both often. For example, baseball thrives on statistics. One of the most common is the batting average. An average is calculated by adding up a list of numbers and dividing the sum by the total number of items on the list. A batting average is calculated by dividing the number of hits by the total number of times at bat. Hall of Famer Roberto Clemente, an outfielder for the Pittsburgh Pirates, had a lifetime batting average of .317. He had 3,000 hits in 9,454 times at bat. Using his career numbers, retrospectively, this means he had a 31.7% chance of getting a hit each time he stepped up to the plate.

Repeat this analysis for each of the crimes listed in Table 1.4. Next, return to the table to determine if a pattern exists.

1. Examine the percentage change for each type of crime. What happened here?

2. What is the overall (Total) pattern?

3. Which type of crime declined the most? The least? How do the violent crimes compare to the property crimes?

4. What do these figures say about Compstat? Has it been effective in reaching its goal of reducing crime in New York City?

This rather simple method of analysis is capable of conveying a great deal of information. The construction and interpretation of a table can provide a way to analyze and make sense of data. The detection and interpretation of a pattern is what statistical analysis is all about.

Lying with Statistics

One of the widely held myths about quantitative analysis is that you can lie with statistics. This belief has a long history. In the 1800s, British political mathematicians viewed their work as a way to promote certain reforms, such as the abolition of capital punishment, rather than as an objective report on social conditions. They collected only data that would support their conclusions and interpreted them accordingly. Such presentations led to the famous quote by Prime Minister Benjamin Disraeli, "There are lies, damned lies, and statistics."[39]

Our goal is to assist students in their development in becoming informed consumers of research. Lying occurs, but the educated, informed consumer is more difficult to deceive. If you know how statistics are calculated and presented, you are less likely to fall victim to a charlatan. Actually, the source of any lying is not statistical analysis. Fraudulent researchers typically falsify or alter the data to reach a desired conclusion. After all, 2 + 2 = 4, no matter which way we add two and two together. To make 2 + 2 = 5, one of the twos must be changed to a three. The statistics are not the source of the deception.

Problems with data do occur. In this chapter, we have cited and used data from official sources of crime statistics. The problem with official statistics is that the researcher has no quality control over the accuracy of the data. We did not collect or record the information; someone else did. When the data are from sources such as police records, many police officers collected the data. You have no idea how accurate they were. As Sir Josiah Stamp noted in the past:

> The government is very keen on amassing statistics. They collect, raise them to the nth power, take the cube root and prepare wonderful diagrams. But you must never forget that every one of these figures comes from the village watchman, who just puts down what he damn pleases.[40]

In fact, many police departments recorded a huge increase in the number of crimes once they began to rely on computerized record keeping.[41] As a result, while computers made the police more efficient, they also contributed to a perceived crime wave.

Some evidence suggests that the police respond to political pressure to alter crime data. For example, crime in the streets became a major political theme in two presidential campaigns. In 1968, candidate Richard Nixon proposed the use of the District of Columbia as a site for an evaluation of his anti-crime proposals. The goals of the program were evaluated by crime statistics. A 1974 study by David Seidman and Michael Couzens suggested that police administrators purposively misclassified crimes to alter crime patterns and bring them into line with the goals of the program. After all, patrol officers had the discretionary authority to classify crimes in a certain way. Apparently, they responded to these pressures, downgrading larcenies and burglaries to misdemeanors rather than reporting them as felonies.[42]

Jim Galvin and Kenneth Polk offered several guidelines to prevent the misuse or misrepresentation of crime statistics, particularly in the determination of crime waves.

1. *Obtain data over as many data points and years as is feasible.* You can then assess the pattern of crime in an accurate fashion and are less likely to jump to conclusions based upon a short-term fluctuation.

2. *Increase the number of indicators.* For example, use UCR and NCVS data to analyze the extent of crime in society. While one focuses upon reported crime and the other upon victimization, they can supplement each other.

3. *Use current data, particularly for public policy research.* Researchers must overcome the time lag between the recording and publication of data.[43]

Careful consideration of these points will lead to more accurate crime analysis.

Summary

This text stresses the development of students as consumers of research. We are preparing students to be managers. Good managers are analysts before they can be decision makers. They must be able to construct management information systems that are decision (problem-solving) oriented. You need to tease out what the analysis means to you when you are a practitioner. Research provides data for informed planning and decision making, rather than hip-shooting. In order to be informed consumers and professionals, students need to study research methods and statistics.

Crime statistics are a source of information. Our review covered several basic sources of data: crimes reported to the police (the Uniform Crime Reports), the National Incident-Based Reporting System (NIBRS), the National Crime Victimization Survey, the calls for service data, and Compstat. Each source has its own strengths and weaknesses and provides different perspectives on the amount of crime in society. Each source uncovers particular aspects of crime and can also serve as a basis for action.

The term statistics has two meanings. You are probably most familiar with the first—statistics as data and information that describe the nature of a phenomenon such as crime. In this text, we learn that statistics are tools—methods of analysis to understand what is happening regarding crime.

Again, we stress that we use statistics to provide information. They can serve as a basis for rational planning in the criminal justice system. Analysis of data can help guide investigation and enforcement policies and programs. As one police chief put it, "I want our decisions data driven, not intuition driven. This isn't new; it's just smart police work."[44] Statistics provide information about the nature of crime and exactly which factors should be addressed in the attempt to minimize its occurrence.

Key Terms

Data Set: information that has been collected and organized by the researcher

Validity: the degree to which the crime measure accurately gauges the amount of crime in society. Does the measure of crime accurately gauge the amount of crime in society or does it tally something else?

Reliability: the extent to which the crime measure is a consistent and dependable indicator of the level of crime in society. Are the crime measures consistent over time and do they yield consistent results?

Part I or Index Offenses: serious crimes highlighted in the FBI's *Crime in the United States*. Together, these crimes (murder, rape, robbery, assault, burglary, larceny-theft, motor vehicle theft, and arson) make up the crime index.

Crime Index: an indicator of the level of serious crime in America

National Incident-Based Reporting System (NIBRS): Established in 1991, this system is designed to collect more detailed information on crimes. NIBRS will report both crimes and arrests. It will eventually replace the Uniform Crime Report as the source of official FBI counts of crimes reported to law enforcement agencies.

National Crime Victimization Survey (NCVS): The Bureau of Justice Statistics has conducted the NCVS since 1972. Its aim is to uncover unreported crime and learn the actual level of crime in the country. The NCVS is a scientifically designed survey of U.S. households. Approximately 60,000 households respond to the survey each year. Information in this report is also presented as a population rate: the number of victims per 1,000 households.

Compstat: The abbreviation "Compstat" stands for computer statistics. In the New York City Police Department, statistics are compiled at the precinct level and sent to headquarters for analysis. These data are used as information to provide operational guidance. The timely flow of information allows precinct commanders to make effective use of their resources.

Exercises

1. Analyze the following table of data from the New York Police Department.

New York City Police Department Narcotics Arrests in Bronx Precincts, 1997–1998

Precinct	1997	1998	Percentage Change
47th	426	647	
46th	1292	1053	
44th	965	812	
43rd	977	1021	
41st	929	1801	
40th	1169	1680	
Total			

Calculate the percentage change for this distribution. First, calculate the total number of narcotics arrests for 1997 and 1998. Second, calculate the percentage change between these totals. What happened in the Bronx overall to the amount of narcotics arrests between 1997 and 1998? Third, calculate the percentage change for each precinct. Using the percentage change column, do you detect a pattern? Which precincts increased?

Which decreased? Which one went up the most? Down the most? How do you think these data would be used in a Compstat meeting?

2. In response to rising rates of violent crime, the Louisville Police Department in Kentucky implemented "more aggressive tactics" in its 4th police district. The measures include a crackdown on "nuisance" crimes such as loitering, drinking in public, and trespassing; a juvenile curfew; neighborhood road blocks; and the use of traffic stops as a pretense for searching occupants for drugs and weapons. In addition, Mayor Jerry Abramson offered a series of anticrime proposals. His suggestions included expanding youth programs, adding block watches, and making it easier for people to turn in criminals anonymously.

These policy changes took place in early 1997. One year later, the mayor's office compiled the following data for the period January 1–October 4, 1997 and 1998 in the 4th police district:

- The number of homicides was 31 for the 1997 period and 13 for the 1998 period.
- The number of rapes was 24 for the 1997 period and 29 for the 1998 period.
- The number of robberies was 341 for the 1997 period and 264 for the 1998 period.
- The number of assaults was 379 for the 1997 period and 269 for the 1998 period.
- The number of burglaries was 805 for the 1997 period and 804 for the 1998 period.
- The number of thefts was 929 for the 1997 period and 801 for the 1998 period.
- The number of auto thefts was 907 for the 1997 period and 739 for the 1998 period.

In the space provided, make a table for these data. The table should be fully labeled (use the table from question 1 as an example). Calculate the percentage trend for this distribution. First, calculate the total trend between the 1997 and 1998 time periods, then calculate the trend between the 1997 and 1998 time periods crime by crime. What is the pattern? Would you say that the program measures have been effective? Why or why not?

3. Car break-ins are becoming a problem in Jefferson County, Kentucky. The police chief, William Carcara, aims to stop them. Here are the data concerning the problem:

Car Break-ins in Jefferson County, Kentucky, 1996–1997, by Zip Code

Zip Code	1996	1997	Percentage Change
40023	0	0	
40025	0	1	
40059	11	15	
40118	45	46	
40205	10	9	
40207	20	62	
40211	8	11	
40213	101	76	
40214	159	170	
40216	156	189	
40218	45	46	
40219	164	170	
40258	456	421	
40220	115	130	
40222	132	146	
40223	78	111	
40225	2	3	
40228	64	98	
40229	138	165	
40241	111	145	
40242	74	60	
40243	43	69	
40245	42	72	
40272	279	245	
40291	123	164	
40299	28	35	
Total			

a. Calculate the percentage change for each zip code area.

b. What is the pattern? How many zip codes had a percent decrease in car break-ins? Which areas had the largest increase and decrease?

c. Which zip code(s) should the police target?

d. What do your answers in part b suggest with regard to the chief's goal of decreasing car break-ins?

4. The murder rate is on the rise in Louisville, Kentucky. The following table presents data on homicides in Louisville, Jefferson County, the Commonwealth of Kentucky, and the United States.

Homicides at a Glance

Year	Louisville	Kentucky	United States
2000	39	193	15,586
2001	25	191	16,037
2002	35	184	16,229
2003	42	188	16,503
2004	66	216	16,137
2005	55	190	16,692

a. How do these trends compare?

b. Does the trend in Louisville match that of the county, state, and nation?

5. Using the following data from the Miami-Dade Police Department on Visitor Robberies, calculate the percentage change from one year to the next and for the period 2001 to 2005. What is the nature of these trends?

Miami Dade Police Department Visitor Robberies

Year	Number of Visitor Robberies Reported	Percentage Change
2001	25	
2002	10	
2003	16	
2004	30	
2005	12	

6. Using the following data from the Minneapolis Police Department on Homicides, calculate the percentage change from one year to the next and for the period 1995 to 2000. What is the nature of these trends?

Minneapolis Police Department Homicides

Year	Number of Reported Homicides	Percentage Change
1995	99	
1996	86	
1997	58	
1998	58	
1999	48	
2000	50	

7. Analyze the following data from the Chicago Police Department, January 2005 and January 2006:

Chicago Police Department Index Crimes,
January 2005 and January 2006

Index Crime	January 2005	January 2006	% Change
Murder	20	28	
Robbery	131	108	
Burglary	1811	1994	
Theft	5842	6407	
Motor Vehicle Theft	1778	2089	
Totals			

a. Calculate the percentage change for each type of crime and discuss the percentage change trend for each crime.

b. Calculate the totals for all types of crime for each column and the percentage change. What has happened overall?

8. Analyze the following data from the Los Angeles Police Department, January–March 2004 and January–March 2006:

Los Angeles Police Department Index Crimes,
January–March 2004 and January–March 2006

Category	Jan.–March 2004	Jan.–March 2006	% Change
Weapons Arrests (Possession)	542	551	
Shots Fired	1227	1081	
Shooting Victims	506	424	

a. Calculate the percentage change for each type of category and discuss them.

b. Do you think that these trends are related? If so, how and if not, why not?

9. Analyze the data from the New York City Police Department on p. 26:

a. Calculate the Crime Totals for each year.

b. Calculate the Percentage Changes listed in the table:

   i. 2005 vs. 2001

  ii. 2005 vs. 1998

 iii. 2005 vs. 1995

 iv. 2005 vs. 1990

c. What is the nature of these trends? By Type of Crime? What do you think they mean about Compstat?

New York City Police Department

Index Crime	1990	1995	1998	2001	2005	% Change 05 vs. 01	% Change 05 vs. 98	% Change 05 vs. 95	% Change 05 vs. 90
Murder	2262	1181	629	649	540				
Rape	3126	3018	2476	1930	1638				
Robbery	100,280	59,733	39,003	27,873	24,422				
Assault	44,122	35,528	28,848	23,020	17,337				
Burglary	122,055	75,649	47,181	32,694	23,983				
Theft	108,487	65,425	51,461	46,291	47,642				
Totals									

Notes

[1] Margaret Vandiver and David Giacopassi, "One Million and Counting: Students' Perceptions of the Annual Number of Homicides in the U.S.," *Journal of Criminal Justice Education,* Vol. 8 (1997), pp. 135–144.

[2] John Kitsuse and Aaron Cicourel, "A Note on the Use of Official Statistics," *Social Problems,* Vol. 10 (1963), pp. 131–139.

[3] Gennaro F. Vito, Edward J. Latessa, and Deborah G. Wilson, *Introduction to Criminal Justice Research Methods* (Springfield, IL: Charles C. Thomas, 1988).

[4] Mark Lanier and Stuart Henry, *Essential Criminology* (Boulder, CO: Westview Press, 1998), p. 47.

[5] Paula H. Kleinman and Irving F. Lukoff, "Official Crime Data: Lag in Recording Time as a Threat to Validity," *Criminology,* Vol. 19 (1981), pp. 449–454.

[6] Richard Quinney, "What Do Crime Rates Mean?" in Leon Radzinowicz and Marvin E. Wolfgang, eds., *Crime and Justice, Volume I: The Criminal in Society* (New York: Basic Books, 1977), pp. 107–111.

[7] Alan S. Bruce and Scott A. Desmond, "A Classroom Exercise for Teaching the Problems of Offense Classification and Tabulation Associated with the UCR," *Journal of Criminal Justice Education,* Vol. 9 (1998), p. 119.

[8] Walter R. Gove, Michael Hughes, and Michael Geerken, "Are Uniform Crime Reports a Valid Indicator of the Index Crimes? An Affirmative Answer with Minor Qualifications," *Criminology,* Vol. 23 (1985), p. 453.

[9] Michael Gottfredson and Don Gottfredson, *Decisionmaking in Criminal Justice* (Cambridge: Ballinger, 1980), p. 35.

[10] Ibid., p. 489.

[11] Ibid., pp. 474–475.

[12] Ibid., pp. 465–466.

[13] James Alan Fox and Marianne W. Zawitz, *Homicide Trends in the United States* (Washington, DC: Bureau of Justice Statistics, 2006). www.ojp.usdoj.gov/bjs/

[14] J. P. Levine, "The Potential for Crime Overreporting in Criminal Victimization Surveys," *Criminology* Vol. 14 (1976), pp. 307–330.

[15] Gove et al., "Are Uniform Crime Reports a Valid Indicator," p. 459.

[16] H. M. Eigenberg, "The National Crime Survey and Rape: The Case of the Missing Question," *Justice Quarterly,* Vol. 7 (1990), 655–672; Gove et al., "Are Uniform Crime Reports a Valid Indicator," p. 465.

[17] Gove et al., "Are Uniform Crime Reports a Valid Indicator," p. 455.

[18] Ibid., pp. 462–464.

[19] Marianne W. Zawitz, *Highlights from 20 Years of Surveying Crime Victims: The National Crime Victimization Survey, 1973–92* (Washington, DC: U.S. Department of Justice, Office of Justice Programs, Bureau of Justice Statistics, 1993), p. 32.

[20] Ibid.

[21] Ibid., p. 33.

[22] Ibid.

[23] Ibid.

[24] Wesley G. Skogan, "Citizen Reporting of Crime: Some National Panel Data," *Criminology,* Vol. 13 (1976), pp. 535–549.

[25] Barbara D. Warner and Glenn L. Pierce, "Reexamining Social Disorganization Theory: Using Calls to the Police as a Measure of Crime," *Criminology,* Vol. 31 (1993), p. 503.

[26] Robert J. Bursik and Harold G. Grasmick, "The Use of Multiple Indicators to Estimate Crime Trends in American Cities," *Journal of Criminal Justice,* Vol. 21 (1993), p. 511.

[27] Pamela I. Jackson and Leo Carroll, "Race and the War on Crime: The Sociopolitical Determinants of Municipal Police Expenditures in 90 Non-Southern U.S. Cities," *American Sociological Review,* Vol. 46 (1981), pp. 290–305; Allen E. Liska and Mitchell B. Chamlin, "Social Structure and Crime Control Among Macrosocial Units," *American Journal of Sociology,* Vol. 98 (1984), pp. 383–395.

[28] Warner and Pierce, "Reexamining Social Disorganization Theory," pp. 494, 512–513. Robert J. Sampson, "Effects of Socioeconomic Context on Official Reaction to Juvenile Delinquency," *American Sociological Review,* Vol. 51 (1986), pp. 876–885; Douglas A. Smith, "The Neighborhood Context of Police Behavior," in Albert J. Reiss and Michael Tonry, eds., *Communities and Crime* (Chicago: University of Chicago Press, 1986), pp. 313–342.

[29] Lawrence W. Sherman and Barry D. Glick, *Police Foundation Reports: The Quality of Police Arrest Statistics* (Washington, DC: Police Foundation, 1984).

[30] James Q. Wilson, *Varieties of Police Behavior: The Management of Law and Order in Eight Communities.* (Cambridge, MA: Harvard University Press, 1968).

[31] Warner and Pierce, "Reexamining Social Disorganization Theory," p. 504.

[32] Bursik and Grasmick, "The Use of Multiple Indicators to Estimate Crime Trends in American Cities," p. 512.

[33] Marcus Felson, "Routine Activities and Crime Prevention in the Developing Metropolis," *Criminology,* Vol. 25 (1987), pp. 911–931. For more information about routine activities and crime prevention, see Ronald V. Clarke, ed., *Situational Crime Prevention: Successful Case Studies,* 2nd ed. (Monsey, NY: Criminal Justice Press, 1997); Ronald V. Clarke and Marcus Felson, eds., *Routine Activity and Rational Choice, Advances in Criminological Theory, Volume 5* (New Brunswick, NJ: Transaction Books, 1993); and Marcus Felson, *Crime and Everyday Life,* 3rd ed. (Thousand Oaks, CA: Sage, 2002).

[34] Terrance D. Miethe, Michael C. Stafford, and James S. Long, "Social Differentiation in Criminal Victimization: A Test of Routine Activities/Lifestyle Theories," *American Sociological Review,* Vol. 52 (1987), pp. 184–194.

[35] Lawrence W. Sherman, Patrick R. Gartin, and Michael E. Buerger, "Hot Spots of Predatory Crime: Routine Activities and the Criminology of Place," *Criminology,* Vol. 27 (1989), pp. 27–56.

[36] D. W. Roncek and P. A. Maier, "Bars, Blocks, and Crimes Revisited: Linking the Theory of Routine Activities to the Empiricism of 'Hot Spots,'" *Criminology,* Vol. 29 (1991), p. 742.

[37] William Bratton with Peter Knobler, *Turnaround: How America's Top Cop Reversed the Crime Epidemic* (New York: Random House, 1998); Howard Safir, "Goal-Oriented Community Policing: The NYPD Approach," *The Police Chief* (December 1997), pp. 31–58.

[38] Bratton, *Turnaround,* p. 239.

[39] Patricia Loveless, "The History of Criminal Justice Statistics: A Cautionary Tale," in M. L. Dantzker, Arthur J. Lurigio, Mangus J. Seng, and James M. Sinacore, eds., *Practical Applications for Criminal Justice Statistics* (Woburn, MA: Butterworth-Heinemann, 1998), p. 11.

[40] Gwynn Nettler, *Explaining Crime* (New York: McGraw-Hill, 1974), p. 45.

[41] Lanier and Henry, *Essential Criminology,* p. 46.

[42] David Seidman and Michael Couzens, "Getting the Crime Rate Down: Political Pressure and Crime Reporting," *Law and Society Review,* Vol. 8, No. 3 (1974), pp. 457–493.

[43] Jim Galvin and Kenneth Polk, "Any Truth You Want: The Use and Abuse of Crime and Criminal Justice Statistics," *Journal of Research in Crime and Delinquency,* Vol. 19, No. 1 (1982), pp. 135–165.

[44] Scott Wade, "County Forms Squad to Fight Car Break-ins." *Louisville Courier Journal,* February 14, 1999, p. 2 (B).

chapter 2 ———————————————————

Basic Elements of
Criminal Justice Research

In chapter 1, Compstat was used as an example of a data-driven strategy to analyze crime patterns. This method has also been termed "intelligence policing": using data analysis to identify key problems. It is dependent upon the flow of information—accurate and timely intelligence on crime and community conditions—to get the job done. It also features a public health or "epidemiological" perspective on crime. Crime, like physical disease, cannot be completely eliminated. It must be managed, and outbreaks of dangerous conditions must be dealt with to protect the public. Compstat is a good example of how research can inform policy and guide operations.

Research results can inform decision making in several ways. Through its problem-solving focus, research provides direction and focus for crime prevention efforts. It can promote the efficient utilization of resources. The research results can help identify what works in a program or policy and what does not. In that manner, it helps develop and support policies and modify or drop them. Thus, the ultimate purpose of criminal justice research is to provide information to solve problems and prevent crime. It is important to provide accurate findings so that the decision making is properly informed.

To accomplish this task, criminal justice research follows elements of the scientific method. Methods are nothing more than a plan to ensure the accuracy of the information generated by the research. In this chapter, we review several basic elements of the criminal justice research process. We also introduce you to SPSS (Statistical Package for the Social Sciences), a statistical analysis software program that provides a number of statistical functions that can be used to analyze data.

Elements of the Research Process

The research process in criminal justice typically is designed to examine crime problems. It is presented in the outline below.

I. Problem Identification
   A. Concepts
   B. Hypotheses
   C. Variables
II. Research Design
   A. Type of Design
   B. Sampling
   C. Data Collection
III. Data Analysis
   A. Selection of Statistical Method
   B. Calculation of Statistic
   C. Interpretation of Statistic
IV. Interpretation and Presentation of Research Results

The scientific method outlines the manner in which research should be conducted. Methods deal with the design of the research: how data are measured, where data will come from, how data are collected, and what methods—**quantitative analysis,** which deals with numbers and statistical analyses, or **qualitative analysis,** which deals with words and descriptions drawn from interviews, direct observations, and documents—will be used to analyze the data. Research begins with **theory**—ideas and concepts about the nature of crime. Criminological theories attempt to explain the causes of crime. Theories have the following functions:

• They define scientific questions.

• They provide a means for selecting variables and measures.

• They make possible the interpretations of results.[1]

Programs and policies in criminal justice are not divorced from theory. Theory provides the reason why a program or policy is expected to work. Theory leads to the development of hypotheses that can be tested and examined.

Problem Identification

At this stage, we must state why research is needed to address a certain problem. The problem must be clearly identified and described. You must specify the concept(s), hypothesis, and variable(s) you are studying.

Concepts are abstractions (such as deviance and socioeconomic status) that are not directly observable but that you wish to measure.[2] A **variable** is designed to measure these observations or concepts. It has more than one possible value. We categorize variables according to their level of measurement (levels of measurement are discussed later in the chapter). If we were studying the relationship between substance abuse and crime, both substance abuse and crime would be considered variables. The measurement of a variable must be clearly specified or given an **operational definition.** Measures must be assigned according to some rules. Measures must be both valid and reliable. Recall from chapter 1 that validity is the degree to which the measure accurately gauges the variable and its underlying concept. Is the selected measure a clear indicator of the concept in question? Reliability is the extent to which the variable is a consistent and dependable indicator of the concept.

A **hypothesis** is stated in the form of a relationship between variables. In terms of problem solving, the hypothesis outlines the manner in which a problem can be potentially solved. In research, the **independent variable (X)** produces an effect or impact upon the **dependent variable (Y)**. The dependent variable (Y) may change due to the presence of the independent variable. In effect, the hypothesis is a prediction. We are expecting the independent variable to produce an effect in the dependent variable.

For example, let us examine the relationship between the execution of inmates convicted of murder and the homicide rate. One of the policy goals of the death penalty is the prevention of future homicides. According to the theory of *general deterrence,* the execution will protect society from future homicides by potential offenders. The execution sends a message to citizens who are thinking of committing murder. If you kill someone and you are caught and convicted, you will be executed by the state. Therefore, rational people will weigh the cost (losing their life) and the benefit (getting rid of someone whom they wish to dispose of) of committing the murder and decide not to commit the crime. In short, the execution of an inmate convicted of murder will deter other people from committing a murder.

Comparing this example with the research process outline above, *deterrence* is the concept (IA). Note that it is not directly observable. We cannot see when someone is deterred. The independent variable (X) is the execution of the inmate convicted of homicide. The dependent variable is the homicide rate in the state (Y) in the period following the execution. The independent and dependent variables correspond to IC. Based upon deterrence theory, the research hypothesis is a **directional hypothesis**—the independent variable is expected to influence the dependent variable in a certain manner. If the execution of a convicted murderer is a deterrent to other people, the homicide rate should go down in the period following an execution (IB).

Examples such as this will be given throughout the text as we use statistical analysis to answer such questions. Remember that the aim is to generate information that can guide programs and policies.

A Note on the Language of Science

Science has its own vocabulary. You have already been introduced to several key terms, and there are many more to follow. We speak of hypothesis testing, but what we really mean is that we are testing the **null hypothesis**. Like the hypothesis, it is a theoretical statement about the expected relationship or difference between the independent and dependent variables. However, the null hypothesis is always stated in the form of no relationship or no difference. It is not the opposite of the hypothesis.

This format might seem a bit awkward or unnecessary. In fact, much of the research you will read never mentions the null hypothesis because it is understood that we are testing it instead of the hypothesis. The reason that we test the null hypothesis is that it is difficult, if not impossible, to prove that the hypothesis is true. We only have to find one example where the hypothesis is not true in order for us to reject it.

If we conducted a study in Idaho, and the results confirmed our original hypothesis, would we obtain the same results if we conducted the study in Kentucky? Our research is both valid and reliable, but the possibility remains that we could obtain different results because of factors that are present in Kentucky that were not present in Idaho. The same problem arises with regard to different time periods—would we obtain the same results if we repeated our study 20 years from now?

Thus the quest for knowledge is never ending due, in part, to the nature of hypothesis testing. We cannot control for every factor that might influence our results, so in essence, we can never prove a hypothesis to be true. What we can say, however, is that in this instance we failed to reject the null hypothesis. The implication is that the hypothesis is true.

The concepts behind hypothesis testing are part of the formal language of science. It is a language that you will become more comfortable with and conversant in by the time you successfully complete this course.

Research Design

Several elements of the research design especially relate to the process of statistical analysis. They all play a key role in the logic of statistics. Research design helps us to determine whether the program or policy would be effective if it were attempted at other places and times.

The Classical Experiment

The goal of the research is to demonstrate whether or not the intervention had the desired impact. To make this determination, the research design attempts to isolate the effect of the treatment (policy or program) upon the problem. The best way to accomplish this is through the use of the classical experiment. The **classical experiment** involves the assignment of subjects to the experimental (receives the treatment) and control (does not receive treatment) groups. The key element in the process is **random selection**. Random selection means that every member of the target population has an equal chance of being selected for the experimental group. Also, members must be selected in an independent manner. The selection of any one member must not influence the chance that another member is selected. If every member of a population does not have an equal chance of selection, the resulting sample is biased. It does not represent the population from which it was drawn. Random selection ensures that the two groups are comparable—the same in every relevant aspect.

For example, consider a drug treatment program for probationers. The target population is probationers who have an admitted problem with drug abuse. The county health department, in conjunction with the probation department, has established a treatment program to help these probationers.

The program features individual counseling, drug testing, and group therapy sessions for its clients. To evaluate the effectiveness of this program, we intend to use the classical experiment. After screening the probationer population, it is determined that there are 500 potential clients for the drug treatment program. We use random selection to assign 250 clients to the program (our independent variable) and 250 to the control group.

The classical experiment is outlined in Figure 2.1.

Random selection ensures that the placement of one subject in the drug treatment program does not affect the chance that any other member of the target population will be selected. All members of the original target population (probationers with an admitted drug problem) have an equal chance of getting into the program. Random selection thus ensures that the members of the experimental and control groups are alike in every respect except one—the experimental group is subjected to the treatment and the control group is not. All of the attributes of our target population are equally distributed across the groups. Here, we use drug test results (positive or negative) as an outcome measure for the program.

The pre-test determines whether the experimental and control groups are the same before the treatment is given. The two groups should be equal before the treatment begins. Otherwise, the experiment will be inaccurate. Any results could be due to the fact that one group had a lower rate of positive drug tests (failure to stay clean) than the other. Therefore, the results due to the treatment program could not be determined.

If the pre-test does not show a difference between the groups, then the effectiveness of the treatment can be determined. If there is a positive difference in outcomes between the two groups after treatment (the post-test), it can be assumed to be due to the treatment. For example, if a greater number of probationers in the treatment group pass their final drug test (come up negative for drug use), than the control group, then the treatment will be judged effective. Statistical tests allow us to make such determinations on the pre- and post-tests.

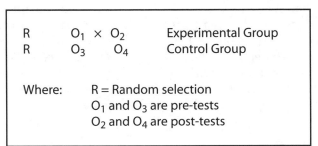

Figure 2.1   The Classical Experimental Design

Quasi-Experimental Design

What can the researcher do when random selection is impossible? For example, the member of the target population may not wish to participate in the program. This is where the **quasi-experimental design** comes into play. Here, a comparison group is established in some other way than random selection. Both groups are drawn from a pool of like cases. For example, a drug treatment program is developed to treat delinquents who smoke marijuana. The pool of individuals (or program eligibles) are delinquents who smoke marijuana regularly. Suppose that this is further defined by delinquents who smoke marijuana three or more times per week. One way of constructing the comparison group of delinquent, regular marijuana smokers is by **matching** their other demographic and social characteristics with those juveniles who have already entered the program. If the experimental group is 50 percent male and 30 percent white, the comparison group should reflect these same characteristics. Figure 2.2 presents the elements of a quasi-experimental design.

$$O_1 \times O_2 \qquad \text{Experimental Group}$$
$$O_3 \qquad O_4 \qquad \text{Comparison Group}$$

Where: O_1 and O_3 are pre-tests
O_2 and O_4 are post-tests

Figure 2.2   The Quasi-Experimental Design

Here, you would also compare the pre-test scores of the two groups to ensure that the experimental and comparison groups were alike. In our example, let us say that the pre- and post-test outcome measures are drug tests for marijuana. If the pre-test levels between the groups are comparable, we would assume that they are alike in the nature of their marijuana problem. At the conclusion of the treatment program, if the experimental group had a lower rate of positive (post-)tests for marijuana, we would say that the treatment program was effective. The only difference between the experimental and quasi-experimental designs is that the groups are constructed by some other means than random selection. Without random selection, it is more difficult to conclude that treatment differences (on the post-test especially) are due to the effectiveness of the program.

Probability Sampling

We want to select participants who are as representative as possible of the population being studied. It is usually impossible for a researcher to examine every element of a population. For example, suppose that you wished to conduct a victimization study in your state. You could not contact every person who lived there. The defining characteristic of this population is residence in the state at the time of your study. Most research is conducted by selecting a sample from the population. The sample is a smaller, yet representative, replacement for the entire population. You conduct your victimization survey on a sample of state residents. The most common method of selecting a sample is to draw it at random from the population. **Random sampling** (like random selection) ensures that the sample is an accurate representation of the population from which it was drawn.

Typically, the larger the sample is, the greater the likelihood that it is representative of the population from which it was drawn. When a sample is not randomly selected, however, the probability that it is representative of the population is greatly reduced. Your ability to make generalizations about your sample findings is in jeopardy. The survey sample stands in place of the entire population. Statistical analysis helps us make the determination that the research findings can be attributed to the entire population from which the sample was drawn. Randomization assures us that the results are representative of the population.

Generalizability

Once the survey is administered and the data are analyzed, you want to know what the victimization level is for the entire state, not just this sample. The purpose of the survey is to make generalizations about the population based upon our analysis of the sample survey results. Statistical analysis allows us to determine the probability that the sample findings are representative of the population. Because you do not know the state level of victimization, you would use the sample data to make inferences about the population level of victimization based upon your analysis of the sample. As we see later, statistical tests allow us to make inferences from sample to population values by measuring the probability that the inferences are correct. In this manner, statistical analysis performs an important function, giving us the ability to extend our research findings beyond the sample itself.

A Note on Human Subjects

We want to inject a word of caution and a reminder. Whenever research is conducted, whether it be in a university setting or for a criminal justice agency, we urge you to observe the highest ethical standards and to comply with existing laws and policies. Most universities have units that specialize in compliance, especially if humans are the subject of the research. Before starting any research project, we suggest that you check with the appropriate research unit at your college or university to be sure that you are in compliance with all applicable requirements.

Some of the data used in this text are derived from archival resources. For example, UCR data are offenses reported to the police. The identity of the victims and the offenders is not contained in the data sets. This sort of data represents one of the least intrusive methods of gathering data. As a general rule, the more intrusive the research becomes, the greater the level of oversight.

The other data used in this text were generated from survey data. You might think that asking questions is not very intrusive, and in most cases you would be right. However, survey research may bring you into contact with human subjects, and we urge you to exercise utmost caution even with seemingly innocuous surveys.

No matter how bureaucratic these requirements may seem to you, they exist in order to protect the safety and dignity of the participants. We don't have to look to far in the annals of research to find examples where human subjects were harmed as a result of the supposed quest for knowledge.

Data Collection

Data collection involves the identification and selection of data sources. The data source could be a survey, official records, or official statistics.

Data Analysis

Once the data are collected, the analysis begins. The proper selection and use of statistical methods are the focus of this text. Statistics are tools that only work well when they are used appropriately. The research uses the statistic that fits the task at hand. Think of statistics as both a universal language and a form of "shorthand" communication. You can describe the population of the U.S. in a language that nearly everyone will understand. For example, according to the U.S. Census Bureau, the mean travel time to work for people over the age of 16 was 25.5 minutes. Notice that we did not say that it takes everyone 25 minutes to commute to work, but that the average for everyone was 25 minutes. We did not have to list every individual who fits the category (thank goodness!). Instead we used shorthand that virtually everyone understands.

Interpretation and Presentation of the Research Results

Here, it is important to consider the audience for the research results. Typically, decision makers want information to be presented clearly and crisply. The criminal justice researcher must pay careful attention to the policy implications of the results. What do the conclusions mean in terms of criminal justice policy? How do they direct potential solutions to the problem under study?

Program Evaluation

As the previous examples demonstrate, much of the research conducted in criminal justice is for the purpose of **program evaluation.** Evaluation research addresses the ability of a program or policy to accomplish its goals. It is action-oriented policy research that is specifically designed to guide decision making.

R. O. Washington[3] identified six basic steps the evaluator should follow in the design and execution of evaluation research. Here, we use the example of a drug court program in Louisville, Kentucky:[4]

1. State the problem.
2. Select the evaluation goals and the standard or criteria against which judgments are to be made. What do you hope to accomplish by the end of the project?
3. Identify the indicators that will permit measurement of the changes to be brought about.
4. Collect data on the indicators, including baseline data.
5. Analyze data for
    a. rates of change
    b. direction of change
    c. nature of change
    d. amount of change
6. Interpret the data in terms of the public interest:
    a. Was the predetermined goal met?
    b. Did the program activity make a significant impact upon society in general?
    c. Was it worth the cost in terms of effort, resources, and time?
7. What were the critical factors that determined the outcome?

The goal of drug court is to establish an alternative to prison and jail for drug offenders. The drug court model diverts first-time drug possession offenders into a community treatment program that features the development of social and educational skills. Drug court breaks down the traditional adversarial roles assumed by defense attorneys and prosecutors. The aim is to provide a treatment regimen that holds the offenders responsible for their sobriety. If the judge believes that the offender is trying to break the pattern of addiction, he or she can remain in treatment indefinitely.

Indicators of the Louisville, Kentucky, program performance were successful completion of the treatment program and recidivism (defined as reconviction for a new felony, including probation violation) over a one-year period. Since participation in the program was voluntary, a quasi-experimental research design was used in the drug court program evaluation. The research compared performance of clients who (1) completed the program successfully, (2) could have entered the program but (for reasons of their own—a "self-drop" comparison group) did not, and (3) did not complete the program.

The research findings determined that the completion rate of clients was low (23.8 percent) but were comparable to other drug court programs around the country. With regard to recidivism rates, the drug court graduates had the lowest rate (13.2 percent) followed by the "self-drop" comparison group (55.4 percent), and the drug court nongraduates (59.5 percent). The statistical analysis revealed that this difference in recidivism rates was greater than would be expected by chance. It also found that graduating from drug court was the strongest predictor of success even when other independent variables (such as extent and type of drug use) were taken into account. Clearly, completion of the drug court program led to improved performance among drug offenders in the community.

Levels of Measurement

Often, we assign numbers to measure a concept, such as fear of crime or support for the police or capital punishment. Numbers are assigned in order to make the data amenable to statistical analysis. The numbers are used as a code. Statistically, the question is "Can we use mathematics to now analyze this code that we have established?" Does it make sense to treat the numbers as such and perform arithmetic operations on them?

This code is called the **level of measurement.** It involves converting concepts to numerical data. There are four levels and each has different attributes. The levels of measurement are cumulative, however, like the steps on a ladder. You have to step on the first step to reach the second, and so on. Each succeeding level automatically possesses the attributes of the level preceding it, plus another distinct one.

The Nominal Level of Measurement

The nominal level involves the process of classifying data into categories. When we classify respondents by race or sex, we are using nominal measurement (i.e., 1 for male, 2 for female). The nominal level of measurement follows three basic rules:

1. The list of categories must be exhaustive and cover all the types of observations made.
2. The categories must be mutually exclusive. Each observation can only be classified in one way.
3. No ordering is present in the list of categories. The order is arbitrary, and no one classification is superior to another.

At the nominal level, the numbers are actually substitutes for names and serve as a numerical label. It does not make sense to add them together or perform any other mathematical function on them. The only legitimate summarizing statistic is the largest category (or mode). It does not make sense to discuss the mean (average) or median (midpoint) with nominal data. It cannot be summed and divided, nor can it be ranked in order from highest to lowest.

For an example of nominal data, let us examine the sex of the respondents in the National Crime Survey. The **frequency distribution**, a table or count that displays the number of times a data value is obtained in a sample of scores, is listed in Table 2.1. Here we see that the majority of the respondents are female (51.8 percent). Although everyone knows that women are smarter, we cannot say that the mutually exclusive categories of sex are in rank order, nor can we say that one sex is "average."

A word of caution. Researchers must absolutely understand the concept of levels of measurement. With nominal and ordinal levels of measurement, the numbers are merely labels. Changing the labels does nothing to change the statistical output. However, if you instruct SPSS (or any other program) to perform any mathematical function, the program will produce the requested output. But it will

Table 2.1 Sex of Respondents in the National Crime Survey

Sex of Respondents	Frequency	Percentage
Male	484	48.2
Female	521	51.8
Total	1005	100

have no meaning. The adage "garbage in and garbage out" applies in this circumstance, which is one of many opportunities to introduce error that researchers face. As a consumer of research, you must be aware of this and other pitfalls.

The Ordinal Level of Measurement

Ordinal measurement exists when we can also detect degrees of difference between the categories on the scale. The values of the variable indicate order or ranking. For example, in the National Crime Survey, respondents were asked "Do you favor or oppose the death penalty for persons convicted of murder?"[5] and were provided these choices for their level of support: (1) Favor, (2) Oppose, (3) Neither, and (4) Don't Know.

An ordinal scale has the property of **transitivity.** For the items on the scale, if A > B and B > C, A must be greater than C or ordinal level measurement is not present. In our example, "Favor" > "Oppose," "Oppose" > "Neither," "Neither" > "Don't Know," and "Favor" > "Don't Know." The frequency distribution of responses is presented in Table 2.2.

Here, "Favor" is the first response category. It ranks higher than "Oppose," "Neither," and "Don't Know." The response categories are ordered in terms of the positive nature of the response. In the frequency distribution, it also turns out to be the majority (selected by more than 50 percent of the respondents) category. Almost 71 percent of the respondents favored

Table 2.2 Responses to the Question "Do You Favor the Death Penalty for Persons Convicted of Murder?"

Response	Frequency	Percentage
Favor	707	70.6
Oppose	189	18.9
Neither	82	8.2
Don't Know	24	2.3
Total	1002	100

capital punishment for murderers. The categories are ordered and ranked but we cannot say anything about the distance between the categories on the scale—only that they are one item apart.

The Interval Level of Measurement

It is very difficult to reach the requirements of interval level measurement when assigning numbers to a scale. In addition to all the properties of nominal and ordinal levels of measurement, the interval level assumes that all the items on the scale have equal units (or intervals) of measurement between them. It also assumes that these units have a commonly recognized meaning.

In the National Crime Survey, respondents were asked, "How safe do you feel on neighborhood streets?" (See Table 2.3.) The response categories were (4) safer, (3) not as safe, (2) about the same, and (1) don't know.[6] The frequency distribution reveals that a majority of respondents do not feel any safer on neighborhood streets than they have in the past (71 percent).

Ordinal level measurement is present here, but can we say anything about the distance (or interval) between items on the scale? Do they represent units of "fear"? If they do, then we can add and subtract the different items on the scale.

Obviously, our scale does not meet the requirements of interval level measurement. But scales are often treated as though they contain interval measurement. For example, the Intelligence Quotient (IQ) scale that is used to measure intelligence is usually treated as an interval scale. The IQ scale does not have equal intervals of measurements between items on the scale. The higher score values represent greater leaps in intelligence than those earlier in the scale. Although persons who score higher on the IQ scale than others can be said to be "smarter," the absence of a true zero point ("no intelligence") does not permit us to say that a person with a score of 130 is "twice as intelligent" as a person who scores 65.

Table 2.3 Responses to the Question "How Safe Do You Feel on Neighborhood Streets?"

Response	Frequency	Percentage
Safer	95	9.5
Not As Safe	186	18.5
About the Same	704	70.0
Total	995	98

In mathematical terms, we can perform functions and change the meaning of the labels. On a number line, for every two points, there is another point in between. An example is temperature measured in degrees Fahrenheit. It was 105 degrees F in Boise this week, but was in the 50-degree F range at night in Stanley, ID (one of the coldest spots in the continental U.S. during winter!). While we can state that it was warmer in Boise by 55 degrees, we cannot state that it was twice as hot in Boise (but it is a dry heat!) as it was in Stanley. If we use another scale to measure temperature, such as Kelvin, then we have an example of our next level of measurement, the ratio level.

The Ratio Level of Measurement

The distinguishing feature of a ratio scale is a true zero point that is the point of origin for the scale. Zero represents the total absence of the concept being measured. The zero point makes it possible to consider the manner in which the points on the scale stand in relation to each other via ratios. Statements such as "twice as great" can now be made legitimately.

A standard example of a ratio scale is time. A year is a common, constant unit of measurement. Before birth, a person is considered to be zero years of age. For example, analysis of the age of the respondents to the National Crime

Survey revealed that the mean was 41.93 years. The median or midpoint was 39. The mode was 18. All measures of central tendency can be considered with ratio level measurement.

We can also compare groups of respondents according to their age. Eighteen survey respondents were 44 (group A), and 19 respondents were 22 (group B). We draw the following conclusions about respondents from groups A and B:

1. They have different ages (nominal measurement).
2. Members of group A are 22 years older than members of group B (ordinal and interval measurement).
3. Members of group A are twice as old as members of group B (ratio measurement).

Of course, any statistical test can be performed under the ratio level of measurement. The numbers that have been assigned truly can be treated as numbers, not just a code. The attributes of the levels of measurement are summarized in Figure 2.3.

			Ratio
		Interval	Zero point
		Equal space	Equal space
	Ordinal	Fixed order	Fixed order
	Fixed order	Mutually exclusive and exhaustive	Mutually exclusive and exhaustive
	Mutually exclusive and exhaustive	Continuous variable	Continuous variable
Nominal Categorical	Property of transitivity	Property of transitivity	Property of transitivity
Mutually exclusive and exhaustive	Discrete variable	Powerful statistics can be applied	Powerful statistics can be applied
Descriptive statistics can be applied	Limited statistics can be applied	Histogram	Histogram
Bar, pie, and line graphs	Histogram	Scatter plot	Scatter plot
No arithmetic functions possible	Limited arithmetic functions possible	Arithmetic functions possible	Arithmetic functions possible

Figure 2.3 Attributes of the Levels of Measurement. You can convert from higher (ratio) to lower (nominal), but not the other direction.

Measurement and Types of Variables

Another characteristic that affects the manner in which data can be analyzed is the type of variable—discrete or continuous. A **discrete variable** is categorical. It assumes a finite number of values between two points. Variables at the nominal and ordinal levels are discrete. In the National Crime Survey, respondents were asked whether "To discourage youth gangs there should be stiffer sentences for juvenile offenders."[7] The response pattern for this variable was (1) strongly agree, (2) agree, (3) neither, (4) disagree, and (5) strongly disagree. More than 82 percent of the respondents agreed or strongly agreed with this statement. A discrete variable cannot be split into smaller units or fractions.

Continuous variables can take an infinite number of values between points. Again, age is a good example of a continuous variable. Time can be broken down into increasingly smaller units: years, days, hours, minutes, seconds, and so on. Variables at the interval and ratio levels are continuous. As with the levels of measurement, different statistical tests are permissible with discrete and continuous variables.

Using SPSS: An Introduction

This section serves as an introduction to one of the data sets, NCSD, that accompany this textbook and also as a means of introducing you to the SPSS (Statistical Package for Social Science) program. (We assume the four data sets on the CD accompanying this book have been installed on your computer.) NCSD is the result of a national opinion survey. It was conducted in 1995 by the Criminal Justice Research Center at Sam Houston State University.[8] The purpose of the survey was to provide legislators, public officials, and the public with a reliable source of information about citizens' attitudes toward crime and criminal justice-related topics. The survey questions are concerned with neighborhood atmosphere, worries regarding possible attacks (robbery and physical attacks), confidence in and opinions of the police and their effectiveness, attitudes concerning the death penalty, and other topics. Demographic information on the respondents includes sex, age, race, income, education, marital status, political party, and religion. Once you have installed SPSS on your computer, open it. The first screen (Figure 2.4) is a menu of the things you can do when you open the program. "Run the tutorial" is highly recommended for first-time users of SPSS. The tutorial familiarizes you with all the elements of SPSS and what the program can do. Also on the menu is the option "Open an existing file." Click on this and then select the NCSD data set.

When you have familiarized yourself with SPSS, complete the following items:

1. Switch between "variable view" and "data view" (bottom left-hand corner tabs) to see what the following mean: n9, w7, d7

2. Using the toolbar across the top, click on "Analyze," then "Descriptive Statistics," and then "Frequencies." A small "Frequencies" screen will pop up.

   a. Click on "Last Grade of School Completed." (Make sure the "Display frequency tables" box is checked.) Then click on the arrow. The variable now appears in the Variable(s) box. Next, click "OK." Answer the following question:

   How many respondents are college educated? What percentage is this?

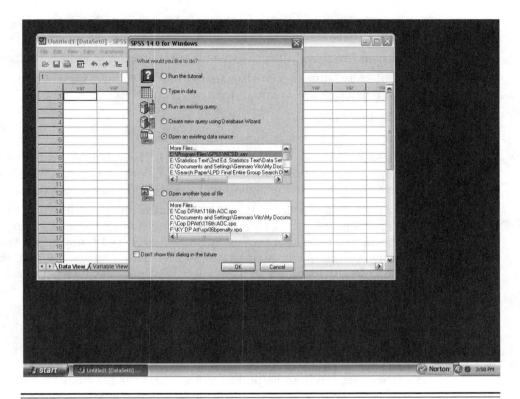

Figure 2.4

b. Go back to the "Frequencies" screen. Click on "Last Grade . . ." and click on the arrow to move it back to the listing box. Then click on "What if: DP not Deterrent to Murderer" and move it to the Variable(s) box. Click "OK."

How many respondents (more) favor the statement, "The death penalty is not a deterrent to murder"?

c. Go back to the "Frequencies" screen. Move the "What if: DP . . ." variable back to the listing box. Then click on "What if: Poor More Likely to Get DP" from the list and move it to the Variable(s) box. Click "OK."

How many respondents (more) oppose the statement, "Poor people are more likely to get the death penalty"?

For the next series of questions, we will not repeat instructions for locating and moving the variable to be analyzed from the listing box to the variable(s) box.

3. Do you think more republican respondents would have guns in the household than democrats? Why?

a. Look at "Party Affiliation" in the variable view. What is the number for Republican? What is the number for Democrat?

b. Identify the variable (using the variable view) that represents "guns in household."

c. Click on "Analyze," then "Descriptive Statistics," and then "Crosstabs":

• Put "Any Guns in Your Household" as the column variable.

• Put "Party Affiliation" as the row variable.

• Click on "OK."

d. Can you interpret anything from the tables?

4. Do the same analysis for "Any Guns in Your Household" by "Ideological Alignment." Do you find anything that corroborates the initial finding? Is there any literature or "agreement reality" that supports this?

In reviewing the items above, it is easy to realize the potential that SPSS has in testing proposed relationships between or among variables (this, of course, is known as hypothesis testing and will be covered later in this text). In the previous exercises we analyzed secondary data; that is, we analyzed data that were already available in a data set. SPSS can also be used to create a data set using survey data. For example, consider the following set of questions used by a human resources officer in a local police department:

1. Why did you call the police department?

1. Call for Service; 2. Report a Crime; 3. Make a Complaint; 4. Information; 5. Other

2. Was the officer/civilian helpful in addressing your question(s)?

1. Very Helpful; 2. Somewhat Helpful; 3. Helpful; 4. Not Helpful

3. Did the officer/civilian treat you with respect?

1. Yes; 2. No

4. Would you feel comfortable calling the police department again?

1. Yes; 2. No

5. What is your sex?

1. Male; 2. Female

6. What is your age?

7. What is your race?

1. White; 2. Black; 3. Hispanic; 4. Other

8. What is your home zip code?

Each of the above questions represents a variable that will be measured (or answered) when an individual completes the survey. Suppose for the first 10 people, the responses were as follows:

Case	Why Call	Helpful	Respect	Try Again	Sex	Age	Race	Zip Code
1	1	2	2	1	2	24	1	32514
2	1	1	1	1	2	45	1	32514
3	1	2	2	2	1	56	1	32504
4	2	1	1	1	1	62	1	32509
5	3	3	2	2	1	16	1	32509
6	5	4	2	2	1	28	2	32507
7	1	4	2	2	2	33	2	32560
8	1	4	2	2	2	33	3	32509
9	1	2	2	2	1	65	2	32508
10	2	1	1	1	1	57	1	32507

Open SPSS to a new data set. You are going to create a new data set using the data above. First, begin by switching between "variable view" and "data view" (bottom left-hand corner tabs). You will begin creating the data set in "variable view." Each row represents a separate variable and each column represents the characteristics of the variable (e.g., "name," "type," "width," etc.). In row 1, column 1, type in the name of the first variable which is "case." Once you type the variable name in and press "return" or "tab," the remaining columns fill in with default information. Since you are not working with decimals with the case number, you should set decimals to "zero." The only thing left to do for this variable is add a label for it; this allows you to know what the variable "case" represents. Continue adding the name and label for each of the variables.

It is also important for you to complete the "values" column for each variable. This allows you to enter the meaning for each numerical code being used. For example, the variable "sex" is represented by the numbers 1 and 2, which really makes no sense unless we know that "1" represents "male," and "2" represents "female." This is the information that should be included in the "values" column. Again, you should enter this information for the remaining variables (i.e., why call, helpful, respect, try again, and race).

Once you have completed entering the data in the variable view, switch back to the data view. You have just completed the creation of your very first data set! See if you can use SPSS (analyze, descriptive statistics, frequencies) to answer the following questions:

1. What percentage of the customers thought that the service was "very helpful"?

2. What was the main reason that individuals contacted the police department?

3. What was the average age of the customers?

Of course, one cannot do much with such a small data set with only 10 cases, but this offers a good exercise for you to see how data sets are created, as well as how data sets might be connected to survey/data collection and data analysis.

Summary

Research in criminal justice typically addresses policy questions. Research is used to identify a problem. Problem solving is the key element. The nature of the problem must be specified: its seriousness, magnitude, and direction. Research attempts to identify effective policies and programs to deal with crime and delinquency. The research design outlines the nature of the problem and sets up the data collection, analysis, and conclusions. The research design includes the collection, the method of obtaining and conducting statistical analysis of the data. The goal is to ensure the accuracy of the research findings.

Variables and hypotheses provide the framework for analysis. The basic research design that is followed is the classical experiment. Research in criminal justice tends to be conducted under the program evaluation model. When we assign numbers to a variable in an attempt to measure a concept, we are using the levels of measurement. These numbers form a code. Our ability to analyze the assigned scores depends upon the level of measurement that our scale values represent.

Key Terms

Quantitative Analysis: deals with numbers and statistical analysis

Qualitative Analysis: deals with words and descriptions drawn from interviews, direct observations, and documents

Theory: ideas and concepts about the nature of crime. Criminological theories attempt to explain the causes of crime. Theories have the following functions: (1) They define scientific questions. (2) They provide a means for selecting variables and measures. (3) They make possible the interpretations of results. Programs and policies in criminal justice are not divorced from theory. Theory provides the reason why a program or policy is expected to work. Theory leads to the development of hypotheses that can be tested and examined.

Concept: abstraction that is not directly observable but that the researcher wishes to measure

Variable: designed to measure an attribute. It usually has more than one possible value.

Operational Definition: The measurement of a variable must be clearly specified.

Hypothesis: stated in the form of a relationship between variables. In terms of problem solving, the hypothesis outlines the manner in which a problem can be potentially solved.

Independent Variable (X): produces an effect or impact upon the dependent variable

Dependent Variable (Y): may change due to the presence of the independent variable

Directional Hypothesis: The independent variable is expected to influence the dependent variable in a certain manner.

Null Hypothesis: a theoretical statement of no relationship or no difference between the independent and dependent variables. It is *not* the opposite of the hypothesis statement. We always test for the null hypothesis.

Classical Experiment: involves the assignment of subjects to the experimental (receives the treatment) and control (does not receive treatment) groups via random selection

Random Selection: a crucial element of the classical experiment. It provides every member of the target population (subjects who are the target of the program or policy) with an equal chance of being selected for the experimental group. In addition, random selection ensures that the selection of one subject does not affect the chance that any other member of the target population is selected. Random selection thus ensures that the members of the experimental and control groups are alike in every respect.

Quasi-Experimental Design: follows the same basic pattern of the classical experiment. Here, a comparison group is established in some other way than random selection. Both the experimental and comparison groups are drawn from a pool of like cases.

Matching: Under the quasi-experimental design, the comparison group can be established by matching the sociodemographic characteristics of the experimental group with other program eligibles.

Random Sampling: ensures that the sample is an accurate representation of the population from which it was drawn

Program Evaluation: addresses the ability of a program or policy to accomplish its goals. It is action-oriented policy research that is specifically designed to guide decision making.

Level of Measurement: involves converting the concepts to numerical data. There are four categories and each have different attributes: nominal, ordinal, interval, and ratio.

Nominal Level Measurement: involves the process of classifying data into categories. At the nominal level, the numbers are actually substitutes for names and serve as numerical labels. At this level, it does not make sense to add values together or perform any other mathematical function on them. The only legitimate summarizing statistic is the majority category (or mode).

Frequency Distribution: a table or count that displays the number of times that a data value is obtained in a sample of scores. The sum of the frequencies is the size of the sample.

Ordinal Level Measurement: exists when we can also detect degrees of difference between the categories on the scale. An ordinal scale has the property of transitivity. With an ordinal scale, the categories are ranked, but we cannot say anything about the distance between the categories on the scale.

Interval Level Measurement: assumes that all the items on the scale have equal units of measurement between them. It also assumes that these units have a commonly recognized meaning.

Ratio Level Measurement: has a true zero point. Zero represents the total absence of the concept being measured. The zero point makes it possible to consider the manner in which the points on the scale stand in relation to one another via ratios. Statements such as "twice as great" can now be made legitimately.

Transitivity: For items on a scale, if A > B and B > C, A must be greater than C.

Discrete Variables: are categorical. A discrete variable assumes a finite number of values between two points. Variables at the nominal and ordinal levels are discrete.

Continuous Variables: can take an infinite number of values between points. Age is a good example of a continuous variable. Time can be broken down into increasingly smaller units: years, days, hours, minutes, seconds, and so on. Variables at the interval and ratio levels are continuous.

Exercises

1. A researcher was interested in the reasons why juveniles become gang members. She tested the hypothesis that juveniles from broken homes were more likely to join gangs. She randomly selected 100 juveniles incarcerated in state institutions, interviewed them, and examined their sociodemographic attributes (including family status).

   a. What is the independent variable in this study?

   b. What is the dependent variable?

   c. Is the research hypothesis directional?

2. A researcher was hired to conduct an evaluation of an educational program designed for jail inmates. The program features individualized, computerized instruction to improve the reading and mathematical performance of below-average students. Jail inmates with low educational levels were randomly assigned to the experimental and control groups. The reading and math ability of the two groups was measured at the beginning and end of the program.

   a. What is the independent variable in this study?

   b. What is the dependent variable?

   c. Is the research hypothesis directional?

3. You want to research college students' opinion of the death penalty. Your hypothesis is that there is a relationship between enrollment in higher education institutions and an individual's opinion of the death penalty (for or against). With this in mind,

   a. What type of *probability* sample would you select? Why (i.e., who is your population)?

   b. How would you obtain your sample? Discuss steps fully!

4. In 2002, the City of Louisville passed a curfew that required youngsters below the age of 16 be off city streets after 10 o'clock at night. The ordinance proved controversial and was repealed in 2003. In late 2004, however, the ordinance was reenacted and has been enforced up to the

present time. City officials would now like to know if the ordinance has actually reduced youth crime and violence in the city. How will you address this?

5. You are examining traffic stop data that have been collected by your local police department. After examining the variables from the collected data, you decide to address the question of racial profiling by examining the relationship between the "productivity of the search" (Did the search of the vehicle uncover illegal substances or weapons) and the race of the driver. In order to address this question, which variable should be your independent and which should be your dependent variable and why?

Notes

[1] Thomas J. Bernard and R. Richard Ritti, "The Role of Theory in Scientific Research," in Kimberly L. Kempf, ed., *Measurement Issues in Criminology* (New York: Springer-Verlag, 1990), pp. 1–2.

[2] Ibid., p. 4.

[3] R. O. Washington, *Program Evaluation in the Human Services* (Madison: University of Wisconsin, 1971), p. 16.

[4] Gennaro F. Vito and Richard Tewksbury, "The Impact of Treatment: The Jefferson County (KY) Drug Court Program," *Federal Probation,* Vol. 62 (1998), pp. 46–51.

[5] Timothy J. Flanagan and Dennis R. Longmire, *Americans View Crime and Justice: A National Public Opinion Survey* (Thousand Oaks, CA: Sage Publications, 1996), p. 193.

[6] Ibid, p. 182.

[7] Ibid, p. 199.

[8] Timothy J. Flanagan and Dennis R. Longmire, eds., *Americans View Crime and Justice: A National Public Opinion Survey* (Thousand Oaks, CA: Sage, 1996).

chapter 3

Summarizing Data and Presenting the Results

A list of raw numbers yields little in the way of valuable information. However, by arranging or sorting the data according to some sort of format, and by displaying that format, we may begin the process of describing our data. We begin our study of **descriptive statistics** by effectively summarizing a data set. We next introduce several formats for arranging and displaying data, including graphical displays. We conclude with a section on how to present research using multimedia software such as Microsoft PowerPoint.

Frequency Distributions

As we saw in chapter 2, the most common means of sorting data is by producing a frequency distribution. In order to show how the data are distributed, nonoverlapping categories (sometimes referred to as "groups") are created that contain the number of observations in each category. Figure 3.1 is an example of a frequency distribution created with SPSS. We opened the NCSD data set, selected "Analyze" from the top menu, and clicked on "Descriptive Statistics" from the menu choices. After selecting "Frequencies," we highlighted "How Safe Feel on Neighborhood Streets" and clicked on the arrow. The variable moved to the "Variable(s)" box. We then clicked on OK.

The smaller table in Figure 3.1 reveals that there are 1005 cases (responses) to this question—985 valid observations and 20 missing. The larger table has five columns of information: the nonoverlapping categories, the frequencies, the percentages, the valid percentages, and the cumulative percentages.

We can see that participants in the study had four options in responding to the question in the survey. Twenty of the respondents failed to answer the question for reasons unknown; 95 of the participants indicated that they felt safer; 186 responded that they were not as safe; and 704 said they were about the same. Thus, the frequency column is the number of observations (in this instance the responses of the participants) for each possible category.

Another way to interpret these results is found in the column that reports the percentages. For example, 9.5 percent of the respondents indicated that

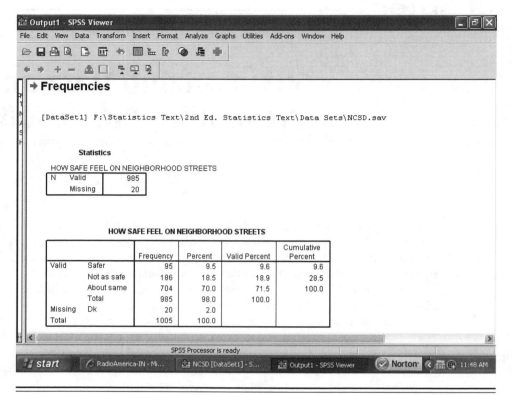

Figure 3.1

they felt safer. This figure was obtained by dividing the number of observations in a particular category by the total number of observations. In this instance, 95/1005 = .0945273. Multiply this figure by 100 to obtain a rounded value of 9.5 percent.

But how do we account for the 2 percent of the survey participants who failed to provide a valid response to the question? The "Valid Percent" column reports the percentage of valid responses. We take the 95 respondents who said they felt safer and divide those observations by the total number of valid observations (95/985 = .0964467) and then multiply by 100 to obtain the percentage of valid responses, which is 9.6 percent.

The last column, "Cumulative Percent," is simply each category added together as we move down the column. We start with 9.6 percent, then add 18.9 percent to obtain a cumulative percentage of 28.5. We add the next category of 71.5 percent to obtain 100 percent of all the observations in the data set. Other conventions used when writing frequency distributions are presented in the text box.

Elements of Frequency Distributions

Robert Mason and others make the following recommendations about frequency distributions:

1. *Overlapping categories:* The categories must be mutually exclusive; that is, an observation must fall into one, and only one, category.

2. *Equal-sized categories:* Sometimes it is necessary to reduce the number of categories by collapsing them into a smaller number of categories that contain a range of observations. The intervals between the ranges should be equal.

3. *Open-ended categories:* Avoid open-ended categories at every opportunity. An open-ended category prohibits the calculation of an important statistic, the arithmetic mean.

4. *Number of categories:* Generally, no fewer than 5 and no more than 20 categories should be created.

5. *Category size:* A common practice is to base the size of the range on multiples of 5 or 10.

6. *Category limits:* Another common practice is to make the lower limit of the first category a multiple of the category interval.

Robert D. Mason, Douglas A. Lind, and William G. Marchal, *Statistics: An Introduction* (Belmont, CA: Thomson Brooks/Cole, 1998), p. 29.

Displaying Frequency Distributions Graphically

Although we work with frequency distributions constantly, try explaining a table similar to the one generated for "How safe feel on neighborhood streets" to a group of criminal justice practitioners. Now you can better appreciate the proverb, "a picture is worth a thousand words." The table of the frequency distribution presented in Figure 3.1 does not portray the shape of the distribution. It is much easier to see how scores are spread in a distribution when they are presented in a graph.

Fortunately for us, software programs such as SPSS can easily portray frequency distributions graphically. Several types of graphs can be prepared depending upon whether the variable is discrete (categorical—like our safety variable above) or continuous (where the variable can assume an infinite number of values, such as age), and whether we are looking at one variable independently or comparing 2 or more variables. In this section, we will examine the use of bar charts, pie charts, histograms, and line graphs to graphically portray frequency distributions.

Frequency distributions of data represent several categories/groups, or they may simply represent a single category of a finite variable. Think about the variable "age." Age is a continuous variable, and if you were to ask a roomful of individuals their age, you are likely to get many different responses. If you were to ask the 1,005 respondents from the NCSD data set, then you are likely to get a full-range of ages; specifically, you're likely to get every age between 1 and 90! Given this situation, it makes sense to group or categorize the ages when displaying in a table.

Thus, with the age variable as well as most other continuous variables, categories would be created using a grouped frequency distribution (e.g., 0–9, 10–19, 20–29, etc.). Notice how the categories are mutually exclusive (e.g., 0–9 and 10–19) and exhaustive (we would continue categories of 10 through 110 to be certain that each respondent could list his/her age). Basically, what we are doing when we categorize the age variable is shift it from a ratio-level continuous variable to an ordinal-level categorical variable. Consider length of sentence, time until recidivism, or even your GPA; like other ratio-level variables, these data would benefit from a grouped frequency distribution when being displayed.

One might suggest that categorical or finite variables (nominal or ordinal level) are already in groups or in categories that allow for easy and clear representation of the data. Consider a letter grading scale using A, B, C, D, and F to represent grades earned by students. Though we may consider collapsing the categories even further (e.g., pass or fail), it is not necessary that we do so in order to clearly display the data. A similar example is the question "How safe feel on neighborhood streets" from the NCSD data set.

Creating Bar Charts with SPSS

One of the most frequent ways to display data graphically is to create a bar chart. A **bar chart** is used to compare the size of different items on a scale. It is a most appropriate method when data are presented in categories (the bars do not touch). Our NCSD question, "How safe feel on neighborhood streets," is discrete and categorical. Respondents said that they felt either (1) safer, (2) not as safe, or (3) about the same. The heights of the bars on the graph correspond to the frequencies (size of) the different categories.

Take the following steps to obtain a bar graph using SPSS:

1. Open the NCSD data set (Figure 3.2).
2. On the top menu, highlight "Graphs." In the pop-down menu, highlight and click on "Bar."
3. The "Bar Charts" menu now appears. The type of bar chart graph that you want ("Simple") is already highlighted, so click the "Define" button.
4. The "Define Simple Bar: Summaries for Groups of Cases" menu now appears. The left side of the window reveals all of the variables in the NCSD data set. Move down this window until you see the variable "How Safe Feel on Neighborhood Streets." Highlight this variable and then click on the box containing an arrow pointing to the right to paste it into the "Category Axis" window.
5. Click the "OK" button.

You have now produced a bar chart like that presented in Figure 3.3, in which we can now actually see that the greatest number of respondents feel "about the same" about their safety on neighborhood streets. This example compares respondents' feelings across one variable/question. When response categories used are the same for multiple questions (e.g., Likert scale), then cluster bar graphs may be utilized to compare participant responses to multiple questions.

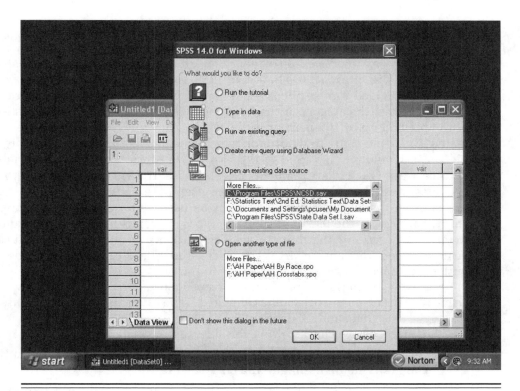

Figure 3.2

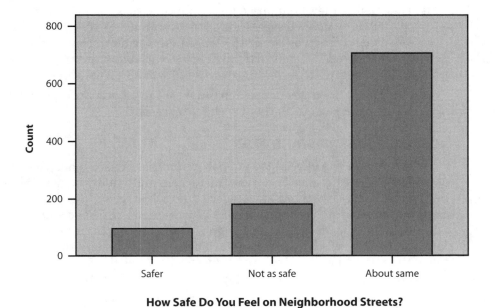

How Safe Do You Feel on Neighborhood Streets?

Figure 3.3   How Safe Do You Feel on Neighborhood Streets?

Creating Pie Charts with SPSS

Another way to present a frequency distribution graphically is to create a pie chart. A **pie chart** shows how a variable can be divided into parts—a circle that is divided into segments that correspond to the percentage of cases that fall into each category of the frequency distribution. Together, the slices of the pie add up to 100 percent of the cases. You can then compare the segments of the pie chart to determine which category is the largest. Finally, a pie chart should only be used to represent a categorical or discrete variable with between two and six segments or categories. If a variable has more than six categories, then the utility of the pie graph (i.e., easy comparison, clear presentation) is lost. A bar graph might be used as an alternative. The pie chart, however, is the least useful of the types of graphs listed in this chapter in terms of describing the shape of the distribution. The only measure that can be determined from a pie chart is the mode—the largest category in the distribution will have the greatest percentage in the pie.

For example, in the NCSD data set, respondents were also asked "How the crime rate in the neighborhood has changed." The categories are (1) increased, (2) stayed the same, and (3) decreased.

To generate a pie chart for this variable, take the following steps:

1. On the top menu in the data window, highlight "Graphs" again. In the pop-down menu, highlight and click on "Pie."

2. The "Pie Charts" menu now appears. Under the "Data in Chart Are" section, the entry "Summaries for groups of cases" is already marked, so click the "Define" button.

3. The "Define Pie: Summaries for Groups of Cases" menu is next. The left side of the window reveals all of the variables in the NCSD data set. Move down this window until you see the variable "How Crime Rate in Neighborhood Change." Highlight this variable and then click on the arrow pointing to the "Define Slices by" window. Then click "OK."

You have now produced a pie chart like that presented in Figure 3.4 on p. 57. What does the pattern in this pie chart represent?

Creating Histograms with SPSS

A **histogram** is a special type of bar graph that is used when the data are continuous. The difference between a histogram and the first type of bar chart we covered is that the bars or categories in a histogram directly touch one another, representing that the variable is continuous, thus showing the shape of the distribution (discussed in chapter 4). For example, if you open State Data Set I, there are a number of variables that represent an actual count. One of them is "Prisoners Executed Between 1977 and 1995."

To create a histogram using SPSS, take the following steps:

1. Open State Data Set I. On the top menu in the data window, highlight "Graphs" again. In the pop-down menu, highlight and click on "Histogram."

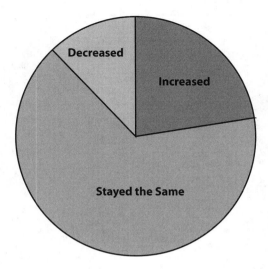

How Has the Crime Rate in the Neighborhood Changed?

Figure 3.4   How Has the Crime Rate in the Neighborhood Changed?

2. The "Histogram" menu appears. The left side of the window reveals all of the variables in State Data Set I. Move down this window until you see the variable "Prisoners Executed Between 1977 and 1995." Highlight this variable and then click on the box containing an arrow pointing to the right to paste it into the "Variable" window. Click on OK.

You have now created a histogram like that presented in Figure 3.5 on p. 58. The histogram represents a continuum. The bars of the histogram represent a range of values. The number of observations that fall within each value determines the height of the bars. Some states did not execute a prisoner during this time period while some executed more than 100.

Creating Line Graphs with SPSS

A related method of presenting continuous data in graphic form is the **line graph** (or frequency polygon). It also demonstrates the flow of the variable from its lowest to its highest value. You will see that the line graph uses the same measurements on the vertical and horizontal axes that were used for the bar histogram about executed prisoners.

Actually, if we place a dot in the midpoint of each interval in the histogram and connect them all, we can form the line graph. Instead, we again summon SPSS to help us with this task.

1. In State Data Set I, on the top menu in the data window, highlight "Graphs" again. In the pop-down menu, highlight and click on "Line." "Simple" is already selected. Click on "Define."

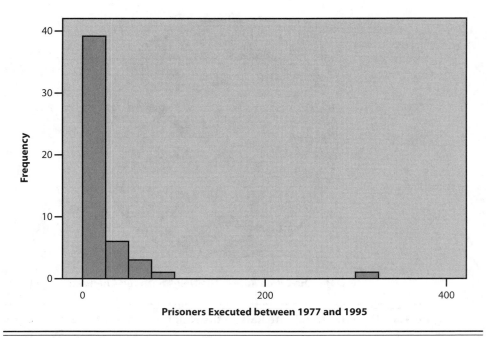

Figure 3.5   Histogram

2. The "Line Charts" menu now appears. The type of line chart graph that we want ("Simple") is already highlighted, so click the "Define" button.

3. The "Define Simple Line: Summaries for Groups of Cases" menu pops up. The left side of the window reveals all of the variables in State Data Set I. Move down this window until you see the variable "Prisoners Executed Between 1977 and 1995." Highlight this variable and then click on the box containing an arrow pointing to the right to paste it into the "Category Axis" window and click on OK.

You have now created a line chart like that presented in Figure 3.6 on p. 59. Does this pattern differ from that of the histogram?

A line graph (frequency polygon) is useful for describing the shape of how the data are distributed. When we work with continuous data, the shape of the distribution becomes very important. We explore this topic more fully in chapter 4. For now, we should note that most of the data fall to the left of the center of the distribution.

Presenting Your Results

After you have concluded your analysis and drawn your conclusions, you may be required to present your findings to an audience. A short time ago, it was common to hand out pieces of paper with charts and tables and ask your audience to refer to a particular item while you provide an explanation. Then,

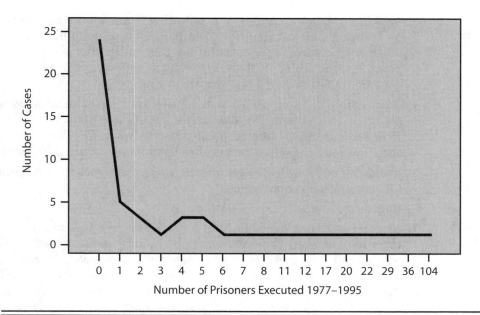

Figure 3.6   Prisoners Executed between 1977 and 1995

we started to utilize transparencies and overhead projectors in our presentations. Now there are more sophisticated methods of presenting data.

One of the more effective ways of making presentations is to use multimedia software programs such as Microsoft PowerPoint. You need to master a few simple skills in order to make successful presentations. The software is relatively easy to use effectively. Making effective presentations, however, is an art form that takes greater skills and preparation.

The following are some tips for making successful presentations using programs such as PowerPoint. The tips basically cover delivery of the presentation and creation of the content.

1. *Avoid placing too much information on a slide, and don't make too many slides.* A general rule we follow is no more than seven lines of text per slide. You don't want your audience concentrating on reading the slide and not listening to you. You also want to keep your presentation focused within the time allotted for the presentations, so keep the number of slides to a minimum. If needed, you can create slides and then hide them until you need to reveal them to the audience.

2. *Make the slides legible.* Use backgrounds that contrast with the text. We prefer to use darker (not black) backgrounds and lighter text. Also, make the fonts large enough to be seen from the back of a large room. We generally use 60-point type for major headings and 40-point for the main text. We also suggest that you use *sans serif* fonts (Helvetica is a good example) as serifs may appear fuzzy when projected.

3. *Avoid too much animation.* It is tempting to use all the tools that exist for creating slides. Animation to emphasize your point is great, but too much detracts from the presentation. Remember that you are the focal point, not the slides. If there is too much activity, your audience may not remain focused on what you are saying.

4. *Don't read from your slide.* Instead, use your slides to emphasize the points of your speech. We like to use bullets to emphasize our points. Talk around these bulleted points. Don't turn your back to the audience and read the slides—a surefire formula for losing your audience.

5. *Avoid complete sentences and paragraphs.* Be terse! One exception to this suggestion is quotations.

6. *Encourage audience participation.*

7. *Have a beginning, a middle, and a closing to your presentation.* Inform the audience what you are going to be talking about, make your main points, and then make your summary and conclusions. It is important to make a good impression with your opening sentence—why should they listen to you? Tell them what they will gain by listening, and then deliver! Some presenters suggest that the closing is the most important part of the presentation.

8. *Use handouts, when economically feasible.* PowerPoint has a wonderful feature for making handouts in the print menu. Inside PowerPoint, go to the drop-down menu, select which slides you want to print, then select "Handouts." Be sure to select "Print Pure Black and White" to remove backgrounds.

9. *Have a backup plan.* This technology is fragile and subject to malfunction and disruption. We suggest that you store your presentation on several different media (a CD and a server, for example) in case one fails. Depending on the importance of the presentation, you might want to consider making transparencies or printing copies of the slides.

10. *Check additional resources.* Time spent looking for additional resources can pay dividends in terms of improved presentations. Many Web sites offer training, tips, and additional PowerPoint backgrounds.

11. *Practice your delivery.*

Summary

Researchers must have a means of summarizing certain features of the data with which they are working. In this chapter, several methods of visually presenting data are introduced. Graphics can present data quickly, efficiently, and powerfully. Multimedia presentations are especially effective ways of presenting data.

Key Terms

Descriptive Statistics: measures that provide various ways of summarizing the data. We can count data (frequencies), as well as explain how the data are distributed (measures of central tendency and dispersion).

Bar Chart: a series of unconnected bars in a graph, with height representing the frequency of cases in each category

Pie Chart: a graphic circle in which each segment corresponds to the percentage of frequencies in each category. Like the bar chart, it is used with discrete data.

Histogram: a series of bars connected in a sequence. The height of the bars represents the frequencies of the values.

Line Graph: a series of connected points. The distance of each point from the baseline of the graph represents the frequency of the values. Like the histogram, it is used with continuous data.

Data Analysis

1. Using the NCSD data set, construct a bar chart using the following variables. Write a few sentences to describe what the chart represents. Be sure to present percentages on the bar chart from the SPSS program.

   a. Worry: Getting Mugged

   b. Police Confidence: Prevent Crime

   c. Rate Police: Respond Quickly to Calls

   d. How Satisfied with That Contact (Police)

2. Using the NCSD data set, construct a pie chart using the following variables. Write a few sentences to describe what the chart represents.

   a. Favor/Oppose Plea Bargaining

   b. Favor: Death Penalty for Murderers

   c. Which Marijuana Policy Do You Favor

   d. Armed 5 Best Defense Against Criminals

3. Using State Data Set I, construct a histogram for each Region of the country using the following variables and interpret the results.

   a. Crime Index Total per 100,000

   b. Prison Population, 12/31/95

   c. Number of Adults on Probation per 100,000 Adult Residents

   d. Number of Adults on Parole per 100,000 Adult Residents

4. Using the following table from chapter 1 on visitor robberies reported to the Miami-Dade Police Department, 2001–2005, go into SPSS and enter the data, both year and number of visitor robberies reported. Using SPSS, construct a line graph for each year. Be sure to fully label your graph. Print it out and write a paragraph to describe what the pat-

tern of visitor robberies over this time period represents. MAKE SURE THAT YOU NAME AND SAVE THIS DATA SET.

Miami Dade Police Department Visitor Robberies

Year	Number of Visitor Robberies Reported
2001	25
2002	10
2003	16
2004	30
2005	12

5. Using the following table from chapter 1 on homicides reported to the Minneapolis Police Department, 1995–2000, go into SPSS and enter the data, both year and number of homicides reported. Using SPSS, construct a line graph for each year. Be sure to fully label your graph. Print it out and write a paragraph to describe what the pattern of homicides over this time period represents. MAKE SURE THAT YOU NAME AND SAVE THIS DATA SET.

Minneapolis Police Department Homicides

Year	Number of Reported Homicides
1995	99
1996	86
1997	58
1998	58
1999	48
2000	50

chapter 4

Measures of Central Tendency

Statistical analysis provides information by organizing and summarizing data. Think of statistics as a way to describe the characteristics of a variable or sample efficiently and (we hope) effectively. Without them, data would be a jumbled mess, waiting to be somehow sorted out. The description of a data set involves the use of those measures that best represent a frequency distribution. We must determine the scores that are most "typical." These measures describe scores that are the most frequent, occupy the middle of the distribution, or represent the average score. These measures are the mode, the median, and the mean.

Measures of Central Tendency

Constructing a Frequency Distribution

To introduce the measures of central tendency, we use a variable from our State Data Set I. In State Data Set I, one of the variables is the number of prisoners executed between 1977 and 1995. The data are from all 50 states. The **frequency distribution** on the number of executions is presented in Table 4.1.

A number of standard methods are used to present data in a frequency distribution. The symbol X stands for the value of the variable. In this case, X is the number of prisoners executed. In the X column, the items are listed in order from the highest to the lowest value.

In the second column, f (which stands for "frequency") is the number of cases that assume a certain value; f is the number of states that have executed a number "X" of prisoners. Here, we see that one state has executed 104 prisoners (it happens to be Texas). This is by far the highest number. We also see at the bottom of the table that 24 states did not execute a prisoner during this time period. The total for the f column is labeled, for the number of cases—in this case the 50 states.

In the third column, fX is the total number of cases that assumes a value times the value itself. In this example, it would equal the number of prisoners executed, times the number of states that executed that many prisoners.

Table 4.1 Frequency Distribution—Prisoners Executed 1977–1995

X (Number of Prisoners Executed)	f (Number of States that Executed X Prisoners)	fX (f times X)
104	1	104
36	1	36
29	1	29
22	1	22
20	1	20
17	1	17
12	1	12
11	1	11
8	1	8
7	1	7
6	1	6
5	3	15
4	3	12
3	1	3
2	3	6
1	5	5
0	24	0
	$N = 50$	$\Sigma fX = 313$

Again, on the first line, one state executed 104 prisoners for a total of 104 executions. ΣfX is the sum of scores. Σ (sigma) is a Greek letter that represents "the sum of" in statistical terms. ΣfX indicates that we have multiplied all the X scores times f and then added the results together to arrive at the total number of prisoners executed during 1977–1995—313.

The Mode

The **mode** is the score that occurs most frequently in a distribution. In Table 4.1, zero (0) is the mode. Twenty-four states (0 under the X column, 24 under the f column) did not execute a single convicted offender between 1977 and 1995. Note the mode *is not* 104! That is, it is not the highest number. The mode *is also not* 24! That is, it is not the number of respondents/cases in a category. Zero is the mode because it is the score that has the greatest number of cases under the f column. Thus, the mode is the score that has the greatest number of cases under the f column, or the response/answer that occurs most often. It is the most frequently occurring category.

Consider, for example, that most states or "cases" ($f = 24$) reported zero executions as opposed to an alternative number or category of executions. In this example, the mode is determined for a continuous or ratio-level variable. While the mode (and median and mean) may all be calculated for ratio-level variables, the mode is the only measure of central tendency that is meaningful for nominal-level data. Consider, for example car colors (e.g., red, green, yellow, and black). There is no meaning to a mean or median color as each color has no numerical value (i.e., a code of "1" to represent "red" has simply a label meaning versus a scale meaning). However, suppose we know that 25 people own red cars, 15 people own yellow cars, 27 own green cars, and 30 own black cars. Then, we know that the majority of the individuals own black cars, and therefore the mode is black. Thus, the mode provides information about nominal-level data (e.g., car color) that has some meaning.

A frequency distribution may have more than one mode. If another value (number of executions) had a frequency of 24 in Table 4.1, it would also have been the mode. If a frequency distribution has two modes, it is termed bimodal. If it has more than two modes, it is called multimodal.

The mode does not necessarily occur in or near the center of a distribution. The mode can occur anywhere in a distribution. It does not indicate the range or variability between scores in a distribution. The mode simply indicates the response value(s) or categories that occur most frequently.

The Median

In a frequency distribution, when scores are placed in order from lowest to highest, the **median** is the middle of the distribution. Just like the middle of a road, the median divides the distribution in half. It is the 50th percentile. Fifty percent of the scores in the frequency distribution fall below it. This is the way that percentiles are always presented: the percentage of scores falling *below* that point. For example, if you took standardized tests in school growing up and scored in the 50th percentile, then you scored higher than one-half or 50 percent of the individuals taking the exam. Likewise, if you scored in the 95th percentile, only 5 percent of test takers scored higher than you! In SPSS, the values in the cumulative percentage column of a frequency distribution are interpreted in this way.

The median can be calculated easily and determined by inspection. In Table 4.1, we have data on executions in the 50 states. With the median, we must determine where the middle case lies. The median is computed by taking the total number of cases, adding one to the total and dividing by two. Here, $50 + 1 = 51$ and 51 divided by $2 = 25.5$. Counting up from the bottom of the frequency distribution, we see that 24 jurisdictions executed zero prisoners. Since we are looking for the 25.5th case, we need to keep moving up. Next, we see that 5 jurisdictions executed one prisoner during this period. Therefore, the median (here, the 25.5th case) falls in the category one (1). One is the median of this distribution. Half of the jurisdictions (about 26) executed one or zero prisoners between 1977 and 1995.

The median gives more information about the nature of the distribution than the mode. It tells us the score that divides the distribution into two equal halves. The mode tells us nothing about the center of the distribution. With this variable, the median tells us that half of the jurisdictions executed one prisoner or less during this period. Therefore, executions were rare in half of the states at this time.

One of the attributes of the median is stability. The median is unaffected by extreme scores. If one jurisdiction had executed 1,000 prisoners, it would just be one more state in the distribution. The median is calculated by counting the number of cases. It does not consider the value of the case. Although 1,000 prisoners would make this jurisdiction the leader in the number of executions, it would not affect the median.

The Mean

The **mean** is a statistic that you should be most familiar with. It is the average score in a distribution. We encounter averages on a regular basis. You have a grade point average that illustrates your average grade for the total number of credit hours that you have taken to this point. The sports pages bury us with statistics daily, and averages (i.e., batting averages, scoring averages per game in basketball) figure prominently in their coverage. The mean is one statistic that needs no introduction.

The formula for the mean is $\Sigma fX/N$. The mean is derived by adding all the scores in a distribution and dividing the total by the number of cases. Table 4.1 shows that a total of 313 prisoners ($\Sigma fX = 313$) were executed in the United States between 1977 and 1995. There were 50 jurisdictions ($N = 50$). The mean is 6.26 (313/50). Since we are talking about people here, it is simpler to interpret the mean this way: each state executed an average of six prisoners during the period 1977–1995.

Unlike the mode and median, the mean is sensitive to extreme scores (either very high or very low) in a distribution. Table 4.1 provides an excellent example of this sensitivity. One jurisdiction (Texas) executed 104 prisoners between 1977 and 1995. The next closest jurisdiction executed 36 prisoners, a difference of 68 prisoners. Therefore, 104 executions (Texas) was an extreme score in this distribution. Remember that the median for this distribution was only one. Half of the jurisdictions executed one or no prisoners during this time period. Yet our mean is 6.26—five points above the median. The number of executions in Texas drove up the average number of prisoners executed over the time period.

This occurs because the mean is computed using the value of each score in the distribution. The mode and median fail to use the value of each score in a distribution. The mode is derived from the frequency of the scores. The median is based on the position of the scores, regardless of their values. In addition, the mean is amenable to statistical analysis and comparisons between samples while the mode and median are not. Finally, the sum of the deviations from the mean (how far each score stands in relation to the mean) is zero—a concept we demonstrate fully in chapter 5.

The "Three Ms" text box presents a summary of all three measures of central tendency.

Calculation Formulas: The Three Ms

1. Mode: the most frequent score in a distribution.
2. Median: the midpoint of a distribution.
$$(N+1)/2$$
Where: N = the total number of cases
3. Mean: the average score in a distribution
$$\Sigma f X / N$$
Where: X = the score value
f = the number of times the score value occurred
Σ = the total value of the f times X

A Measure of Shape

The values of the measures of central tendency also determine the shape of a distribution. Figure 4.1 represents a **symmetrical distribution** in which the mean, median, and mode are equal in value. When this situation occurs, we see that half of the values fall to one side or the other when we plot the distribution.

Figure 4.2 is a **positively skewed** curve because the tail of the distribution follows the positive values along the X-axis of the distribution (toward the higher numbers on the X-axis). Here, the median falls to the right of the mode and the mean falls even further to the right of the median. If graphed, a variable representing the number of days it takes for someone to recidivate following release from incarceration would be an example of a positively skewed distribution. Consider, for example, that the majority of individuals released recidivate within two years, and as time passes individuals are less likely to recidivate. This means the majority of individuals will recidivate "immedi-

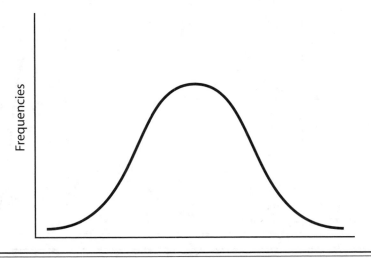

Figure 4.1   Symmetrical Distribution

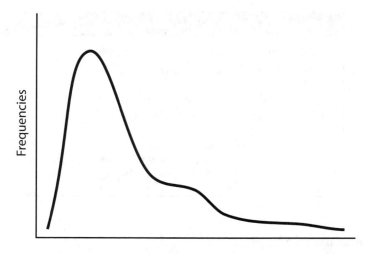

Figure 4.2   Positively Skewed Curve

ately" following release, while some will recidivate after a few years, some after additional years, and some (represented in the extreme positive tail) will never recidivate. Think about where the mode is located in the distribution. The mode in our recidivist example, representing the value that occurs most often, matches the majority of individuals who recidivate immediately or within the first 2 years of being released.

Figure 4.3 is a **negatively skewed** curve. The tail of the distribution follows the zero point of the *X*-axis (toward the negative values on the axis). The order of the measures of central tendency is reversed from that in a positively

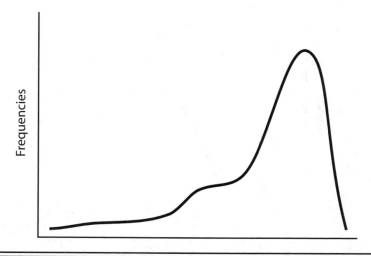

Figure 4.3   Negatively Skewed Curve

skewed curve. The median falls to the left of the mode and the mean falls even further to the left, past the median. Think about a variable whose distribution, when graphed, would be negatively skewed. Although not a criminal justice example, one's grades on exams could present a clear example of a negatively skewed distribution. Consider the following exam grades: 95, 97, 88, 92, 93, and 60. No mode exists in this distribution; however, the majority are "high" grades. These scores are represented in the "hump" on the positive/right side of the distribution. What happens to the average exam grade when the 60 is included? The average will decrease or be "skewed" by the inclusion of the 60 and therefore will move the distribution toward the negative values/left side of the distribution.

Why is the shape of the distribution important? In later chapters, we will see that the shape of the distribution is very important to our selection of the appropriate statistical test. Some of these tests are based on the assumption that the shape of the distribution is normal (also a concept that we will take up in chapter 7) or symmetrical. If we violate this assumption and use the wrong test for our analysis, we run the risk of making a Type II error with regard to the null hypothesis.

The basic point to remember is the relationship between the skewness of the distribution and the values of the mean, median, and mode. Remember how we pointed out that the study of methods of statistical analysis is linear? We have two good examples in this chapter. First, the mean is a very important measure that will be used extensively in upcoming chapters. The other example is skewness. Failure to understand these two concepts now will mean more difficulty in the future.

Using SPSS to Analyze Data

In this chapter, the frequency distributions were set up as tables, and we calculated the measures of central tendency by hand. However, we can use the computer and SPSS to analyze our two data sets throughout this text.

1. The first screen (Figure 4.4) is a menu of the actions you can take when you start the program. Our screen highlights State Data Set I.sav. Open the file.

2. On the second screen (Figure 4.5), you see the data set. On the top menu, highlight "Analyze." On the pop-down menu, highlight "Descriptive Statistics" and then "Frequencies." This is the method to obtain a frequency distribution and calculate the measures of central tendency.

3. The "Frequencies" menu now appears (Figure 4.6). The first window presents all of the variables in State Data Set I. Move down the window until you see "Prisoners Executed Between 1977 and 1995." Click on the arrow pointing to the right to paste this variable into the "Variables" window.

4. After the pasting is completed, you are ready to conduct analysis of this variable. Click on the "Statistics" button.

5. The "Frequencies: Statistics" menu appears (Figure 4.7). The measures of Central Tendency are on the right side of the menu. Click on the Mean, Median, Mode, and Sum boxes, and a check mark appears. Click on the "Continue" button.

6. Now return to the original "Frequencies" menu (Figure 4.8). Click on the "Format" button.

7. This takes you to the "Frequencies: Format" menu (Figure 4.9). Click on "Descending values" button. This arranges the distribution from the highest to the lowest values. Click the "Continue" button.

8. Go back to the "Frequencies" menu again (Figure 4.10). Click on "OK" button to generate the output.

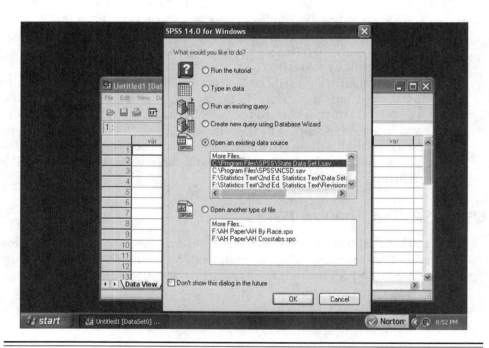

Figure 4.4

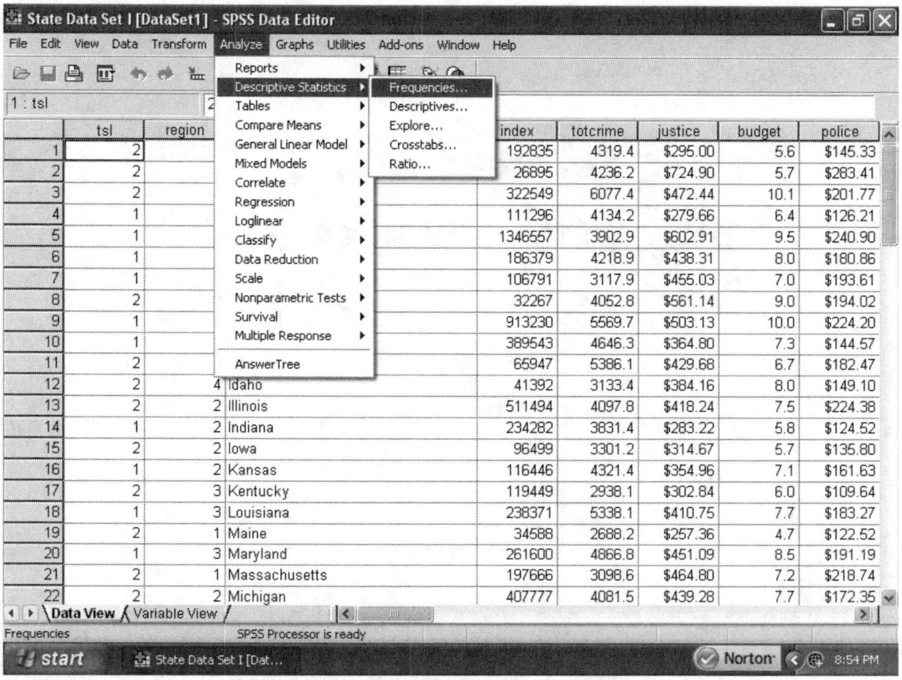

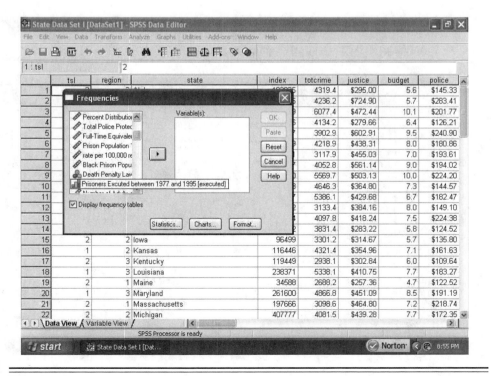

Figure 4.5

Figure 4.6

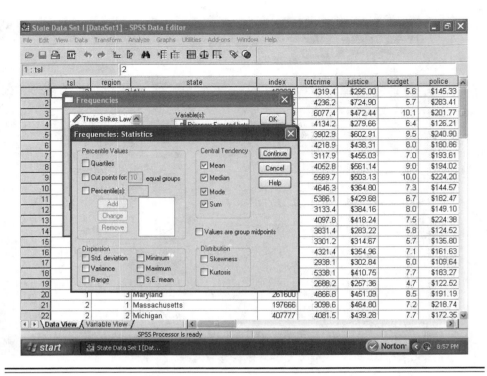

Figure 4.7

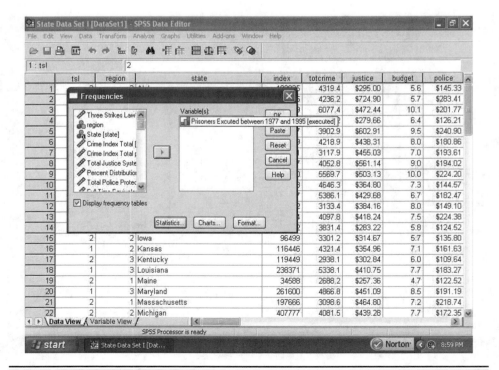

Figure 4.8

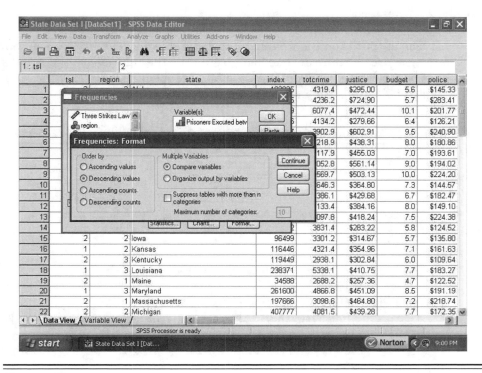

Figure 4.9

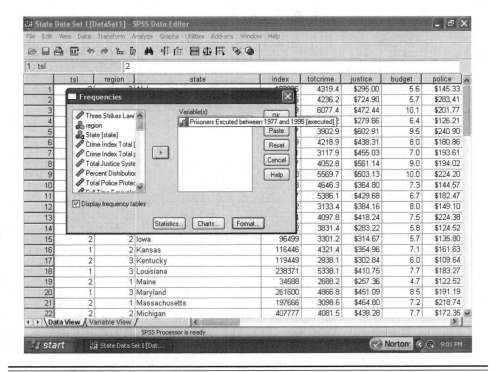

Figure 4.10

The output is on the final list, labeled Table 4.2. The first section contains our measures of central tendency. Note that the figures are the same as the ones we calculated earlier. Our N is 50. The mean is 6.26. It is the sum (313) divided by N (50). The median is one and the mode is zero.

Table 4.2   Measures of Central Tendency—Prisoners Executed 1977–1995

	Statistics		
N	Valid		50
	Missing		0
	Mean		6.26
	Median		1.00
	Mode		0
	Sum		313

Frequency Distribution

		Frequency	**Percent**	**Valid Percent**	**Cumulative Percent**
	104	1	2.0	2.0	2.0
	36	1	2.0	2.0	4.0
	29	1	2.0	2.0	6.0
	22	1	2.0	2.0	8.0
	20	1	2.0	2.0	10.0
	17	1	2.0	2.0	12.0
	12	1	2.0	2.0	14.0
	11	1	2.0	2.0	16.0
VALID	8	1	2.0	2.0	18.0
	7	1	2.0	2.0	20.0
	6	1	2.0	2.0	22.0
	5	3	6.0	6.0	28.0
	4	3	6.0	6.0	34.0
	3	1	2.0	2.0	36.0
	2	3	6.0	6.0	42.0
	1	5	10.0	10.0	52.0
	0	24	48.0	48.0	100.0
	Total	50	100.0	100.0	

The second section is our frequency distribution. The first column shows the X scores (number of prisoners executed). The second column is the f or frequency column, representing the number of states associated with each value. These were the first two columns of our original table.

Instead of the fX column, however, we now have three percentage columns: percent, valid percent, and cumulative percent. In the first column, we see that the mode (zero) accounts for 48 percent of all the cases (24/50). The valid percent column repeats this information. We have no missing cases on this variable. If we did, we would interpret this valid column because it would calculate the percentages on the cases that were not missing. The last column, cumulative percent, adds up the percentages from top to bottom. It gives you the percentage for each score, plus the percentage for the frequencies that preceded it. Here, we see how the median works. Note that at the median (one), we have 52 percent of the cases.

In this fashion, we can see just how powerful a PC armed with SPSS can be. It frees us from many tasks, including mathematical calculations and formulas (Thank goodness! More relief from math phobia!). Nevertheless, we must still interpret the findings and state the conclusions.

Summary

This chapter discussed the three measures of central tendency. The mode is the most frequently recurring score in a distribution. The median is the midpoint (50th percentile) of a distribution. Half of the scores in a distribution fall above and below the median. The mean is the average score in a frequency distribution. The measures of central tendency summarize the data in a distribution. They also provide an indication of how the scores fall in a distribution. Measures of shape reveal how far the distribution extends to the left (negative) or to the right (positive).

Key Terms

Frequency Distribution: a table that organizes a set of scores. The symbols used in a frequency distribution are

X Value of a score (raw score)

f Frequency of scores

N Total number of scores

$\Sigma f X$ The sum (total value) of scores

Mode: the score that occurs most frequently in a distribution. A frequency distribution may have more than one mode. If a frequency distribution has two modes, it is termed bimodal. If it has more than two modes, it is called multimodal.

Median: the midpoint in a distribution. The median divides the distribution in half. It is the 50th percentile. Fifty percent of the scores in the frequency distribution fall above and below it. The median is more stable than the mean because it is determined by position (and not value) in a distribution. It is less affected by extreme scores.

Mean: the average score in a distribution. Unlike the mode and median, the mean is sensitive to extreme scores (either very high or very low) in a distribution. It is computed by using the value of each score in the distribution. The mean is amenable to statistical analysis and comparisons between distributions. The sum of the deviations from the mean (how far each score stands in relation to the mean) is zero.

Symmetrical Distribution: the mean, median, and mode are equal in value

Positively Skewed Distribution: the tail of the distribution follows the positive values along the X-axis of the distribution (toward the higher numbers on the X-axis). Here, the median falls to the right of the mode and the mean falls even further to the right of the median.

Negatively Skewed Distribution: the tail of the distribution follows the zero point of the X-axis (toward the negative values on the axis). The order of the measures of central tendency is reversed from that in a positively skewed curve. The median falls to the left of the mode and the mean falls even further to the left, past the median.

Exercises

1. The following frequency distribution presents the number of prior drug arrests for a sample of probationers and parolees who are enrolled in a drug testing program. Compute the mode, median, and mean for this distribution. Write a concluding statement concerning the mean and what it represents.

Number of Prior Drug Arrests for Probationers and Parolees

X	f
10	1
9	2
7	2
6	6
5	16
4	16
3	24
2	59
1	128
0	311

2. The following frequency distribution presents the number of executions conducted in the "top ten" states between 1976 and 1995. Compute the mean of this distribution. Write a concluding statement concerning the mean and what it represents.

Executions in the "Top Ten" States between 1976 and 1995

	X	f
IL	7	1
NC	8	1
AR	11	1
AL	12	1
MO	17	1
GA	20	1
LA	22	1
VA	29	1
FL	36	1
TX	104	1

Data Analysis

1. With State Data Set I, use SPSS to get a frequency distribution and measures of central tendency for the following variables:

   a. Number of Juveniles Arrested (Under 18), 1997

   b. Number of Adults Arrested, 1997

   c. Number of Juveniles Arrested Violent Crimes (Under 18), 1997

   d. Number of Juveniles Arrested Property Crimes (Under 18), 1997

   e. Number of Adults Arrested Property Crimes, 1997

   f. Number of Adults Arrested Violent Crimes, 1997

   Read each table and write a few sentences about the mean and median of each distribution and what they represent.

2. With the NCSD set, use SPSS to get a frequency distribution and measure of central tendency for the variable Respondent's Age. Read the table and write a sentence about the mean and median of the distribution and what they represent.

3. Using State Data Set II, use SPSS to get a frequency distribution and measures of central tendency for the following variables:

   a. Number of Juveniles Arrested (Under 18), 2003

   b. Number of Adults Arrested, 2003

   c. Number of Juveniles Arrested Violent Crimes (Under 18), 2003

   d. Number of Juveniles Arrested Property Crimes (Under 18), 2003

   e. Number of Adults Arrested Property Crimes, 2003

   f. Number of Adults Arrested Violent Crimes, 2003

   Read each table and write a few sentences about the mean and median of each distribution and what they represent. How do the means from 1997 for these variables compare to those from 2003? What is the pattern—Which means are higher? Which means are lower? Did any means remain the same or very close in value?

4. With the data set that you saved in the last chapter (See below: Miami Dade Police Department Visitor Robberies), use SPSS to get a frequency distribution and the measures of central tendency from these data. Read the table and write a few sentences about the mean and median of the distribution and what they represent.

Miami Dade Police Department Visitor Robberies

Year	Number of Visitor Robberies Reported
2001	25
2002	10
2003	16
2004	30
2005	12

5. With the data set that you saved in the last chapter (See below: Minneapolis Police Department Homicides), use SPSS to get a frequency distribution and the measures of central tendency from these data. Read
the table and write a few sentences about the mean and median of the
distribution and what they represent.

Minneapolis Police Department Homicides

Year	Number of Reported Homicides
1995	99
1996	86
1997	58
1998	58
1999	48
2000	50

chapter 5

Measures of Dispersion

The fundamental task of social science research is to determine if variation exists. Once we have determined that it does, our goal is to answer the questions of how and why this variation occurs. For example, if a set of scores (e.g., crime statistics across different cities) had no variation, then it would not be necessary to do statistical analysis. No difference would exist among the crime rates in the cities. No variation would need to be explained. Any score would describe the distribution. That is, it would not matter whether one city had a lower unemployment rate, less drug abuse, or better-educated populace.

Measures of central tendency do not describe how scores stand in relation to one another. One measure of central tendency, however, the mean, provides the starting point for such analysis through the creation of a benchmark. How scores stand in relation to the mean provides one measure of dispersion. Measures of dispersion consider the spread or distance between scores. This chapter explores dispersion of variability and how it is used to describe the variation in a data set.

Measures of Dispersion Defined

Measures of dispersion, also known sometimes as measures of variability, are a type of descriptive statistics that, as the name suggests, provide information concerning the extent of how the values (or scores) for each case in any given variable are distributed. We can combine this information with other descriptive statistics, such as measures of central tendency and shape, to improve our ability to describe our variable efficiently and effectively. When we perform other types of statistical analysis, the measures of central tendency, shape, and dispersion are the foundation for the calculations.

The following explanation of measures of dispersion are arranged in terms of the level of measurement that you should be familiar with: index of dispersion for nominal levels of measurement, the range for ordinal levels of measurement, and standard deviation for internal-ration levels of measurement.

The Index of Dispersion

The index of dispersion is used to analyze nominal level data and is a value from 0 to 1. When one category of a variable contains the majority of cases, then the index of dispersion would be zero or close to zero. This result means the data have minimal dispersion or variability. When the value is one or near one, then the frequencies of the variable categories are more equally dispersed. This result means the cases have maximum dispersion or variability. Suppose there were 20 individuals in a room. If all 20 were male, then the index of dispersion would be 0; there is no variability since all 20 cases are male. However, if there were 10 males and 10 females in the room, then the index of dispersion would be 1, as each category (male and female) contain an equal number for maximum variability across the categories. Although the index of dispersion also provides a measure of dispersion for ordinal level data, it is rarely used.

The Range

The simplest measure of variability in a set of scores is the **range,** which is the distance between the highest and lowest scores in a distribution. Ordinal or higher data are required; otherwise, it would be impossible to rank the scores in this fashion. Of course, one may want to compute the range between frequencies of ordinal level data. The interpretation of this range computation for ordinal level data is a difference in categorical occurrences versus a difference in raw data scores. The formula for the range is presented next.

$$\text{The Range} = H - L$$
$$\text{Where:} \quad H = \text{the highest score in the data set}$$
$$L = \text{the lowest score in the data set}$$

Table 5.1 shows a frequency distribution of the number of prior arrests for drug offenses among Tuesday's drug court clients. In the score (X) column, we see that the greatest number of prior arrests for drug offenses was six and the fewest was two, so the range was four $(6 - 2 = 4)$.

Table 5.2 presents an example of data on the number of homicides committed in 30 cities in the state (pop. > 50,000). Here, the highest number of homicides was 10 and the lowest was zero, so the range was ten $(10 - 0 = 10)$.

Both of the examples above involve range calculations using ratio level data, that is, the "number of prior arrests" and the "number of homicides committed." Suppose the data presented in Table 5.2 were grouped (in categories) by city population: 50,001–60,000; 60,001–70,000; and so on up until 150,001–160,000. Though the range in number of homicides

Table 5.1   Number of Prior Arrests for Drug Offenses Among Tuesday's Drug Court Clients

X	f	fX	x $(X - \text{the Mean})$	fx^2
6	1	6	2	4
5	1	5	1	1
4	1	4	0	0
3	1	3	−1	1
2	1	2	−2	4
	$N = 5$	$\Sigma fX = 20$	$\Sigma x = 0$	$\Sigma fx^2 = 10$

Table 5.2 Number of Homicides Committed in 30 Cities in the State (pop. > 50,000)

X	f	fx	x (X – the mean)	x^2	fx^2
10	1	10	5.1	26.01	26.01
9	2	18	4.1	16.81	33.62
8	3	24	3.1	9.61	28.83
7	1	7	2.1	4.41	4.41
6	2	12	1.1	1.21	2.42
5	12	60	0.1	0.01	0.12
4	1	4	– 0.9	0.81	0.81
3	1	3	– 1.9	3.61	3.61
2	3	6	– 2.9	8.41	25.23
1	2	2	– 3.9	15.21	30.42
0	2	0	– 4.9	24.01	48.02
	N = 30	ΣfX = 146			Σfx² = 203.5

among these cities is 10, we may also interpret the range by city population. For example, "The greatest difference in number of homicides is between cities with 70–80,000 and 100–110,000 people." This interpretation is possible when data are ordinal level or frequencies are presented using grouped data.

The range is a limited measure of variability. It uses only the scores at the extreme ends (the highest and the lowest) of the distribution. Like the mean, the range responds to these extreme scores. It tells us nothing about how the scores between them fall. There could be a great difference between the ends of the distribution but little variation within the extremes. Similarly, there might be very little difference between highest and lowest scores in the data set, with a majority of cases falling into one category. Additionally, the range does not tell us "where" the data are. For example, if the range of test scores equals "10," we are not sure whether the scores ranged from 100 to 90 or from 70 to 60. The range does not deal with these possibilities.

The Variance and Standard Deviation

The most commonly used measures of dispersion are the **variance** (designated by σ^2, lowercase Greek sigma, in the case of populations, or s^2 for samples) and the **standard deviation**. The mean is used as the reference point, rather than the ends of the distribution. These measures are based upon the distance of each score from the mean of the distribution. Therefore, all of the scores in the data set are used. Because they are based upon the mean, the variance and standard deviation require interval or ratio level data.

The first step in this process is the calculation of deviation scores—how each score stands in relation to the mean. If you think about it, this is a very common process. You do this naturally, comparing your performance to the average. Everyone wants to know how he or she is doing compared to the average score. When tests are returned to you, your instructor typically reports the mean or average score. What is the very first thing you do in response to this information? Naturally, you calculate how well you did in relation to the mean. Is your score above or below average? Your calculation here is a deviation score—how your score stands in relation to the mean.

The data set in Table 5.1 reveals how this process works. Here, we have the number of prior drug arrests for five clients who appeared in Tuesday's drug court. The mean number of prior drug arrests was four ($\Sigma fx/N = 4$ or $20/5 = 4$). Our next step is to calculate how far each score (person in this case) stood in relation to this mean of four. The deviation score (x) is calculated by subtracting the mean from each score in the distribution.

On the first line of Table 5.1 is the score six. If we subtract the mean of four from six, we get a deviation score of two. This person had two more prior drug arrests than the average person appearing before the drug court on Tuesday. This process is repeated for each score in the distribution.

Now, we run into a bit of a problem. Remember that in chapter 4 we said that one of the characteristics of the mean is that the sum of the deviations from the mean equals zero ($\Sigma x = 0$). In the fourth column of Table 5.1, we see this "magic" at work. When we sum up the deviation scores in the fourth column ($x = X -$ the Mean), the total is zero. The sum of the deviations from the mean in this distribution does indeed equal zero. This is a point in the process to check your calculations if you are doing so by hand. The sum of the deviations will always equal zero.

What can we do now? In the fourth column, note that the positive deviation scores of the values above the mean are cancelled out by the negative deviation scores of the values that fell below the mean. This is precisely why we are always left with zero when we sum up the deviation scores in a distribution.

The remedy for this dilemma is to square every deviation score. Remember from your early math course that a negative value times a negative value equals a positive value. Squaring each deviation score cancels out the negative numbers.

When we take this step (in the fifth column of Table 5.1—fx^2), we have positive numbers that add up to 10 ($\Sigma fx^2 = 10$). This total is called the **sum of squares** because it represents the total number of squared deviation scores from the mean of the distribution. This step is a crucial part of the calculation of the variance and standard deviation.

Actually, we have created a new frequency distribution. It is based upon how each case stands in relation to the mean through the use of the deviation score (x). Just as we have done before, we can now calculate another average score (or mean)—the variance. The variance is the mean of the squared deviations from the mean. This definition is actually a verbal formula—a description of how the variance is calculated. The variance represents the average squared deviations that each score stands in relation to the mean of the distribution.

A slight difference in the computation of these two measures of dispersion exists in terms of the divisor. The formulas are shown in the box on the following page.

Calculation Formulas: Variance and Standard Deviation

1. Deviation Score: $x = (X - \bar{X})$
2. Population Variance:

$$\sigma^2 = \frac{\Sigma(X - \bar{X})^2}{N}$$

Where:

X = the value of each element or observation in the population

$\bar{X}$ = the sample mean

N = the number of cases or observations in the population

3. Sample Variance: The formula for the variance of a sample is

$$s^2 = \frac{\Sigma(X - \bar{X})^2}{n-1}$$

Where:

X = the value of each element or observation in the sample

$\bar{X}$ = the sample mean

n = the number of cases or observations in the sample

4. Standard Deviation: $\sqrt{s^2}$

To summarize, here are the steps involved in calculating the variance:

1. Calculate the deviation score (x) for each score by subtracting the score from the mean of the distribution.

2. Square each deviation score to remove negative numbers.

3. Multiply each deviation score by its frequency (f).

4. Calculate the sum of squares (Σfx^2).

5. Divide the sum of squares by the number of cases.

The variance is a measure of the spread of scores in a distribution around its mean. The larger the variance, the greater the spread of scores around the mean. The smaller the variance, the more closely the scores are distributed around the mean. In Table 5.1, the variance equals two ($\Sigma fx^2/N = 2$ or $10/5 = 2$).

Because we squared the deviation scores around the mean in order to clear the negative numbers and arrive at a number other than zero, it is necessary to take one more step to determine a meaningful measure of dispersion. The standard deviation is the square root of the variance. Taking the square root of the variance compensates for the fact that we had to square all the deviation scores in order to clear the negative numbers (step 2 above). In Table 5.1, the standard deviation equals 1.41 ($\sqrt{2}$). Like the variance, the definition of the standard deviation is actually a verbal formula. It tells us how to calculate the standard deviation.

The standard deviation is a measure of dispersion of the scores around the mean. Remember that the key to the measurement of variation is the deviation score—how each score stands in relation to the mean of the distribution. If the score is equal to the mean, the deviation score will be zero. The higher the standard deviation, the greater is the spread in the scores. The lower the standard deviation, the closer the scores are on average from the mean of the distribution.

Let's do another example, from Table 5.2, using the steps to calculate the variance.

1. Calculate the deviation score (x) for each score by subtracting the score from the mean of the distribution. The mean of this distribution is 4.9. See the first line of the table; the score is 10. The deviation score is 5.1 This process is repeated for each score in the distribution.

2. Square each deviation score to remove negative numbers. Again, on the first line of Table 5.2, when we square the deviation score of 5.1, we get 26.01. This process is repeated for the entire distribution.

3. Multiply each deviation score by its frequency (f). The score 10 occurred once in the distribution, so 26.01 times one equals 26.01. This process is repeated for the entire distribution.

4. Calculate the sum of squares ($\Sigma f x^2$). When we sum the figures in the last column, we get 203.5.

5. Divide the sum of squares by the number of cases (Variance = $\Sigma f x^2 / N$ = 6.8 or 203.5/30 = 6.8).

Beginning with the deviation score (x) column, we have created a new frequency distribution based upon the deviation score values. The x column is simply another version of the X (score) column with which we began. But we then had to square each x value to clear the negative numbers and end up with a number that we work with—unlike zero! The variance is the mean of the distribution of squared deviation scores.

The standard deviation is the square root of the variance. In Table 5.2, the variance is 6.8. The square root of 6.8 is 2.6. This is the standard deviation for this distribution.

Calculating Measures of Dispersion with SPSS

Naturally, we can generate measures of dispersion for a data set using our SPSS software. For example, let us calculate these measures for the variable "Prisoners executed between 1977 and 1995" from State Data Set I.

Follow these steps:

1. The first screen is a menu of the actions we can take when we start the program. Our screen highlights "Open an existing file" and the file that we wish to use is State Data Set I. Open the file.

2. On the second screen (Figure 5.1), we see the data set. On the top menu, highlight "Analyze." On the pop-down menu, highlight "Descriptive Statistics" and then "Frequencies."

3. The "Frequencies" menu now appears (Figure 5.2). The first window presents all of the variables in the State Data Set I. Move down the window until you see "Prisoners Executed Between 1977 and 1995." Click on the arrow pointing to the right to paste this variable into the "Variables" window.

4. After the pasting is completed, you are ready to conduct some analysis of this variable. Click on the "Statistics" button.

5. The "Frequencies: Statistics" menu appears (Figure 5.3). The measures of central tendency are on the right side of the menu. Click on the "Mean," "Median," "Mode," and "Sum" boxes and a check mark will appear.

6. The measures are in the "Dispersion" box in the lower left-hand corner of the menu. Click on the "Std. deviation," "Variance," and "Range" boxes. A check mark will appear in each box. Click on the "Continue" button.

7. You now return to the original "Frequencies" menu (Figure 5.4). Click on "OK" button to generate the output.

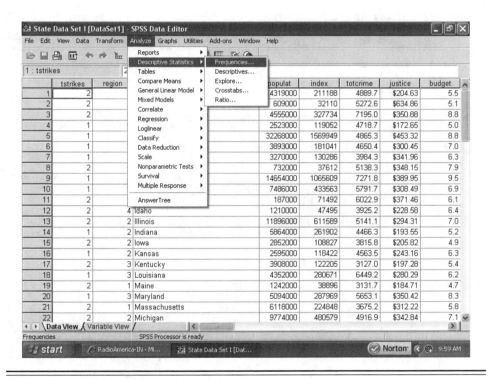

Figure 5.1

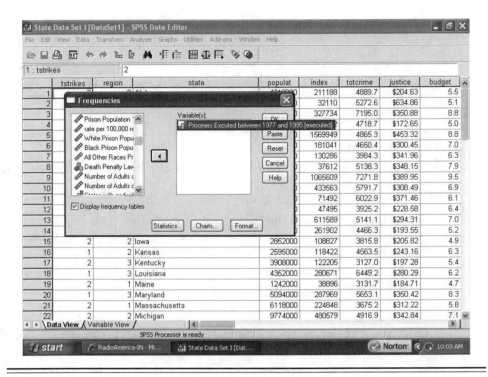

Figure 5.2

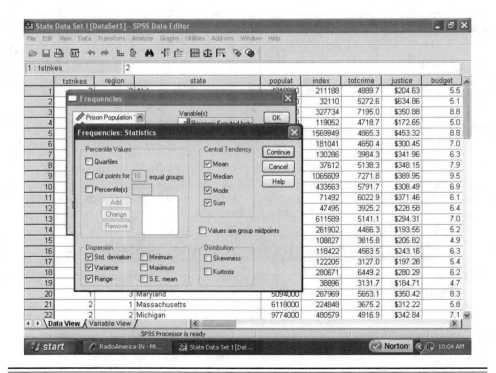

Figure 5.3

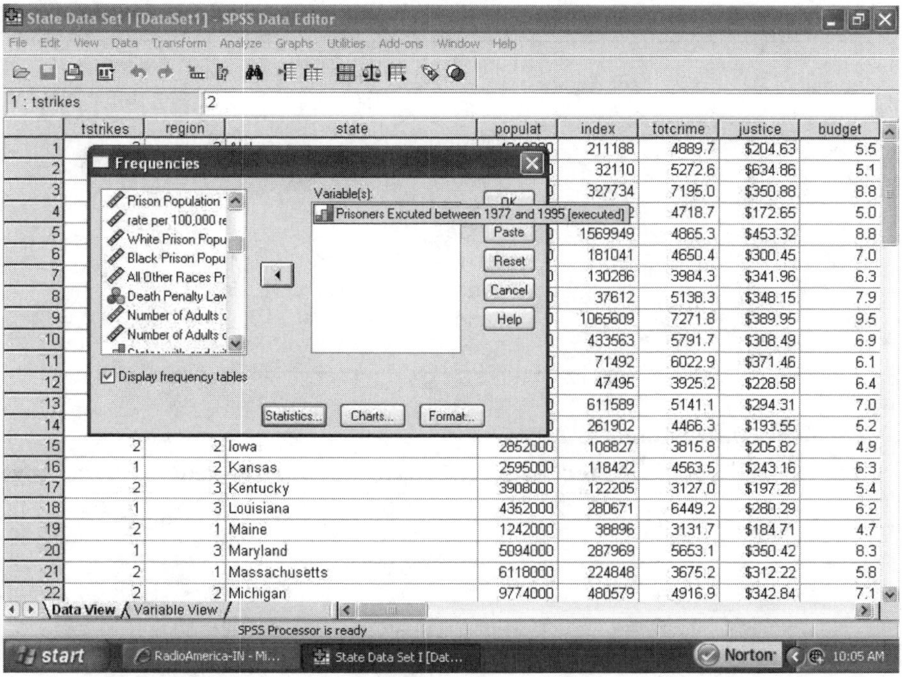

Figure 5.4

The output is on the final list. It is labeled Table 5.3 and appears on p. 88. The first section contains the measures of central tendency. Our N is 50. The mean is 6.26. It is the sum (313) divided by N (50). The median is one and the mode is zero.

The measures of dispersion are also in the first section. The range (104) is the value that results from subtracting the lowest score in the distribution (0) from the highest score (104). The variance (259.79) was calculated by the program in the same steps that we have reviewed. The program does not show us all of these calculations. The standard deviation is the square root of the variance The second box is our frequency distribution.

Once again, the use of the SPSS program spares you a number of fairly tedious calculations. The steps taken to calculate the variance and standard deviation, however, give you a better indication of what they represent. You must be able to run the program and interpret the results.

Table 5.3   Measures of Dispersion—Prisoners Executed 1977–1995

Statistics

N	Valid	50
	Missing	0
	Mean	6.26
	Median	1.00
	Mode	0
	Standard Deviation	16.12
	Variance	259.79
	Range	104
	Sum	313

Frequency Distribution

		Frequency	Percent	Valid Percent	Cumulative Percent
	0	24	48.0	48.0	48.0
	1	5	10.0	10.0	58.0
	2	3	6.0	6.0	64.0
	3	1	2.0	2.0	66.0
	4	3	6.0	6.0	72.0
	5	3	6.0	6.0	78.0
	6	1	2.0	2.0	80.0
	7	1	2.0	2.0	82.0
VALID	8	1	2.0	2.0	84.0
	11	1	2.0	2.0	86.0
	12	1	2.0	2.0	88.0
	17	1	2.0	2.0	90.0
	20	1	2.0	2.0	92.0
	22	1	2.0	2.0	94.0
	29	1	2.0	2.0	96.0
	36	1	2.0	2.0	98.0
	104	1	2.0	2.0	100.0
	Total	50	100.0	100.0	

Summary

To determine the spread in scores, the most accurate measures are based upon the deviation score—the distance between the mean of the distribution and each score in it. In this chapter, we calculate deviation scores, the variance, and the standard deviation. Further analysis of the variance is the heart of statistical explanation in criminal justice.

Unlike the index of dispersion and the range, the variance and standard deviation are calculated for every score in the distribution. For this reason, they are much more useful measures of dispersion.

These measures are used later when we attempt to determine the source of variability. Such an analysis can help us determine the factors that contribute to crime or to the success or failure of a program or policy. We discuss how these measures are used in the next chapter.

Key Terms

Index of Dispersion: used to analyze dispersion of nominal level data and varies between 0 and 1

Range: $(H - L)$. used to analyze dispersion of ordinal or higher data and is the distance between the highest and lowest scores in a distribution

Variance: the mean of the squared deviations from the mean

Standard Deviation: the square root of the variance

Sum of Squares (Σfx^2): the endpoint of the process involved in calculating the variance and standard deviation. First, you determine the distance between each score and the mean of the distribution. You then square these deviation scores, multiply them by f, and sum these scores to arrive at the sum of squares

Exercises

1. Return to the data for questions 1 and 2 in chapter 3 and calculate the variance and standard deviation.

2. A court administrator wants to examine burglary case disposition times in his city. A random sample of 50 burglary cases disposed of during the previous year is drawn. The numbers that follow represent the number of days needed for each case:

   70 35 86 81 63 71 58 53 99 85 64 56 17 38 94 78 101 71 63 65
   58 49 88 70 51 61 80 67 53 74 73 29 64 48 98 78 67 65 76 59
   50 65 98 91 66 64 69 86 63 74

   a. Construct a frequency distribution from these data. Start with the highest score (X) and proceed down to the lowest score. The f column will indicate the frequency or how often the score occurred.

   b. Calculate the mean, variance, and standard deviation.

3. In chapter 1, question 9 presented data from the New York City Police Department on Index Crimes for the period 1990–2005. The following number of murders was reported:

1990:	2262
1995:	1181
1998:	629
2001:	649
2005:	540

   a. Construct a frequency distribution from these data. Start with the highest score (X) and proceed down to the lowest score. The f column will indicate the frequency or how often the score occurred.

      b. Calculate the mean, variance, and standard deviation.

      c. Construct a line graph using these data. Write a paragraph about the mean and the pattern demonstrated in the graph.

Data Analysis

1. Using the State Data Set I and SPSS, calculate the mean, variance, and standard deviation for the following index crimes for all 50 states in 1997 (murder, rape, robbery, assault, and burglary). What can you say about your results?

2. Using the State Data Set I and SPSS, calculate the mean, variance, and standard deviation for the number of Handgun Homicides in all 50 states. What can you say about your results?

3. With the State Data Set I, use SPSS to get a frequency distribution and measures of dispersion (range, variance, and standard deviation) for the following variables and interpret the results:

      a. Number of Juveniles Arrested (under 18), 1997

      b. Number of Adults Arrested, 1997

      c. Number of Juveniles Arrested Violent Crimes (under 18), 1997

      d. Number of Juveniles Arrested Property Crimes (under 18), 1997

      e. Number of Adults Arrested Property Crimes, 1997

4. Using the State Data Set II and SPSS, calculate the mean, variance, and standard deviation for the following index crimes for all 50 states in 2003 (murder, rape, robbery, assault, and burglary). What can you say about your results?

5. Using the State Data Set II and SPSS, calculate the mean, variance, and standard deviation for the number of Handgun Homicides in all 50 states in 2002. What can you say about your results?

6. With the State Data Set II, use SPSS to get a frequency distribution and measures of dispersion (range, variance, and standard deviation) for the following variables and interpret the results:

      a. Number of Juveniles Arrested (under 18), 2003

      b. Number of Adults Arrested, 2003

      c. Number of Juveniles Arrested Violent Crimes, 2003

      d. Number of Juveniles Arrested Property Crimes (under 18), 2003

      e. Number of Adults Arrested Property Crimes, 2003

7. Compare your answers from State Data Set I to those from State Data Set II. How do these statistics compare? Are there any differences between your 1997 and 2003 results? What do you think they mean?

chapter 6

Contingency Table Analysis

In the preceding chapters, we introduced descriptive statistics. Sometimes referred to as univariate statistics, this type of statistical analysis summarizes the distinguishing characteristics of the data drawn from a sample. In this chapter, we move to inferential statistics. Inferential statistics allow us to go beyond description and attempt to answer this basic question: "Would the research findings be true if we had the data from the entire population rather than just the sample?" Can we have confidence in the results of the research?

Nonparametric statistics make it possible to analyze data that are categorical (measured at the nominal or ordinal levels). In this chapter, we present some statistical measures that are designed to deal with categorical data.

Nonparametric Statistics

One method of examining the relationship between independent (X) and dependent (Y) variables is contingency table analysis. **Parametric statistics** make a number of assumptions about the way that the population that serves as the basis of our research sample is distributed. For example, one assumption is that the variables under study that were drawn from the population are normally distributed.

Other assumptions behind the use of parametric statistics include

1. Independent observations: the measurement or selection of one case does not affect the measurement or selection of another case.

2. The level of measurement for the variables is at least interval in nature.

To conduct a valid analysis, these assumptions must be met before parametric methods can be used. If they cannot be met, then the researcher has the option of using **nonparametric statistics.** They are particularly appropriate when you have nominal or ordinal level data, and they require no assumptions about the population parameters.

Parametric statistics are usually preferred because they are more powerful. The **power of a statistic** involves the acceptance of a false null hypothesis. The null hypothesis (H_0) is a statement of no difference or no relationship between two variables. This is the hypothesis that is tested in hypothesis testing. For example, in the first relationship that we will examine in this chapter, the null hypothesis would be that there is no difference in the death penalty support among persons of different races. A research or alternative hypothesis (H_1) states some relationship between two variables. Both the choice of variables and the "relationship" stated in an alternative hypothesis is grounded in theory or prior research. Research on death penalty attitudes has clearly demonstrated that African Americans are more likely than whites to oppose capital punishment. In this case, the acceptance of a false null hypothesis would lead us to conclude (in error) that there is no difference in support for capital punishment among persons of different races. The likelihood of reaching the conclusion that there are no differences between the sample and the population when, in fact, there are (in other words, committing a Type II error) decreases as the power of a statistic becomes greater. Also, if sample sizes are sufficiently large, the assumptions listed above can be violated because some parametric statistics are **robust.**

It is difficult, however, to overcome the requirement that the variables be measured at least at the interval level. To do a t-test, you must be able to calculate a mean, and you cannot calculate a mean when you have nominal or ordinal data. Under these conditions, nonparametric measures are more appropriate.

In this chapter, we consider one particular nonparametric measure, chi-square (χ^2), and some of the measures of association that are used with nominal and ordinal data. Chi-square is most appropriate when the data is divided into mutually exclusive categories that cannot be legitimately summed up—data measured at the nominal or ordinal level. Chi-square tells us whether the observed distribution is significantly different from the one that we would expect to occur by chance.

Constructing Contingency Tables

A **contingency table** is a joint frequency distribution—a frequency distribution with two categorical variables. Once again, we are concerned with the relationship between an independent and a dependent variable. It is also known as a **crosstabulation** because it counts the cases that fall into each cell of the table. The cells contain those cases that fall into each pairing of the variables—the number of cases that fit the categories described by the cross-listing of the variables. The joint frequencies fall within the cells of the table under the categories for the independent and dependent variables. It is called a contingency table because the cases contained along the rows (the categories of the dependent variable) are contingent upon what is contained along the columns (the categories of the independent variables).

Consider a crosstabulation of race and attitudes toward capital punishment (the death penalty for murderers) from the National Crime Survey Data set (see Table 6.1). Our research hypothesis is that whites are more likely to favor capital punishment for murderers than are minorities.

The examination of a relationship typically begins with a look at the frequency distribution of a variable, including the percentages within each cate-

Table 6.1 Relationship Between Race and Attitudes toward Capital Punishment

Do you favor the death penalty for murderers?	Whites	Minorities	Total
Favor	607 (78.5%)	100 (48.5%)	707 (72.2%)
Oppose	104 (13.5%)	85 (41.3%)	189 (19.3%)
Neither	62 (8.0%)	21 (10.2%)	83 (8.5%)
Total	773 (100%)	206 (100%)	979 (100%)

gory as it relates to the entire group. Note that the fourth column of the table is actually the frequency distribution of the answers to the question "Do you favor the death penalty for murderers?"

In a contingency table, such total frequencies are called **marginals** because they are presented at the margins of the table. The marginal frequencies fall under the total values for each column value and each row value. The table reveals that more than 72 percent of the respondents (707 or 72.2 percent) favor the death penalty for murderers. Almost 20 percent of the respondents (19.3 percent) oppose capital punishment, and 8.5 percent are not certain about its use. The total column frequencies indicate that a total of 773 whites and 206 members of minority groups responded to this survey item. The grand total of survey respondents was 979. What conclusions can we draw from this frequency distribution? The majority of respondents support the death penalty (more than 72 percent). We cannot say any more about this question, but it is a starting point. If we examine the attributes of the respondents, we can examine death penalty opinion more fully.

With this method, we are usually concerned with subgroup analysis. Here, we examine the breakdown of frequencies and percentages of the dependent variable as they are categorized under the independent variable. The assumption is that the independent variable, race of the respondents, produces an effect on the dependent variable, attitude toward the death penalty.

The table lists the independent and dependent variables. The usual procedure is to construct the table so that the independent variable is listed along the columns and the dependent variable follows the rows. Because you are interested in the impact of the independent variable upon the dependent variable, the table is read by comparing the percentage value of the column (the independent variable) for the subgroups under the dependent variable (row values). Tabulate the percentages along the columns of the table and then compare the percentages across the rows to see if the dependent variable totals differ within each category of the independent variable. The typical way to examine a contingency table is to look for patterns in this manner.

A crosstabulation simply breaks down this frequency distribution with the introduction of an independent variable. For example, we can examine whether race has an impact upon attitude toward capital punishment. The crosstabulation of the two variables begins with the first cell of the table, whites that favor capital punishment. All the cells of the table follow the same pattern. They present the frequencies of the two variables taken together.

They sort out and reconfigure the data according to your research question. The table is a joint frequency distribution between race and attitude toward capital punishment.

In a contingency table, comparisons between the groups are made in terms of the percentages of each cell, not the number of cases. It is not necessary for the different groups to be equal in size. The percentages take the difference between group sizes into account and give us a common method of measurement that can serve as a basis for comparison.

In Table 6.1, we can see that a higher percentage of whites favor the death penalty in murder cases by a difference of 30 percentage points (whites, 78.5 percent, minorities, 48.5 percent). Minorities are three times more likely to say that they oppose capital punishment (41.3 versus 13.5 percent). Therefore, our conclusion is that whites are more likely to support and minority group members are more likely to oppose capital punishment. The percentage difference is an indicator of the strength of the relationship between the two variables. Now that we know a difference exists, we are interested in other questions. For example, is this difference "real"; i.e., if we repeated our study, would we obtain the same results, or did we get this result by chance alone? This question will be addressed in the sections that follow.

Summary: Rules for the Construction and Interpretation of Tables

When constructing and interpreting contingency tables, the following steps are recommended:[1]

1. Divide the sample into categories based upon the values of the independent variable.
2. The table should be fully labeled. The categories of the independent and dependent variables should be clearly presented. The variable headings should describe what is contained in the table.
3. The independent variable follows the columns of the table. The dependent variable follows the rows of the table.
4. Each subgroup is described in terms of the categories of the dependent variable.
5. To read the table, compare the percentages of the independent variable subgroups in terms of the percentages of the subgroups of the dependent variable.

Following these steps leads to the correct construction and interpretation of contingency tables. The proper use of percentages reveals the relationship (or lack thereof) between the independent and dependent variables.

Chi-Square Test for Independent Samples

Our conclusions about Table 6.1 are based upon our observation of the survey responses. In statistical analysis, conclusions typically result from a description of the findings. Inferential statistics then allow us to make a decision about the null hypothesis and whether this finding would hold true if we had the data from the entire population. In our example, a statistical test is needed to determine whether we can assume that this difference in attitudes on capital punishment between racial groups also exists in the entire population.

The data are at the nominal (race) and ordinal (support for capital punishment) levels of measurement. The groups and the choices fall into different categories. We can use chi-square to tell us the probability that the frequencies we observed in our survey results **(observed frequencies)** differ from an expected (hypothesized) set of frequencies. With chi-square, these **expected frequencies** represent what we could expect to occur by chance.

The survey results showed that about 79 percent of the white and 53 percent of the minority respondents supported the use of capital punishment for convicted murderers. The possibility exists, however, that these findings were due to sampling error and do not represent an actual difference in the entire population. With chi-square, the question is "Are the observed frequencies significantly different from the expected frequencies?" Can the null hypothesis (no difference in support for capital punishment among racial groups) be rejected?

Chi-square is based upon the differences between observed and expected frequencies. It tells us the level of probability of obtaining the difference between the observed and expected frequencies. If the observed frequencies (in this case, survey results) differ substantially (.05 level of significance) from the expected frequencies (what we expect to occur by chance), then the null hypothesis can be rejected. If they do not substantially differ, the difference between the two sets of frequencies could be due to sampling error. The accompanying boxes present the formulas used to calculate the chi-square statistic.

The difference between the observed and expected frequencies forms the basis for the chi-square test. Chi-square is a popular test because it can be used with any number of samples that are divided into any number of categories (or responses). It can be used with variables at any level of measurement that are divided into categories. Another reason that it is popular is the small number of restrictions placed on its use. The limitations on the use of chi-square are as follows:

1. The sample must be randomly selected.

2. Each category must be **independent**—the way in which one response is categorized does not influence the way that another response is listed. In our example, the opinion of one respondent did not affect another in terms of his/her attitude toward the death penalty.

3. Each cell must have an expected frequency of no less than five.

4. Very large sample sizes tend to produce significant differences.

Chi-square is valuable because it can be used when data are in the form of categories and frequencies rather than scores. It determines the probability that the observed frequencies across a set of categories are significantly different from the expected frequencies that would occur by chance.

Calculation Formulas: The Chi-Square Statistic

Chi-Square

$$\chi^2 = \Sigma \, / \, |O - E|^2 \, / \, E$$

Where:

| | indicates that you should ignore the sign of the calculation and always treat it as a positive value (the absolute value)

O is the observed frequency

E is the expected frequency

Σ means that the formula will be calculated for each cell in the table and then added together (or summed)

Expected Frequencies

$$E = (N \text{ row})(N \text{ column}) \, / \, (N \text{ total})$$

Where:

N row = the observed total row frequency for that cell

N column = the observed total column frequency for that cell

Degrees of Freedom

Under chi-square, degrees of freedom are determined by multiplying the number of rows in the table minus one by the number of columns in the table minus one.

Degrees of Freedom = (Rows − 1)(Columns − 1)

Calculating Chi-Square

Chi-Square Calculations by Hand

Unlike some of the other statistics we discuss, chi-square is relatively easy to calculate by hand, with a calculator. In Table 6.2, we show how to calculate chi-square by hand in our example of the relationship between race and attitude toward capital punishment. Table 6.1 is a 3×2 table, so the data are contained in six cells. The data are presented in the Observed column of Table 6.2.

The expected frequencies are presented in the third column of Table 6.2. They were calculated using the formula $E = (N \text{ row})(N \text{ column}) \, / \, (N \text{ total})$. Thus, the marginals in the table are used to calculate the expected frequencies for each cell. For example, in the first cell (whites who favor the death penalty), the observed frequencies are 607 [$E = (N \text{ row})(N \text{ column}) \, / \, (N \text{ total})$, $E = (707)(773) \, / \, (979) = 558.2$]. By chance, we would expect that about 558 whites would favor the death penalty for murderers. This procedure is repeated for every cell in the table. Here, the null hypothesis is that the proportions of whites and minority group members that favor, oppose, or are not

Table 6.2 Chi Square Calculations—Relationship between Race and Attitude toward Capital Punishment

Cell	Observed (O)	Expected (E)	|O – E|	(|O – E|)²	(|O – E|)² / E
1	607	558.2	48.8	2381.44	4.27
2	100	148.8	48.8	2381.44	16.00
3	104	149.2	45.2	2043.04	13.69
4	85	39.8	45.2	2043.04	51.33
5	62	65.5	3.5	12.25	0.19
6	21	17.5	3.5	12.25	0.7
					$\Sigma = 86.18$

Expected Frequencies: (N row) (N column)/(N total)
Cell 1: (707) (773)/(979) = 558.2
Cell 2: (707) (206)/(979) = 148.8
Cell 3: (189) (773)/(979) = 149.2
Cell 4: (189) (206/(979) = 39.8
Cell 5: (83) (773)/(979) = 65.5
Cell 6: (83) (206)/(979) = 17.5
Degrees of Freedom: (Rows – 1) (Columns – 1) = (3– 1) (2 – 1) = (2)(1) = 2

sure about the death penalty are equal. The research hypothesis is that minorities are more likely to oppose the death penalty.[2]

The next step is to take the absolute value of the observed frequency minus the expected frequency for each cell. For cell 1, this value works out to be 48.8. This value is then squared (2,381.44) and finally divided by the expected frequency value. The chi-square value for cell 1 is 4.27. This procedure is repeated for every cell, and then the values in the last column are summed to calculate the chi-square statistic for the table. Our calculated chi-square value is 86.18. The degrees of freedom for a 3×2 table are 2. Let's now see how to calculate chi-square on the computer.

Calculating Chi-Square Using SPSS

The chi-square option in SPSS makes the calculations that are necessary to determine probability of the statistical value. It calculates the expected frequency for each cell and then calculates the chi-square value for it. To use SPSS to calculate chi-square, take the following steps:

1. Open the NCSD data set. On the Menu bar, click on "Analyze."

2. On the drop down menu, click on "Descriptive Statistics."

3. On the next menu, click on "Crosstabs." These three steps are on the first screen (Figure 6.1).

4. In the "Crosstabs" menu, the variables are listed in the left-hand window. Highlight "Favor: Death Penalty for Murderers" and paste it into the "Rows" window by clicking on the arrow button. This is your depen-

dent variable (Y)—the respondents' attitude toward capital punishment. Remember that Y is always the row variable in a contingency table (Figure 6.2).

5. In the same window, highlight the independent variable (X), "Race Recode," and paste it into the "Column(s)" window by clicking on the arrow button.

6. In the "Crosstabs" window, click on the "Statistics" button. The "Crosstabs: Statistics" menu then appears. Click on the box next to "Chi-square" to include a check mark. Then, click on the "Continue" button (Figure 6.3).

7. When you return to the "Crosstabs" window, click the "Cells" button. The "Crosstabs: Cell Display" window appears. In this window, in the "Counts" section, click the box next to "Observed" to make a check mark. Then, in the "Percentages" section, click on the box next to "Column." Now, your contingency table will give you the observed frequencies for each cell. The table will contain the percentages for the independent variable (Figure 6.4).

8. Click on the "Continue" button. You then return to the "Crosstabs" window. Click on "OK" to generate your contingency table and the chi-square statistic (Figure 6.5).

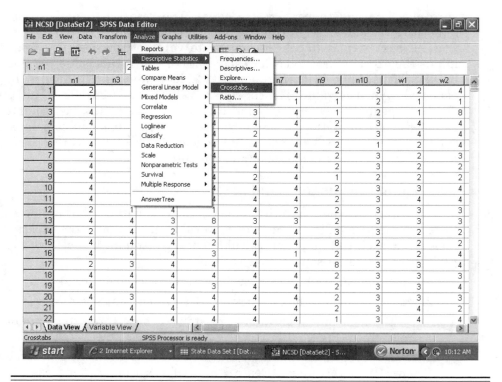

Figure 6.1

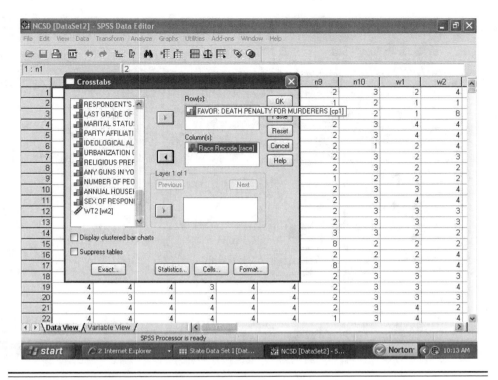

Figure 6.2

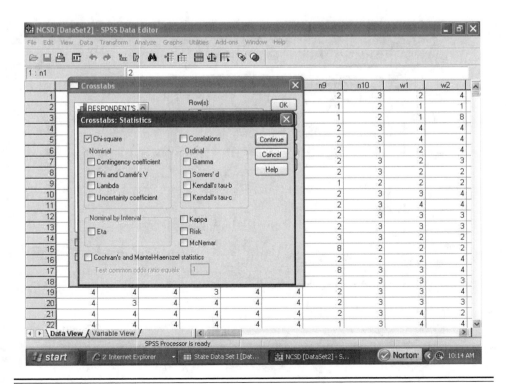

Figure 6.3

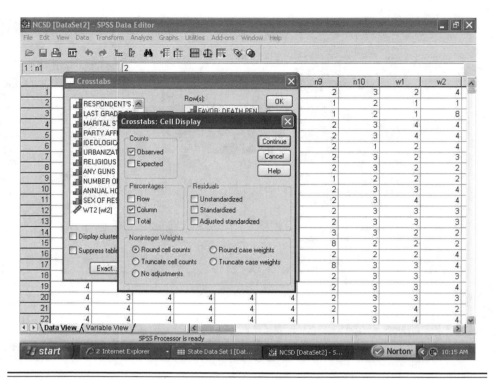

Figure 6.4

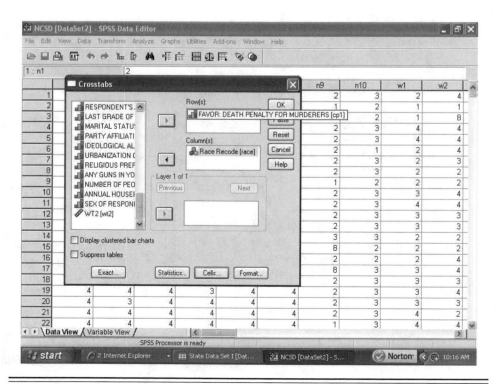

Figure 6.5

The Crosstabs printout contains the contingency table and statistics (Table 6.3). The first table (labeled "Case Processing Summary") tells us the number of cases in the sample that had valid (not missing) information for these variables. The second table is the actual contingency table. Note that it mirrors our Table 6.1. Again, our conclusion is that a higher percentage of whites favor the death penalty in murder cases by a difference of 30 percentage points (whites, 78.5 percent; minorities, 48.5 percent). Minorities are three times more likely to say that they oppose capital punishment (41.3 versus 13.5 percent). Whites are more likely to support and minority group members are more likely to oppose capital punishment.

We still need to decide whether this conclusion would be true if we had data from the entire U.S. population. This is where chi-square, as an inferential statistic, comes in. In the third table (Chi-Square Tests) that appears in Table 6.3, we can see that our hand calculation of the chi-square value for this table was close to the value compiled on the computer. The computer value

Table 6.3 SPSS Output

Case Processing Summary

	Valid		Cases Missing		Total	
	N	Percent	N	Percent	N	Percent
Favor: Death Penalty for Murderers*Race Recode	979	97.4%	26	2.6%	1005	100.0%

Contingency Table

			Race Recode		Total
			Anglo	**Minorities**	**Total**
Favor: Death Penalty for Murderers	**Favor**	Count	607	100	707
		% within Race Recode	78.5%	48.5%	72.2%
	Oppose	Count	104	85	189
		% within Race Recode	13.5%	41.3%	19.3%
	Neither	Count	62	21	83
		% within Race Recode	8.0%	10.2%	8.5%
Total		Count	773	206	979
		% within Race Recode	100.0%	100.0%	100.0%

Chi-Square Tests*

	Value	df	Asymp. Sig. (two-sided)
Pearson Chi-Square	86.304[a]	2	.000
Likelihood Ratio	77.114	2	.000
Linear-by-Linear Association	41.929	1	.000
N of Valid Cases	979		

* No cells (.0%) have expected count less than 5. The minimum expected count is 17.46.

was 86.304, and our hand result was 86.18—the difference is probably due to rounding. In the note at the bottom of the table, we see the one restriction on the use of chi-square of which you must be aware: no cell in the table can have an expected count of less than five. Here, we have no cells with an expected count of less than five. The smallest expected frequency in the table is 17.46. Therefore, our chi-square statistic is valid.

In the Chi-Square Tests table, we see that with two degrees of freedom the Pearson Chi-Square Value of 86.304 is significant at .000. Because .000 is less than .05, we reject the null hypothesis. Our research conclusion is statistically significant. Statistical significance means that there is a good chance (at the .05 level, 95% chance) that the difference that you have discovered in your findings based on your research sample is present in the population. For example, the NCSD is a survey data set from a sample of U.S. residents. If you find in the NCSD data that a higher percentage of African Americans is opposed to the death penalty and the statistical test shows that the difference between their response percentage and those of other groups is statistically significant, then there is a good chance that this is true of all Americans. A substantial probability exists that, in the entire U.S. population, whites are more likely to support and minorities are more likely to oppose capital punishment.

Measures of Association with Chi-Square

Another aspect of chi-square analysis involves measures of association. These measures indicate the strength of a relationship between the independent and dependent variables. They are comparable to the correlation measures that we discuss in chapter 10. The type of measure used is dependent upon the size of the contingency table and the level of measurement of the variables.

The measures of association available under SPSS are listed in the "Crosstabs: Statistics" screen. The following measures are listed under the "Nominal" section[3] (see box).

Let's return to our previous analysis of the relationship between race and attitude toward capital punishment. We have already determined that the relationship is statistically significant. Now, we use Cramer's V to see how strong the relationship is. We repeat some of the same steps in the program that we did before.

Cramer's V and SPSS

1. On the Menu bar, click on "Analyze."

2. On the drop down menu, click on "Descriptive Statistics."

3. On the next menu, click on "Crosstabs."

4. In the "Crosstabs" menu, the variables are listed in the left-hand window. Highlight "Favor: Death Penalty for Murderers" and paste it into the "Row(s)" window by clicking on the arrow button. This is your dependent variable (Y)—the respondents' attitude toward capital punishment. Remember that Y is always the row variable in a contingency table.

5. In the same window, highlight the independent variable (X), "Race Recode," and paste it into the "Column(s)" window by clicking on the arrow button.

6. In the "Crosstabs" window, click on the "Statistics" button. The "Crosstabs: Statistics" menu then appears. Click on the box next to

---

Calculation Formulas: Nonparametric Measures of Association for Use with Chi-Square with Nominal Data

Once you have determined that the chi-square value in your analysis is statistically significant, it is important to know how strong the relationship between X and Y is. Several measures are available to accomplish this task.

1. Contingency Coefficient:

$$C = \sqrt{\chi^2 / N + \chi^2}$$

Where:

$\sqrt{}$ is the square root symbol

χ^2 is the calculated chi-square value

N is the size of the sample

C is particularly useful when one (or both) of the variables is measured at the nominal level. The lower limit of the contingency coefficient is 0 (no association). The upper limit of C, however, must be calculated with the following formula:

$$\sqrt{k-1/k}$$

Where: k = the number of rows in the table

Of course, the closer the computed value of C is to this upper limit, the stronger the relationship between X and Y.

2. Phi:

$$Phi = \sqrt{\chi^2 / N}$$

Phi is used with 2 × 2 tables only—when both X and Y are nominal measures that are dichotomized. If Phi has a value of zero, there is no relationship between X and Y. You must calculate the upper limit of Phi: return to your original table, make the cell with the lowest observed frequency equal to zero, and recalculate the chi-square value. Then, recalculate the value of Phi using the formula above. This is the upper limit of Phi for your analysis. Compare your first Phi value to this upper limit to judge the strength of the association between X and Y.

3. Cramer's V:

$$V = \sqrt{\chi^2 / N(L-1)}$$

Where: L is the number of either rows or columns, whichever is smaller

Cramer's V is also used with nominal data. It is probably the most popular of the three measures we have discussed because it has a lower limit of 0 (no relationship) and an upper limit of 1 (perfect relationship). Unlike C and Phi, there is no need to do further calculations to determine the upper limit of Cramer's V.

"Chi-square" to include a check mark. Then, click on the box next to "Phi and Cramer's *V*." Finally, click on the "Continue" button.

7. When you return to the "Crosstabs" window, click the "Cells" button. The "Crosstabs: Cell Display" window appears. In this window, in the "Counts" section, click the box next to "Observed" to make a check-mark. Then, in the "Percentages" section, click on the box next to "Column." Now, your contingency table will give you the observed frequencies for each cell. The table will contain the percentages for the independent variable.

8. Click on the "Continue" button. You then return to the "Crosstabs" window. Click on "OK" to generate your contingency table, the chi-square statistic, and Cramer's *V*.

Now a fourth box appears in the SPSS output (Table 6.4).

Using Cramer's *V* as our measure, we can see that the relationship between race and attitude toward capital punishment has a value of .297. This would be considered somewhat weak because it is closer to zero (no relationship) than it is to one (strong relationship).

Table 6.4   Symmetric Measures

	Value	Approx. Sig.
Nominal by Phi	.297	.000
Nominal Cramer's *V*	.297	.000
N of Valid Cases	979	

Introducing a Third Variable

Multivariate analysis involves the consideration of the effects of more than one independent variable upon a dependent variable. Naturally, crime analysts prefer such a method because it provides a more complete attempt at explanation. For example, recidivism following a prison term could be due to several factors in addition to prior record. Ability to find and keep a job or to maintain sobriety may be more important. We are unable to consider such questions unless we examine the effect of variables in combination.

Here, we introduce this concept by constructing contingency tables with a third variable. Actually, we are considering the impact of a second independent or *control* variable. We re-examine the relationship between the original two variables (*X* and *Y*) within each of the categories of the control variable and then compare the results across the categories of the control variable.[4] As before, we examine the column percentages (along the independent variable) to reach a conclusion. We use chi-square and the measures of association (in this case, Cramer's *V*).

Returning to our examination of the forces that influence attitudes toward capital punishment, another key independent variable is sex. Traditionally, women tend to oppose capital punishment while men tend to support it.[5] For this reason, we first examine the relationship between sex and attitude toward capital punishment in the NCSD data set. Using the steps we listed previously, we obtained the output from SPSS as shown in Table 6.5.

In this table, the percentages in the contingency table reveal some differences between the sexes in attitude toward capital punishment. While both expressed majority support, a slightly higher proportion of men (more than 75 percent) than women (about 69 percent) favored the death penalty. A higher percentage of women (about 11 percent) also were uncertain about capital punishment compared to males (about 6 percent). The sexes were roughly equal in their opposition to the death penalty.

With two degrees of freedom, the chi-square value of 9.066 is statistically significant (significance level of .011 is less than .05). The Cramer's V statistic, however, shows that the relationship between sex and attitude toward capital punishment is very weak (.096).

Next, we use sex as our third (or control) variable and re-examine the relationship between race and attitude toward capital punishment. We use the same steps in SPSS as before with one additional step. In the third window on

Table 6.5   Sex of Respondent and Attitude toward Capital Punishment

Contingency Table

			Sex of Respondent		Total
			Male	Female	
Favor: Death Penalty for Murderers	**Favor**	Count	356	351	707
		% within Sex of Respondent	75.4%	69.4%	72.3%
	Oppose	Count	89	100	189
		% within Sex of Respondent	18.9%	19.8%	19.3%
	Neither	Count	27	55	82
		% within Sex of Respondent	5.7%	10.9%	8.4%
Total		Count	472	506	978
		% within Sex of Respondent	100.0%	100.0%	100.0%

Chi-Square Tests*

	Value	df	Asymp. Sig. (two-sided)
Pearson Chi-Square	9.066[a]	2	.011
Likelihood Ratio	9.250	2	.010
Linear-by-Linear Association	7.689	1	.006
N of Valid Cases	978		

*No cells have expected count less than 5. The minimum expected count is 39.57.

Symmetric Measures

		Value	Approx. Sig.
Nominal by Nominal	**Phi**	.096	.011
	Cramer's V	.096	.011
	Contingency Coefficient	.096	.011
N of Valid Cases		978	

the right, we highlight and paste "sex of respondent" (Figure 6.6). This becomes our control variable.

The concept of control actually means holding X constant. In the contingency table in Table 6.6, we see that we have two tables that portray the relationship between race and capital punishment. The first table is for male respondents and the second is for female respondents.

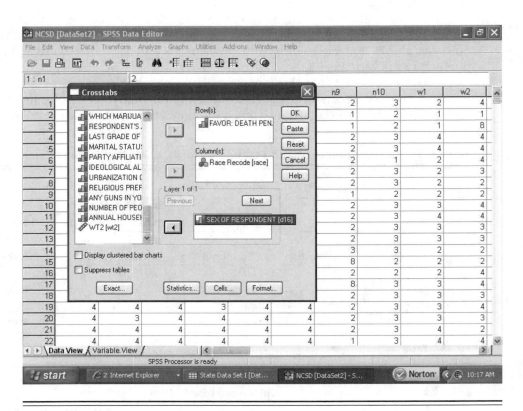

Figure 6.6

Table 6.6   Race and Attitude toward Capital Punishment—Controlling for Sex

	Case Processing Summary					
	Valid		**Cases Missing**		**Total**	
	N	Percent	N	Percent	N	Percent
Favor: Death Penalty for Murderers*Race Recode* Sex of Respondent	978	97.3%	27	2.7%	1005	100.0%

Table 6.6   *(cont'd.)*

Contingency Table

				Race Recode		
				Anglo	**Minorities**	**Total**
Male	**Favor: Death Penalty for Murderers**	**Favor**	Count	310	47	357
			% within Race Recode	82.4%	48.4%	75.5%
		Oppose	Count	48	41	89
			% within Race Recode	12.8%	42.3%	18.8%
		Neither	Count	18	9	27
			% within Race Recode	4.8%	9.3%	5.7%
	Total		Count	376	97	473
			% within Race Recode	100.0%	100.0%	100.0%
Female	**Favor: Death Penalty for Murderers**	**Favor**	Count	297	53	350
			% within Race Recode	74.8%	49.1%	69.3%
		Oppose	Count	56	44	100
			% within Race Recode	14.1%	40.7%	19.8%
		Neither	Count	44	11	55
			% within Race Recode	11.1%	10.2%	10.9%
	Total		Count	397	108	505
			% within Race Recode	100.0%	100.0%	100.0%

Chi-Square Tests[a]

Sex of Respondent		Value	df	Asymp. Sig. (two-sided)
Male	**Pearson Chi-Square**	50.198[a]	2	.000
	Likelihood Ratio	44.644	2	.000
	Linear-by-Linear Association	35.054	1	.000
	N of Valid Cases	473		
Female	**Pearson Chi-Square**	38.594[b]	2	.000
	Likelihood Ratio	34.363	2	.000
	Linear-by-Linear Association	11.347	1	.0001
	N of Valid Cases	505		

[a] No cells have expected count less than 5. The minimum expected count is 5.54.
[b] No cells have expected count less than 5. The minimum expected count is 11.76.

Symmetric Measures

Sex of Respondent			Value	Approx. Sig.
Male	Nominal by Nominal	Phi	.326	.000
		Cramer's *V*	.326	.000
	N of Valid Cases		473	
Female	Nominal by Nominal	Phi	.276	.000
		Cramer's *V*	.276	.000
	N of Valid Cases		505	

In the first contingency table, we can see that white males (about 82 percent) are far more likely than minority group males (about 49 percent) to support the use of capital punishment in murder cases by a difference of more than 30 percentage points. Minority group males are more than three times as likely (42.3 percent) than white males (12.8 percent) to oppose the death penalty.

The second table examines the same question among females. A similar pattern emerges. White females (almost 75 percent) express more support for capital punishment than do minority group females (49 percent). This difference is a little less pronounced than that for males. Minority group females are more than twice as likely (about 41 percent) than white females (about 14 percent) to be against the death penalty.

The overall conclusion is that minority group males are the strongest opponents of capital punishment, although minority group females are close behind. Examining the two tables separately and then comparing the results revealed the patterns.

The statistical analysis found that the relationships in both tables were statistically significant. Among males, the chi-square value of 50.198 with two degrees of freedom was significant at the .000 level. For females, the chi-square value was 38.594 and was significant at the .000 level with two degrees of freedom.

Here, the values of Cramer's V allow us to make comparisons between racial groups and sex and make the final determination as to which relationship is strongest. For males, Cramer's V is .326, and for females, it is .276. The pattern for males is stronger, but .326 is just a moderate measure of association.

Note how the introduction of another independent variable changed or added to the original conclusion. Minority group members are most likely to oppose capital punishment, and the difference is even more pronounced when males and females are examined separately. The minority group males register the strongest opposition to the death penalty. Such analyses and comparisons are a vital aspect of research. They help us move toward causal analysis and inform policy decisions in criminal justice.

Summary

Categorical data measured at the nominal and ordinal levels are very common in criminal justice research. Researchers typically deal with dichotomous data, such as whether or not a probationer recidivates or passes or fails a drug test. Surveys, such as the National Crime Survey, often ask interval level questions about fear of crime or confidence toward the police.

A contingency table is an excellent method to summarize and highlight research findings. If the conventions presented in this chapter are followed, the contingency table is easier to interpret and base conclusions upon. The percentage comparisons between the categories of the independent and dependent variables are the key to the process. Conclusions are drawn from the table and its results.

Chi-square and its accompanying measures of association provide a method to determine statistical significance. A positive decision here extends the findings beyond the sample to the population in the outside world. Thus, research conclusions become crucial and vital.

Another important aspect that we demonstrate is the introduction of a third variable. Consideration of a second independent variable is the first step in conducting multivariate analysis. In order to address complex problems such as crime, multivariate analysis must be conducted. Usually, there is more than one contributing factor to social problems such as crime.

Key Terms

Parametric Statistics: make a number of assumptions about the way that the population that serves as the basis for your research sample is distributed (i.e., the variables under study that were drawn from the population are normally distributed)

Nonparametric Statistics: are particularly appropriate when you have nominal or ordinal level data. They require no assumptions about the population parameters.

Power of a Statistic: involves the acceptance of a false null hypothesis (reaching the conclusion that there are no differences between the sample and the population when, in fact, there are). The greater the power of a statistic is, the lower the probability of accepting a false null hypothesis—committing a Type II error. Think of power of a statistic as the ability to detect variation when it really exists.

Robust: Often, if sample sizes are sufficiently large, the assumptions behind parametric statistics can be violated and not adversely affect the research results.

Contingency Table: a joint frequency distribution—a frequency distribution for two categorical variables. It is also known as a **crosstabulation** because it counts the cases that fall into each cell of the table. The cells contain those cases that fall into each pairing of the variables—the number of cases that fit the categories described by the cross-listing of the variables. It is called a contingency table because the cases organized in rows (the categories of the dependent variable) are contingent upon what is organized in columns (the categories of the independent variables).

Marginals: in a contingency table, the total frequencies presented at the margins of the table. The marginal frequencies fall under the total values for each column value and each row value.

Observed Frequencies: typically, the research results—for example, the respondents' answers in a survey

Expected Frequencies: represent what we could expect to occur by chance. They are calculated for each cell in the contingency table by multiplying the row total by the column total and then dividing that product by the total number of cases in the study.

Independence: a requirement of chi-square, the manner in which one response is categorized should not influence the way that another response is listed.

Data Analysis

Directions: For each of the following exercises, construct a contingency table and obtain the chi-square value and Cramer's *V* using SPSS and the NCSD data set. Be careful to put the independent variables in the correct places and to assign the percentages accordingly. Carefully and fully interpret each contingency table, giving specific attention to the percentage differences in categories between the independent and dependent variables. In the statistical analysis, compare the effect of Cramer's *V*.

1. Examine the relationship between race (*X*—Race Recode) and the issue of whether people feel that the local police use excessive force (*Y*—Problem: Local Police Use Excessive Force).

   a. What is the conclusion based upon the contingency table percentages?

   b. How strong is this relationship?

2. Return to the variables in question 1 and now add "Had Contact with the Police in the Past 2 Years" as a third (control, second independent) variable.

   a. Reconduct the contingency table and statistical analyses.

   b. What is the conclusion based upon the contingency table percentages?

   c. How strong is this relationship?

   d. Have things changed from your conclusion in question 1? How?

3. Researchers have found that opinions toward the death penalty often change when people consider details about the circumstances of the offense or the characteristics of the offender. Examine the relationship between attitude toward the death penalty for murderers (*Y*—"Favor: Death Penalty for Murderers") and "What If Minorities Are More Likely to Get DP?" (*X*)

   a. What is the conclusion based upon the contingency table percentages?

   b. How strong is this relationship?

4. Return to the variables in question 3 and now add race as a third (control, second independent) variable.

   a. Reconduct the contingency table and statistical analyses.

   b. What is the conclusion based upon the contingency table percentages?

   c. How strong is this relationship?

   d. Have things changed from your conclusion in question 3? How?

5. Further examination of death penalty attitudes: Examine the relationship between attitude toward the death penalty for murderers (*Y*—Favor: Death Penalty for Murderers) and each of the following independent variables (*X*):

 a. What If Innocent Have Received DP?

 b. What If Poor More Likely to Get DP?

 c. What If Life Sentence Was Available?

 d. What If Murderer a Teenager Under 18?

 e. What If Murderer Is Severely Retarded?

 Reach your conclusions based upon the percentages in the contingency table and the statistical analyses. Which of these circumstances had the greatest impact upon respondents' original position on the death penalty? What is the basis for your conclusion?

6. Return to the variables in question 5 and now add "Sex of Respondent" as a third (control, second independent) variable.

 a. Reconstruct the contingency table and statistical analyses.

 b. What is the conclusion based upon the contingency table percentages?

 c. How strong is this relationship?

 d. Have things changed from your conclusion in question 5? How?

Use the data set "Public Opinion Study on Courts" to answer Questions 7–16. Use the Crosstab option in SPSS with chi-square and phi as your statistics. Use Race as your as your independent variable (X) and the opinion in question as the dependent variable (Y) to construct the contingency table. Remember to do the percentages along the column (by the independent variable, X—Race).

7. Examine the contingency table for Race and the question "Court Concerned with People's Rights?" Which racial group has the lowest percentage of agreement with this question (feel that the courts are concerned with people's rights)? Which racial group has the highest percentage of disagreement with this question (feel that the courts are not concerned about people's rights)? Is this relationship statistically significant? How strong is this relationship?

8. Examine the contingency table for Race and the question "Court Treat People with Respect?" Which racial group has the lowest percentage of agreement with this question (feel that the courts treat people with respect)? Which racial group has the highest percentage of disagreement with this question (feel that the courts are disrespectful)? Is this relationship statistically significant? How strong is this relationship?

9. Examine the contingency table for Race and the question "Courts Treat People Politely?" Which racial group has the lowest percentage of agreement with this question (feel that the courts treat people politely)? Which racial group has the highest percentage of disagreement with this question (feel that the courts are impolite)? Is this relationship statistically significant? How strong is this relationship?

10. Examine the contingency table for Race and the question "Courts Make Decisions Based on Facts?" Which racial group has the lowest

percentage of agreement with this question (feel that the courts make factual decisions)? Which racial group has the highest percentage of disagreement with this question (feel that the courts fail to make factual decisions)? Is this relationship statistically significant? How strong is this relationship?

11. Examine the contingency table for Race and the question "Judges Honest in Their Case Decisions?" Which racial group has the lowest percentage of agreement with this question (feel that judges are honest in their decision making)? Which racial group has the highest percentage of disagreement with this question (feel that judges make dishonest decisions)? Is this relationship statistically significant? How strong is this relationship?

12. Examine the contingency table for Race and the question "Courts Take People's Needs into Account?" Which racial group has the lowest percentage of agreement with this question (feel that the courts take people's needs into account)? Which racial group has the highest percentage of disagreement with this question (feel that the courts are insensitive to people's needs)? Is this relationship statistically significant? How strong is this relationship?

13. Examine the contingency table for Race and the question "Courts Listen Carefully to People?" Which racial group has the lowest percentage of agreement with this question (feel that the courts listen carefully)? Which racial group has the highest percentage of disagreement with this question (feel that the courts fail to listen to people)? Is this relationship statistically significant? How strong is this relationship?

14. Examine the contingency table for Race and the question "Courts Sensitive to Concerns of Avg. Citizens?" Which racial group has the lowest percentage of agreement with this question (feel that the courts are sensitive to the concerns of average citizens)? Which racial group has the highest percentage of disagreement with this question (feel that the courts are insensitive to the concerns of average citizens)? Is this relationship statistically significant? How strong is this relationship?

15. Examine the contingency table for Race and the question "It Is Affordable to Bring Case to Court?" Which racial group has the lowest percentage of agreement with this question (feel that it is affordable to bring a case to court)? Which racial group has the highest percentage of disagreement with this question (feel that they cannot afford to bring a case to court)? Is this relationship statistically significant? How strong is this relationship?

16. Examine the contingency table for Race and the question "Court Cases Resolved in a Timely Manner?" Which racial group has the lowest percentage of agreement with this question (feel that the courts resolve cases in a timely manner)? Which racial group has the highest percentage of disagreement with this question (feel that the courts are

too slow)? Is this relationship statistically significant? How strong is this relationship?

17. Were the patterns in your answers to Questions 7–16 consistent? Was one racial group consistently dissatisfied with the performance of the courts in this country? Using the value of the phi coefficient, determine which problem was the most severe? Using the value of the phi coefficient, determine which problem was the least severe? What do these results tell us about attitudes toward the courts in this country? Based upon your research results, what do you think should be done about court performance?

Use the data set "Public Opinion Study on Courts" to answer Questions 18–28. Use the Crosstab option in SPSS with chi-square and phi as your statistics. Use Race as your as your independent variable (X), the opinion in question as the dependent variable (Y), and add Sex as the *Control Variable* (second independent variable) to construct the contingency table. Remember to do the percentages along the column (by the first independent variable, X – Race).

18. Examine the contingency tables for Race and the question "Court Concerned with People's Rights?" while controlling for Sex. By Sex, which racial group has the lowest percentage of agreement with this question (feel that the courts are concerned with peoples' rights)? By Sex, which racial group has the highest percentage of disagreement with this question (feel that the courts are not concerned about people's rights)? Are these relationships statistically significant? How strong are these relationships? Which relationship is the strongest?

19. Examine the contingency table for Race and the question "Court Treat People with Respect?" while controlling for Sex. By Sex, which racial group has the lowest percentage of agreement with this question (feel that the courts treat people with respect)? By Sex, which racial group has the highest percentage of disagreement with this question (feel that the courts are disrespectful)? Are these relationships statistically significant? How strong are these relationships? Which relationship is strongest? Did the control for Sex really make any difference?

20. Examine the contingency table for Race and the question "Courts Treat People Politely?" while controlling for Sex. By Sex, which racial group has the lowest percentage of agreement with this question (feel that the courts treat people politely)? By Sex, which racial group has the highest percentage of disagreement with this question (feel that the courts are impolite)? Are these relationships statistically significant? Which relationship is strongest?

21. Examine the contingency table for Race and the question "Courts Make Decisions Based on Facts?" while controlling for Sex. By Sex, which racial group has the lowest percentage of agreement with this question (feel that the courts make factual decisions)? By Sex, which racial group has the highest percentage of disagreement with this

question (feel that the courts fail to make factual decisions)? Are these relationships statistically significant? Which relationship is strongest?

22. Examine the contingency table for Race and the question "Judges Honest in Their Case Decisions?" while controlling for Sex. By Sex, which racial group has the lowest percentage of agreement with this question (feel that judges are honest in their decision making)? By Sex, which racial group has the highest percentage of disagreement with this question (feel that judges make dishonest decisions)? Are these relationships statistically significant? Which relationship is strongest?

23. Examine the contingency table for Race and the question "Courts Take People's Needs Into Account?" while controlling for Sex. By Sex, which racial group has the lowest percentage of agreement with this question (feel that the courts take people's needs into account)? By Sex, which racial group has the highest percentage of disagreement with this question (feel that the courts are insensitive to people's needs)? Are these relationships statistically significant? Which relationship is strongest?

24. Examine the contingency table for Race and the question "Courts Listen Carefully to People?" while controlling for Sex. By Sex, which racial group has the lowest percentage of agreement with this question (feel that the courts listen carefully)? By Sex, which racial group has the highest percentage of disagreement with this question (feel that the courts fail to listen to people)? Are these relationships statistically significant? Which relationship is strongest?

25. Examine the contingency table for Race and the question "Courts Sensitive to Concerns of Avg. Citizens?" while controlling for Sex. By Sex, which racial group has the lowest percentage of agreement with this question (feel that the courts are sensitive to the concerns of average citizens)? By Sex, which racial group has the highest percentage of disagreement with this question (feel that the courts are insensitive to the concerns of average citizens)? Are these relationships statistically significant? Which relationship is strongest?

26. Examine the contingency table for Race and the question "It is affordable to bring a case to court?" while controlling for Sex. By Sex, which racial group has the lowest percentage of agreement with this question (feel that it is affordable to bring a case to court)? By Sex, which racial group has the highest percentage of disagreement with this question (feel that they cannot afford to bring a case to court)? Are these relationships statistically significant? Which relationship is strongest?

27. Examine the contingency table for Race and the question "Court Cases Resolved in a Timely Manner?" while controlling for Sex. By Sex, which racial group has the lowest percentage of agreement with this question (feel that the courts resolve cases in a timely manner)? By Sex, which racial group has the highest percentage of disagreement

with this question (feel that the courts are too slow)? Are these relationships statistically significant? Which relationship is strongest?

28. Were the patterns in your answers to Questions 18–27 consistent? By Sex, was one racial group consistently dissatisfied with the performance of the courts in this country? Using the value of the phi coefficient, which problem was the most severe? Using the value of the phi coefficient, which problem was the least severe? Which question generated the greatest differences in phi values by race and sex? What do these results tell us about attitudes toward the courts in this country? Based upon your research results, what do you think should be done about court performance?

For Questions 29–31, use the 2004 Texas Crime Survey data.

29. Using Gender as your independent variable (X) and the question "Should Those Under 18 at Time of Capital Offense Be Eligible for Death Penalty" as the dependent variable (Y), construct a contingency table. Use chi square and phi as your statistics and be sure to use column percentages (by the independent variable). In the state of Texas in 2004, which sex showed the greatest support for executing juveniles? Which sex showed the least support for the execution of juveniles? Was this relationship statistically significant? How strong was the relationship?

30. Using Dichotomized Race as your independent variable (X) and the question "Should those Under 18 at Time of Capital Offense Be Eligible for Death Penalty" as the dependent variable (Y), construct a contingency table. Use chi-square and phi as your statistics and be sure to use column percentages (by the independent variable). In the state of Texas in 2004, which racial group showed the greatest support for executing juveniles? Which racial group showed the least support for the execution of juveniles? Was this relationship statistically significant? How strong was the relationship?

31. Using Dichotomized Race as your independent variable (X) and the question "Should those Under 18 at Time of Capital Offense Be Eligible for Death Penalty" as the dependent variable (Y), construct a contingency tables while controlling for Gender (as a second independent variable). Use chi-square and phi as your statistics and be sure to use column percentages (by the independent variable). In the state of Texas in 2004, by gender and racial group who showed the greatest support for executing juveniles? Who showed the least support for the execution of juveniles? Was this relationship statistically significant? How strong was the relationship? Which group is the "heart" of support for the execution of juvenile murderers?

Notes

1 Earl Babbie, *Survey Research Methods* (Belmont, CA: Wadsworth, 1990), p. 260; Jerome B. McKean, "A Comparison of Methods for Teaching the Interpretation of Contingency Tables," *Journal of Criminal Justice Education,* Vol. 10 (1999), pp. 327–338.

[2] Robert M. Bohm, "American Death Penalty Opinion, 1936–1986: A Critical Examination of the Gallup Polls," in Robert M. Bohm, ed., *The Death Penalty in America: Current Research* (Cincinnati, OH: Anderson, 1991), pp. 113–145.

[3] Sidney Siegel, *Nonparametric Statistics for the Social Sciences* (New York: McGraw-Hill, 1956), pp. 196–202.

[4] Kenneth J. Meier and Jeffrey L. Brudney, *Applied Statistics for Public Administration* (Fort Worth, TX: Harcourt Brace, 1997), p. 265. See also Babbie, *Survey Research Methods,* p. 264.

[5] Bohm, "American Death Penalty Opinion." See also Dennis R. Longmire, "Americans' Attitudes About the Ultimate Weapon: Capital Punishment," in Timothy J. Flanagan and Dennis R. Longmire, eds., *Americans View Crime and Justice: A National Public Opinion Survey* (Thousand Oaks, CA: Sage, 1997), pp. 101–106.

chapter 7

Probability and the Normal Curve

The outcomes of statistical tests give us is the ability to deal with uncertainty. Statistics can tell us the probability that an event will occur. Anticipation of an event allows for planning. Probability allows us to make inferences about a population on the basis of sample data.

This chapter deals with the basic rules of probability—we use games of chance as examples, and we explain how to calculate probability. Finally, we introduce the concept of estimation through the characteristics and use of the normal curve.

Introduction to Probability

Probability theory is the foundation of inferential statistics. What is the probability of obtaining a certain statistical value? When we examine probability theory we are attempting to estimate the chance that an event will occur. For example:

What is the chance that I will pass a test if I go out partying the night before rather than studying?

What is the likelihood that I will win the Superball Lottery if I buy one ticket today?

We frequently address questions of probability in the criminal justice system. For example, in criminal cases, a jury often determines whether the defendant is guilty "beyond a reasonable doubt" before they make a decision whether or not to convict. The term "beyond a reasonable doubt" implies that there must be a very high probability that the defendant actually committed the offense. In the correctional system, wardens often make a probability judgment regarding the dangerousness of an inmate. The decision on whether an inmate will be placed in a maximum, medium, or minimum security institution is based on probability.

Probability can be used to guide decision making. It involves the calculation of the chance that an event will happen. In criminal justice, you might wish to calculate the chance of victimization or the area of a city where a certain type of crime is likely to occur. The chance of an event taking place ranges from 0 percent (no chance—zero probability) to 100 percent (certainty—a sure thing). Of course, nothing is a sure thing—but that is part of probability as well.

The three types of probability differ in interpretation but are subject to the same rules:[1]

1. **Mathematical probability:** based upon equally likely outcomes that can be calculated

2. **Empirical probability:** based upon observed data or research from the past

3. **Subjective probability:** derived from Italian mathematician Bruno de Finetti, who viewed probability as personal reflections of an individual's opinion about an event

Of these three types, empirical probability is most often used in criminal justice. Research based on past events is used to predict future trends. Mathematical probability is used with outcomes that can be determined beforehand, such as coin flips or rolls of the dice. We consider mathematical probability first by examining the probabilities involved with games of chance.

Mathematical Rules of Probability

The **law of probability** states that the probability of an event is the number of ways it can happen and is expressed as a fraction of the number of all possible things that could happen. This rule applies if all possible outcomes of an event are *equally likely to occur* (e.g., flipping a coin—either heads or tails). The probability that either event will occur is equal to the ratio of "success" (e.g., the coin comes up heads—only one way) to the number of possible outcomes (two—either heads or tails). The probability that you would flip a coin and it would come up heads is one out of two or 50 percent. Note also that the probability of flipping a head extends to the next toss and every toss thereafter. Yet many people mistakenly believe that if you were to toss 10 heads in a row, the probability of tossing another would be astronomical. In fact, it has never changed—it is still 50 percent. This mistake is known as the **Gambler's Fallacy**. (Note that we are discussing the probability of flipping another heads on the eleventh flip. The probability of flipping eleven heads in a row is a different question, and the probability of that event would be much lower than 50 percent.)

Again, the probability of an event has a definite meaning. The probability of an event is defined as the number of times a specific event can occur. As an equation, the probability of event A is written as $P(A)$, where $P(A)$ = the number of times event A can occur / the total number of possible events.

For example, what is the probability of drawing an ace from a deck of playing cards? There are four aces in a standard deck of 52 cards. Therefore, $P(Ace) = 4/52 = .0769$ or approximately 8 percent.

When calculating mathematical probability, one helpful strategy is to write down a complete list of all the possible ways that the process can turn out. For example, you can calculate the probability of any given total that can be thrown in a craps game. Each die has six sides, so there are 36 possible combinations.

Table 7.1 Probability of Shooting Craps

Die #2 Roll	Die #1 Roll					
	1	**2**	**3**	**4**	**5**	**6**
1	2	3	4	5	6	7
2	3	4	5	6	7	8
3	4	5	6	7	8	9
4	5	6	7	8	9	10
5	6	7	8	9	10	11
6	7	8	9	10	11	12

Number of Ways to Roll Each Total	
Total Roll	**N of Ways**
2	1
3	2
4	3
5	4
6	5
7	6
8	5
9	4
10	3
11	2
12	1

Table 7.1 shows the number of ways that we can roll all possible numbers from 2 through 12. Using the basic law of probability, the probability of throwing any particular total is the number of ways to throw it, divided by the number of total outcomes. Using the figures from Table 7.1, here are the probabilities of throwing all possible totals:

Two:	1/36	2.8%	Six:	5/36	13.9%	Ten:	3/36	8.3%
Three:	2/36	5.6%	Seven:	6/36	16.7%	Eleven:	2/36	5.6%
Four:	3/36	8.3%	Eight:	5/36	13.9%	Twelve:	1/36	2.8%
Five:	4/36	11.1%	Nine:	4/36	11.1%			

Based upon these calculations, seven is the most likely roll (16.7%). Notice how low that probability is! If you bet on rolling a seven, you will *lose* 83 percent of the time.

Other Rules of Probability

1. The bounding rule of probability: the probability of any event A can never be less than zero (0) or greater than 1. $0 \leq P(A) \geq 1$

2. The complement of an event is the probability that an event *will not* occur. In our ace example above, the probability that you will not draw an ace is 92% (100% − 8%).

Shooting Craps

In gambling casinos, craps is played on a green felt table with sides shaped like egg cartons. This design ensures that the dice bounce frequently with abandon. We will present some of the basic rules. Each player around the table (going clockwise) takes a roll. The "shooter" stands at one of the shorter ends of the table and rolls the dice hard enough to hit the opposite end. The shooter's first throw is called the "come out" roll.

If you are the shooter in a game of craps, you can win on your first throw if the dice add up to a seven or an eleven (a "natural"). If you are not the shooter, before the first roll you can make a "pass line" bet. If you make such a bet, you are betting with the shooter. If the shooter wins, so do you. The shooter loses if the roll comes up two, three, or twelve ("box cars" or "craps"). If you made a pass line bet and the shooter "craps out," you also lose. If you made a "don't pass" bet, you are betting against the shooter. Therefore, you would win when the shooter loses.

If the shooter's come out roll totals four, five, six, eight, nine, or ten, the particular number rolled establishes the "point," and, to win, the shooter must make his or her "point." The shooter can keep rolling until the shooter makes his or her point and wins. The shooter loses if he or she rolls a seven.

Calculating the probability of winning a craps game requires the use of the addition rule. You use this rule when the events you are trying to predict are **mutually exclusive.** Events are mutually exclusive when the occurrence of one prevents the occurrence of the other. They cannot occur simultaneously.

Dice rolls are mutually exclusive. If you roll a seven, you cannot roll an eight. To calculate the probability of mutually exclusive events, you use the **addition rule:** if two events are mutually exclusive, the probability of their occurrence is equal to the sum of their separate probabilities.

Therefore, the probability of winning a craps game on the first roll of the dice is equal to the probability of rolling a seven plus the probability of rolling an eleven. According to the list on p. 119, the probability of rolling a seven is 6/36 or 1/6 (16.67%). The probability of rolling an eleven is 2/36 or 1/18 (5.6%). Adding these two probabilities gives us the probability of rolling either a seven or an eleven.

$$P(7) + P(11) \quad = \quad 1/6 + 1/18 \quad = \quad 3/18 + 1/18 \quad = \quad 4/18 \quad = \quad 2/9 \quad = \quad 22.2\%$$

What is the probability of losing on the first roll of the dice? To calculate it, you would use the addition rule again. We would add the separate probabilities of rolling a two (1/36), rolling a three (2/36), and rolling a twelve (1/36).

$$P(2) + P(3) + P(12) \quad = \quad 1/36 + 2/36 + 1/36 \quad = \quad 4/36 \quad = \quad 1/9 \quad = \quad 11.1\%$$

What if the shooter does not roll a seven or eleven and also does not crap out? What is the probability of winning when the shooter rolls a ten? The probability of rolling a ten (winning) is 3/36 or 1/12 (8.3%). The probability of losing (rolling a seven) is 6/36 or 1/6 (16.67%). The probability of continuing is 3/4 (75%). "Wait a minute!" you say. "How did you calculate that?" Again, by using the addition rule. Add the probability of rolling a ten to the probability of rolling a seven. 1/12 + 1/6 = 1/12 + 2/12 = 3/12 = 1/4. Then you subtract this probability (of rolling either a ten or a seven) from the probability of rolling any number (1). 1 − 1/4 = 3/4.

According to the rules of craps, the shooter continues to roll until he or she makes the number or loses. The shooter rolls a ten. Now, we must figure the probability of this happening on the first throw or any throw thereafter. Calculating this probability calls for the use of the **multiplication rule.** The multiplication rule covers events that are *not* mutually exclusive. The probability of events that are not mutually exclusive equals the *product* of their separate probabilities. On the second roll of the dice, the shooter could roll any number. Here, we first add to find the chance that at least one of the things will happen (they are mutually exclusive). Then, to find the chance that all of the events could happen, we multiply.

$$P(10) + P \text{ (any number, any roll)} =$$
$$1/12 + (3/4)(1/12) + (3/4) \times 2(1/12) + (3/4) \times 3(1/12) + \ldots$$
$$(1/12)\{1 + (3/4) + (3/4) \times 2 + \ldots \} = (1/12)(1 - 3/4) =$$
$$(1/12)(1 / (1/4)) = 4/12 = 1/3 \text{ (or 33.3\%)}$$

The probability of winning by matching the roll of a ten is (1/12)(1/3) = 1/36 or 2.8 percent. We are not finished yet. This is the probability of rolling a ten. The probability of rolling a four is the same. What about the other numbers?

The probability of winning with two fives or two nines is (1/9)(2/5) = 2/45 = 4.4 percent. The probability of winning with two sixes or two eights is (5/36) (5/11) = 25/396 = 6.3 percent. If you then add up all the probabilities of winning, you would get

$$(2/9) + 2(1/36) + 2(2/45) + 2(25/396) =$$
$$(2/9) + (1/18) + (4/45) + (25/198) = 244/495$$

Note that the house (the casino) wins the majority of the time, 100% − 49.3% = 51.7%.

The multiplication rule may also be used to analyze the probability of empirical data presented in Table 7.2 on p. 124. What is the probability that the victim is either 25–34 years old or that the individual is male? Since the events (being age 25–34 or being male) are not necessarily mutually exclusive, the multiplication rule is used: P(25–34) × P(Male) is 23.6% × 57.4% or .236 × .574 = .135 or 13.5%.

Examples 7.1 and 7.2 (on pp. 122 and 123) present more elements of mathematical probabilities that are typically used in gambling. This is why Las Vegas, Reno, and Atlantic City are lined with enormous, glittery casinos and very few gamblers take their money out of town.

Reading Tables to Determine Empirical Probability

Lifetime Likelihood of Going to State or Federal Prison

The second type of probability (empirical probability) is based upon research findings. Here, we use data from a study of the likelihood of going to state or federal prison conducted by the Bureau of Justice Statistics.

Example 7.1—Odds Versus Probability

A basic difference exists between odds and probability. Again, the probability of an event is the number of ways it can happen, expressed as a fraction of the number of all possible things that could happen. In Table 7.1, we see that the probability of rolling an eleven is 2/36 (or 1/18) or 5.6 percent.

Odds are a different matter. They are listed as the number of chances for (or against) versus the number of chances against (or for). Whether you state the odds as for or against is up to you. It would depend upon what you are interested in determining.

In our example of rolling an eleven, there is 1 chance that you will roll an eleven and 17 chances of your rolling something else. The odds *in favor* of your rolling eleven is 1 to 17. The *odds against* your rolling eleven is 17 to 1. This second statement is the way that gambling odds are typically expressed. Odds are used to compare the unfavorable possibilities (losing) with the favorable possibility (winning).

Here is another gambling example. What are the odds of winning the Powerball Lottery?[a] This is a two-part problem. First, you must determine the probability of matching all five white balls and the red ball (the "Powerball"). Unless the lottery draw is "fixed," these six draws are unrelated or independent.

The probability of drawing the Powerball number is 1/42 (one match out of 42 possible outcomes).

With the white balls, you have 5/49 chance of matching the first number and so on through the five numbers on your ticket. Using the multiplication rule, the probability of matching these five numbers on the white balls is $(5/49) \times (4/48) \times (3/47) \times (2/46) \times (1/45) = .000000524415748$ or odds of 1 in 1,906,884.

To determine the probability of winning the jackpot, you must multiply the probability of drawing the five numbers on the white balls times the probability of drawing the Powerball and get .0000000124861 or odds of 1 in 80,089,128.

[a] Minnesota State Lottery, "General Comments Regarding Odds," http://www.lottery.state.mn.us/odds.html.

According to this study, if incarceration rates from 1991 remain the same, 1 of every 20 persons (5.1%) living in the United States will go to prison in their lifetime. Of course, this probability varies by the sex and race of the person. For example,[2]

- Men (9%) are 8 times more likely than women (1.1%) to go to prison.
- Among men:
  — Blacks (28.5%) are about twice as likely as Hispanics (16%) to go to prison.
  — Blacks are about six times more likely than whites (4.4%) to go to prison.
- Among women:
  — 3.6% of blacks, 1.5% of Hispanics, and 0.5% of whites will enter prison at least once during their lifetime.

Example 7.2—The Birthday Problem*

What is the probability that two people in this class have the same birthday? Remember the basic law of probability: take the number of "successes" and divide it by the total number of possible outcomes.

$$P(A) \text{ was born on any given day} = 1/365$$
$$P(B) \text{ was born on any given day} = 1/365$$

Calculating the probability that persons A and B were born on any one specific day calls for the use of the multiplication rule. Recall that the multiplication rule covers events that are *not* mutually exclusive. That is exactly what we are considering here, the probability that A and B were *born on any one day* (e.g., February 21).

$$P(A) \times P(B) = (1/365)(1/365) = 1/133,225 = .000007506$$

The probability that A and B were *born on another specific day* calls for the use of the addition rule.

$$1/133,225 + 1/133,225 \ldots + 1/133,225 = 365/133,225 = 1/365$$
$$\text{(Jan. 1)} \qquad \text{(Jan. 2)} \qquad \text{(Dec. 31)}$$

Here, we add the fraction 1/133,225 once for every day in the year, or 365 times. This answer gives us the probability that any pair of people can have the same birthday.

For the entire class, the probability that at least one pair of students have the same birthday is as follows:

(The number of pairs of students) (1/365)

To calculate the number of pairs of students, use the following formula:

$$\frac{N(N-1)}{2}$$

For a class of 30:

$$\frac{N(N-1)}{2} \times (1/365) = \frac{30(29)}{2} \times (1/365) = 435/365 = 1.19$$

Because the probability is more than 100 percent, a bet that any two persons in a group of 30 have the same birthday appears to be a "sure thing"—the only one we have uncovered so far!

* This example is a staple when teaching probability. For a published example, see Dennis G. Haack, *Statistical Literacy: A Guide to Interpretation* (North Scituate, MA: Duxbury Press, 1979), pp. 92–94.

Compare these probabilities with the chance that these other events will occur during your lifetime:[3]

- 5 out of 6 persons are expected to be a victim of an attempted or completed violent crime at least once in their lifetime.

- 1 out of every 100 men and of every 323 women are expected to be a murder victim.

- 49.6% of all new marriages are expected to end in divorce.

- 1 in every 8 American women are projected to develop breast cancer in their lifetime.

How do these probabilities compare to the expectation of prison above? Is the likelihood of going to prison independent of these probabilities? Are they mutually exclusive?

Predictors of Victimization

We can use an example of empirical probability based upon research findings. We use data from a study of victimization rates among American Indians conducted by the Bureau of Justice Statistics.

Table 7.2 presents the percentage of violent crime victimization by age, race, and sex of victim for the time period 1992 to 1996. Among race and age groups, we can see that American Indians, ages 18–24, have the greatest rate of violent crime victimization. More than 31 percent of the members of this group had been the victim of a violent crime during this time period. Unless something changes, what would you anticipate about future victimization rates?

Table 7.2   Violent Crime Victimization—By Age, Race, and Sex of Victim, 1992–1996

Victim Age/Sex	Percentage of Violent Crime Victimization				
	American Indian	White	Black	Asian	Total
12–17	20.4%	23.8%	26.8%	24.0%	24.2%
18–24	31.5	23.4	24.0	21.7	23.6
25–34	23.5	23.6	23.2	26.3	23.6
35–44	18.0	17.1	16.6	18.3	17.0
45–54	4.7	7.8	6.1	7.3	7.5
55 and Older	1.9	4.3	3.3	2.4	4.1
Male	58.9	58.4	50.5	62.6	57.4
Female	41.1	41.6	49.5	37.4	42.6

Source: Lawrence A. Greenfeld and Steven Smith, "American Indians and Crime," U.S. Department of Justice, Bureau of Justice Statistics, http://www.ojp.usdoj.gov/bjs/pub/pdf/aic.pdf, p. 5.

How did we determine this? Reading a table is an important skill that researchers must develop. You must examine the labels on the table and look for patterns in the distribution of cases. Analyzing data presented in a table requires analytical thinking, not mathematical calculation. Here, we were looking for the highest percentage of violent crime victimization. From examining the values in Table 7.2, we determined that 31.5 percent was the greatest value. To find what age group had this high rate of violent crime victimization, we followed the row that contained 31.5 percent until we found the label for the age group, 18–24. To find which race had that highest rate of violent crime victimization, we followed the column that contained 31.5 percent until we found the label for the racial group, American Indian.

Using the same method, find the race/age group that had the lowest rate of violent crime victimization. Again, American Indians, ages 55 and older, reported the lowest rate of violent crime victimization (1.9%). Which race/sex group had the highest rate of violent crime victimization?

In this table, values listed in the "Total" column indicate the violent crime victimization rates for age and sex groups, regardless of their race. Among the age groups, who had the highest and lowest rates of violent crime victimization? Is there a pattern here? Follow the same logic to determine violent crime victimization patterns by sex.

In Table 7.3, what were the most dangerous sites for violent crime victimization? For which racial group? Which area could be called "the safest place"?

Research findings such as these can be used to predict future probabilities of crime. Data analysis can help us anticipate where problems will occur for particular segments of the population. We plan for the future and take action against crime, whether we are citizens or criminal justice system operatives.

Table 7.3   Violent Incidents, 1992–1996: By Place and Race of Victim

Place of Occurrence	Race and Percentage of Violent Victimizations				
	American Indian	White	Black	Asian	Total
Home	12%	14%	17%	12%	14%
Near Home	17	11	14	9	11
At, in, or near friend's, relative's, or neighbor's home	14	9	10	7	9
Businesses	13	14	9	19	13
Parking lots and garages	9	8	6	9	8
School	7	13	11	12	13
Open areas, street, or public transportation	19	21	28	24	22
Other	9	10	6	9	10

Source: Lawrence A. Greenfeld and Steven Smith, "American Indians and Crime," U.S. Department of Justice, Bureau of Justice Statistics, http://www.ojp.usdoj.gov/bjs/pub/pdf/aic.pdf, p. 10.

Probability Distributions

In chapter 3, we examined a frequency distribution where variable X has all possible values and f is the symbol for frequencies—how many times variable X (of a certain value) occurred in the distribution.

A probability distribution is directly analogous to a frequency distribution, except that it is based on probability theory rather than what you have observed in the real world (empirical data). In a probability distribution, we specify the possible values of a variable and calculate the probabilities associated with each. The probabilities represent the likelihood of each value—directly analogous to the percentages in a frequency distribution.

Suppose we flip two coins and let X represent the number of heads that we obtain. The variable X has three possible values 0, 1, and 2 (whether we obtain zero, one, or two heads on a flip).

1. Zero heads ($X = 0$) has a probability of P (0 heads) = P (tails on flip 1) P (tails on flip 2) = (.50) (.50) = .25. Thus you have a 25 percent probability of flipping zero heads on two coins.

2. Two heads ($X = 2$) has a probability of P (2 heads) = P (tails on flip 1) P (tails on flip 2) = (.50) (.50) = .25. Thus you have a 25 percent probability of flipping two heads on two coins.

3. Determining the remaining outcome, the probability of obtaining heads on one of the two flips can be expressed in two ways

   a. Heads on flip 1 and tails on flip 2

   b. Tails on flip 1 and heads on flip 2

   c. Using the addition rule, the probability of obtaining heads on one of the two flips can be expressed as: $P(H) P(T) + P(H) P(T) = (.50) (.50) + (.50) (.50) = .25 + .25 = .50$

Thus, the probability distribution for the number of heads in two coin flips looks like this:

X	Probability (P)
2	.25
1	.50
0	.25

Like a frequency distribution, a probability distribution has a mean. Because the mean of a probability distribution is the value that we expect to average in the long run, it is called the *expected value*. In our example of the number of heads obtained in two coin flips, the mean is 1. We use the Greek letter μ (mu) for the mean of a probability distribution (here μ = 1) in order *to distinguish it from X (the mean of the frequency distribution)*. The mean is the average value in a distribution. It is calculated (see chapter 4) from a set of observed data and their frequencies. On the other hand, the mean of our probability distribution (μ) is a quantity that comes from probability theory—our theory of what the distribution should look like or the expected value.

Probability and the Normal Curve

A key statistical tool in determining probability is the normal curve. The normal curve has a long history of development. In 1756, Abraham de Moivre described the normal curve in the first modern book on probability theory. De Moivre was primarily interested in determining the probabilities involved in games of chance, as we did above. In 1777, Jacques Bernoulli proposed a probability curve to describe errors in astronomical measurement. In 1778, Pierre-Simon de Laplace discovered the "bell curve" for the distribution of random errors in measurement. In 1808–1809, Robert Adrian and Carl Fredrich Gauss each developed the normal curve independently.[4]

The normal curve has also been used to interpret data in a theoretical fashion. For example, the Belgian statistician and criminologist Adolphe Quetelet believed that all social and moral data were distributed under the normal curve as a function of nature.[5] In a similar manner, criminologist Ruth Shonle Cavan used the normal curve to describe a "behavior continuum" to explain juvenile delinquency. The bell curve was used by Cavan to describe behavior ranging from the extremes of "underconforming contraculture" to "overconforming conformity." The peak of the curve was represented by "normal conformity." Her major conclusion was that reaction of the "normally conforming" segment of society varied in severity according to the threat to social norms of society. While minor delinquents are drawn back into conformity, serious ones are treated so severely that they are alienated and withdraw into a contraculture.[6]

Here, we are interested in the normal curve as a probability distribution based upon a mathematical model. It is typically used to describe distributions of scores and to infer probability.

The normal curve has a number of useful characteristics. First of all, it is bell shaped and symmetrical. Under the normal curve, the mean, median, and mode are equal. The point at which they lie (the peak of the curve) divides the normal curve into two equal parts. Half the scores lie above and below the mean (known as μ or mu). The second important parameter under the normal curve is the standard deviation (σ or sigma).

Using the normal curve as a probability distribution allows us to predict the areas under the curve. It is possible to calculate different proportions under the distribution. These areas are defined under the empirical rule:

- 68.26 percent of the distribution falls within ±1 standard deviation of the mean (μ).

- 95.46 percent of the distribution falls within ±2 standard deviation of the mean (μ).

The normal curve is interpreted as having a mean of 0 and a standard deviation of 1. Scores from a distribution can be converted or transformed into standard or z scores. The use of a standard score allows us to compare scores from two different distributions. Then, the normal curve is used to estimate areas between the scores. The formula for calculating a *standard score* is:

$$Z = X - \bar{X} / s$$

Where:

X is the score

$\bar{X}$ is the mean of the distribution

s is the standard deviation of the distribution

The standard score or z score indicates how far above or below the mean the score is in units of standard deviation. The normal curve is used to determine the percentage of scores falling below the standard score you have calculated. This interpretation is precisely the same as that made with percentiles (recall that the median is the 50th percentile). This means if you scored in the 50th percentile, 50 percent of individuals scored lower than you; or, of course, you scored better than 50 percent of the "competition." Note the denominator of the z score formula is the standard deviation of the distribution, while the numerator of the z score formula is the deviation for one score in the distribution. If the individual score is greater than the mean of the distribution, the z score is positive. If the score is less than the mean, then the z score is negative. Think about this in terms of an exam grade; you score a 92 percent and the class average is 80 percent. Since your score is greater than the class average, your standard z score is positive.

Consider charting this on Figure 7.1. The mean class score of 80 goes in the middle of the distribution and your positive z score will be somewhere to the right of the mean. In a normal distribution, this means you score better than at least one-half of your classmates (recall the mean, median, and mode in the normal distribution are equal). More specifically, the greater the z score, the greater is the percentage of scores lower than yours in the distribution.

To calculate the exact percentage of scores above or below a z score, use Table A.2 in the appendix. It reveals the distance between the score and μ under the normal curve. Because the normal curve is symmetrical, 50 percent of the scores fall on each side of μ. This is highlighted in Table A-2, as well as Figure 7.1.

Suppose a study of jail inmates revealed that the average years of education for the group was 11.1 years. The standard deviation was 1.4. Using these data, we can determine the z score for the jail inmate who had 9 years of education by using this formula:

$$z = X - \bar{X} / s; z = 9 - 11.1 / 1.4; z = -2 / 1.4 = -1.43$$

This z score is negative because this particular inmate's educational level (9 years) was below the average for the group (11.1 years). Go to Table A.2 (in the appendix). For a z score of 21.43, 42.36 percent of the scores fall between this score and μ. To interpret this as a percentile, we would *subtract* 42.36 per-

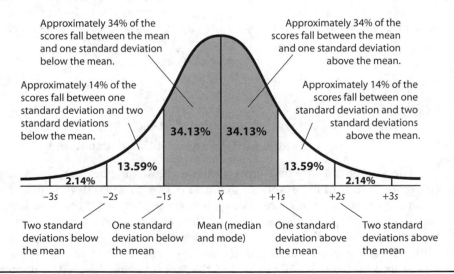

Figure 7.1   Areas under the Normal Curve

cent from 50 percent. We subtract this time since the educational level is below the mean and because we want to find the scores below X. More specifically, recall the number in the chart shows the percentage between the score (X) and the mean; thus, to find the percentage of scores below X, we subtract. Under the normal curve, only 7.64 percent of the jail inmates would have fewer years of education than this inmate (see Figure 7.2).

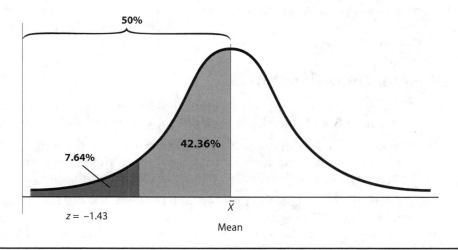

50%

42.36%

7.64%

$z = -1.43$

$\bar{X}$

Mean

Figure 7.2   *z* Score of –1.43

Remember, a negative z score is below the mean while a positive z score is above the mean. The best way to remember this fact is to draw a picture of where the score falls and its value. Then, look up the percentage of scores that fall between the score and the mean under the normal curve and write it in the appropriate area of your sketch. You must remember that the figure always reveals the area between the z score and μ. Always draw the sketch to clarify the area of interest.

The Binomial Distribution

Certain decisions and outcomes in the criminal justice system follow an either/or pattern. In statistical terms, this is known as a **Bernoulli process**, named for the Swiss mathematician Jacques Bernoulli (1654–1705): the outcome can be classified into one of two mutually exclusive categories.[7] There are three aspects to the Bernoulli process: (1) The researcher usually designates one outcome as a "success" (its probability = p) and the other as a "failure" (its probability = q): $p + q = 1$; $1 - p = q$; and $1 - q = p$. In criminal justice research, such outcomes are typically used to evaluate the results of a program or policy. For example, treatment program clients either pass (test negative) or fail (test positive) a drug test. Defendants in court are found guilty (convicted) or not guilty (acquitted). Parolees under a special type of supervision either commit a new crime (failure) or go straight (success). (2) The probability of success is unchanged from one trial to another. (3) The outcomes are *independent*. The probability of any event is not affected by the results of past events. Arguably, in the criminal justice arena, the notion of independent outcomes is not prevalent (e.g., sentencing guidelines). However, an example of the binomial distribution at work is the tossing of coins: the probability of tossing a heads or a tail in one coin flip is 50 percent. Therefore, $p + q = 1$ (50% + 50% = 100%), $1 - p = 50\%$ and $1 - q = 50\%$. See Table A.1 (appendix) for the binomial distribution.

The Central Limit Theorem

The normal curve is not just a theoretical construct. Some variables and functions are normally distributed. For example, the **central limit theorem** states:

If repeated random samples of a given size are drawn from any population (with a mean of μ and a variance of σ), then as the sample size becomes large, the sampling distribution of sample means approaches normality.

If the random samples are large enough (at least $N = 30$) the central limit theorem will hold. The sampling distribution of these sample means will be normally distributed. The population from which the samples are drawn need not be normally distributed.

To demonstrate the central limit theorem in operation, let us return to our distribution of probabilities of rolling dice. From the listed probabilities, we can estimate how many times each number would appear if we rolled the dice 100 times.

Each of the 100 rolls can be considered as a separate sample, and the results for each number can be interpreted as a sample mean. For example, we estimate that the number 12 will come up three times, 11 six times, and so on (see Table 7.4). The results presented in Figure 7.3 mirror the normal distribution (in this case, the distribution of the mean for 100 dice rolls).

We selected a sample of a given size (one roll of the dice) from the population (of possible dice rolls), repeated the procedure several (100) times, and constructed a distribution of numbers (the **sampling**

Table 7.4 Example of the Central Limit Theorem— Results from 100 Dice Rolls

X (Roll)	F (number)
12	3
11	6
10	8
9	11
8	14
7	16
6	14
5	11
4	8
3	6
2	3
	$N = 100$

distribution of the mean). The central limit theorem held true: the sample mean was normally distributed for large values of N.

Another important concept is the **standard error of the mean,** which is simply the standard deviation of the sampling distribution of the mean. It is calculated in the same manner as any standard deviation. Just as with any other standard deviation, it indicates how far (on average) a set of scores varies around

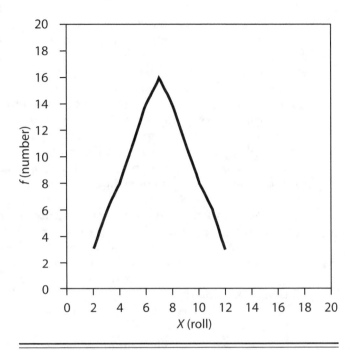

Figure 7.3   Distribution of the Results of 100 Dice Rolls

the mean of the distribution. Because it is drawn from the sampling distribution of the mean, it also indicates how far a sample mean falls from the population mean, a difference known as the "error."

Establishing Confidence Intervals

In criminal justice research, we often draw a sample from a population to study a research question. Typically, the sample results stand in place of the population. In most cases, it would be too expensive (in terms of both time and money) to contact each member of a population. Therefore, the sample stands in place of the population. The research then uses the sample results (sample = statistic) to draw an inference about the actual population value. The purpose of inferential statistics is to make conclusions—research findings drawn from a sample about a population. This decision is based upon probability.

For example, in June of 1997, Gennaro Vito and Thomas Keil conducted a survey of Kentuckians' attitudes toward capital punishment.[8] The survey was conducted a few weeks before Kentucky's first execution since 1962. A telephone survey was conducted with a random sample of Kentucky residents.

Random sampling has two essential components:

1. Each member of the population has an equal chance of being selected.

2. The selection of one element does not affect the probability that any other element will be selected (independence).

In this case, telephone numbers were generated at random by a computer. The phone numbers were random, but even random samples can undersample on certain characteristics of interest to us. So another technique is to include elements from the characteristic—such as rural areas. We can stratify by including area codes and phone prefixes from rural areas. A stratified, proportionate random sample (the difference between sample statistic and population parameter) was drawn so that the sample was representative of federal congressional districts across Kentucky. The sample contained the same percentage of cases for each congressional district that was present in the population. Therefore, if 25 percent of the population resides in the second congressional district, 25 percent of the sample comes from that district (709 × .25 = 175).*

We can use these data to demonstrate another statistical concept, the **confidence interval.** This measure is our first brush with inferential statistics. The confidence interval is an estimate of the population value based upon our sample results. With interval estimation, we use the values from our sample statistics to estimate what the population parameter (in this case, the population mean) could be.

To establish a confidence interval, we use the areas under the normal curve and the following formula:

$$\text{The Sample Mean} \quad \pm \quad (1.96)(S_x)$$

Where:

S_x = the sample standard deviation s' divided by the square root of N

This formula constructs a 95 percent confidence interval around the mean. The 95 percent confidence interval is an estimate. We are 95 percent "confident" that this interval contains the actual mean value from the population. Think of it as a net or fence that "captures" the population mean. Under the normal curve, the z scores or standard deviation values of ± 1.96 contain 95 percent of the scores. This is why 1.96 is in our formula.

For example, in this survey sample, the mean age of the respondents was 47.3. The N = 700 and the standard deviation for age was 16.9. Using our formula for the 95 percent confidence interval:

$$\text{The Sample Mean} \pm (1.96)(S_x)$$
$$(47.3) \pm (1.96)(S_x)$$

We need to calculate the value of S_x using our sample results for age:

S_x = the sample standard deviation s' divided by the square root of N
$$16.9/26.5$$
$$S_x = .64$$

---

* The final sample also overrepresented the number of blacks in the population to permit statistical analysis. This step was taken because only 25 percent of Kentuckians are black, and the research literature on capital punishment opinion indicates that race is related to death penalty support. The sample was then weighted to control for this oversampling so that the final results would be representative of the Kentucky population.

Now, we add this figure to our formula:

$$(47.3) \pm (1.96)(S_x)$$
$$(47.3) \pm (1.96)(.64)$$
$$(47.3) \pm (1.25)$$

Therefore, the 95 percent confidence interval for age is 46.05 to 48.55. This means we are 95 percent confident that the average age of a Kentucky resident in June 1997 fell between 46.05 and 48.55 years of age. We have used the data from our sample to estimate what the population mean for age could be. It is important to construct such confidence intervals because it shows our "confidence" that the sample is representative of the Kentucky population at that time.

Consider the summary of the findings from this survey:

- A majority of Kentucky residents (69.5%) support the use of capital punishment for persons convicted of murder.
- The level of support dropped (38% in favor of capital punishment), however, when life without parole (with restitution) is available as a sentencing option.

The level of support for capital punishment among Kentucky residents generally declined when the personal characteristics of the offender were considered:

- Twenty-eight percent of the respondents supported the execution of the mentally ill.
- Forty-two percent of the respondents favored the execution of juveniles.
- If the offender is under the influence of either alcohol (67%) or drugs (69%), however, a majority of Kentuckians support execution in murder cases.

Support for the death penalty also wavered under certain circumstances.

- Thirty-one percent favor execution when there are two offenders and one receives a lesser sentence.

Kentuckians also believe that a number of procedural issues in capital sentencing should be addressed.

- Fifty-one percent of Kentucky residents favored clemency (by the governor) when new evidence that was not available at trial is discovered.
- Almost 90 percent of the respondents agreed that court-appointed lawyers should meet professional guidelines to ensure they can provide an adequate defense.
- Just more than 50 percent of Kentuckians feel that it is unfair for minorities to be tried and sentenced to death by an all-white jury.
- An overwhelming majority (more than 90%) of the respondents felt that laws should guarantee that there is no racial bias in the application of the death penalty.

- Fifty-eight percent of the respondents favored a review of the prosecutor's decision to seek the death penalty.

Regarding the circumstances surrounding the offense:

- About 75 percent of the respondents favored the death penalty in cases involving more than one victim.
- More than 80 percent of Kentuckians have supported capital punishment when the murder was premeditated and deliberate.

Support for the death penalty varies by race, gender, and congressional district in Kentucky.

- About 57 percent of the African American and 71 percent of the white respondents favored capital punishment.
- Males (79%) were more likely to support the death penalty than females (62%).
- Within congressional districts, support for capital punishment ranged from a high of 77.2 percent in district 2 (Congressman Lewis) to a low of about 60 percent in districts 5 (Congressman Rodgers) and 6 (Congressman Baesler).

The results are a good example of the variation that is revealed when you ask more specific questions about a variable. Death penalty support varied depending upon the circumstances of the offense, the characteristics of the offender, and the availability of other penalties.

These findings are examples of empirical probability. They can be used to predict how future juries will react to homicide cases. They can also determine probable future levels of support for the death penalty, as well as address the reaction to certain policies. For example, if we simply consider the age of the defendant, a jury is less likely to support a death sentence for a juvenile because only 42 percent of the respondents favor the execution of juveniles. The U.S. Supreme Court abolished the death penalty for juveniles in *Roper v. Simmons* (2005) based, in part, on this type of evidence. In future cases, prosecutors would need to stress (aggravating) circumstances that would increase the probability for supporting a death sentence, like stressing the defendant's use of alcohol or drugs (increases to 67% and 69% respectively) or multiple victims (75% favored execution with multiple victims).

Summary

In this chapter, we saw how probabilities can be calculated when certain specified conditions are met. Probabilities help us to determine the likelihood that an event will occur. The different types of probabilities (especially mathematical and empirical) were presented and illustrated.

Probabilities also have another statistical function. They are the basis for statistical inference—using sample data and statistical analysis to estimate what population values may be. In this chapter, we saw how the normal curve can be used to establish confidence intervals and estimate the value of the population mean. This example of estimation is our first brush with statistical inference—the key topic of the following chapter.

The reason we devote attention to probability is not to figure out gambling odds. Probability is at the heart of statistical inference—making generalizations about population values based upon statistical results from a sample. If the sample is randomly selected, then the concept of probability is used to determine whether or not a statistical finding is arrived at by chance alone.

Key Terms

Mathematical Probability: type of probability that is based upon equally likely outcomes that can be calculated, such as coin tosses or dice rolls

Empirical Probability: type of probability based upon observed data or research from the past, such as estimating probabilities based upon survey results from a random sample of respondents

Subjective Probability: individual opinion about the probability of an event

Law of Probability: The probability of an event is the number of ways it can happen, as a fraction of the number of all possible things that could happen. This rule holds if all possible outcomes of an event are *equally likely* (e.g., flipping a coin—either heads or tails). The probability that either event will occur is equal to the ratio of "success" (e.g., the coin comes up heads—only one way) to the number of possible outcomes (two—either heads or tails).

Gambler's Fallacy: The probability that you would flip a coin and it would come up "heads" is one out of two or 50 percent. Note also that the probability of flipping a head extends to the next toss and every toss thereafter. Yet many people mistakenly believe that, if you tossed ten heads in a row, the probability of tossing another is astronomical. In fact, it has never changed—it is still 50 percent.

Mutually Exclusive: The occurrence of one event prevents the occurrence of another. They cannot occur simultaneously. In criminal justice, an example of a mutually exclusive event is a trial outcome: acquitted or guilty; an accused individual or a single trial/offense charge cannot have both outcomes.

Addition Rule: used to calculate the probability of mutually exclusive events. If two events are mutually exclusive, the probability of their occurrence is equal to the sum of their separate probabilities.

Multiplication Rule: covers events that are *not* mutually exclusive, such that the probability of their occurrence is equal to the product of their separate probabilities

Bernoulli Process (Binomial Distribution): The outcome can be classified into one of two mutually exclusive categories. There are three aspects: (1) The researcher usually designates one outcome as a "success" (its probability = p) and the other as a "failure" (its probability = q). (2) The probability of success is unchanged from one trial to another. (3) the outcomes are *independent*.

Central Limit Theorem: If repeated random samples of a given size are drawn from any population (with a mean of μ and a variance of σ), then as the sample size becomes large, the sampling distribution of sample means approaches normality.

Sampling Distribution of the Mean: the distribution of the means of all possible samples drawn from a population. Under the central limit theorem, the sample mean is normally distributed for large values of N.

Standard Error of the Mean: the standard deviation of the sampling distribution of the mean. It indicates how far a sample mean falls from the population mean, a difference known as the "error."

Confidence Interval: an estimate of the population value based upon sample results.

Exercises

1. The Kentucky Legislature passed a law that provides for a sentence of life without parole in homicide cases. Using empirical probability (based upon the Vito and Keil survey results), what do you think will happen in Kentucky?

2. Again, use the survey findings to anticipate the verdict of a Kentucky jury in a death penalty case in which a disgruntled worker has been fired for failing to report for work on time and for poor performance. He threatens his supervisor when he leaves work. He returns to the factory, waits in ambush, and shoots and kills his former supervisor and another office worker. The suspect has a long history of mental illness and drug abuse but no prior record of crime. How would you advise the defense attorneys in this case?

3. A study of persons ($N = 1170$) indicted for murder in Kentucky revealed that each individual had an average number of 1.69 prior felony arrests. The standard deviation was 2.6 (20 points).

   a. Calculate the 95 percent confidence interval for this distribution and write a statement about what it represents.

   b. Determine the z score for a murder defendant who had two prior felony arrests. Under the normal curve, what statement could you make about this z score?

4. You are among 237 citizens who have been selected for jury duty. Using this base, determine the following probabilities:

   a. That you will be one of 45 citizens selected for a jury panel.

   b. That you will then be one of 12 citizens selected to serve as members of the jury.

Notes

[1] Fred Hoppe, "Mathematical Appendix to Maclean's Magazine Article by John Schofield, November 4, 1996." http://www.icarus.mcmaster.ca/fred/lotto (accessed 4/9/07).

[2] Thomas P. Bonczar and Allen J. Beck, "Lifetime Likelihood of Going to State or Federal Prison," U.S. Department of Justice, Bureau of Justice Statistics, March 1997. http://www.ojp.usdoj.gov/bjs/pub/pdf/llgsfp.pdf, p. 1.

[3] *Ibid.*, p. 2.

[4] Deborah J. Bennett, *Randomness Timeline*, Harvard University Press, http://www.hup.harvard.edu/features/benran/timeline.html

[5] John H. Mueller, Karl F. Schuessler, and Herbert L. Costner, *Statistical Reasoning in Sociology* (Boston: Houghton Mifflin Company, 1977), p. 169.

[6] Ruth Shonle Cavan, "The Concepts of Tolerance and Contraculture as Applied to Delinquency." Presidential Address, Midwest Sociological Society, April 28, 1961.

[7] W. Paul Vogt, *Dictionary of Statistics and Methodology*, 2nd ed. (Newbury Park, CA: Sage Publications, 1999).

[8] Gennaro F. Vito and Thomas J. Keil, "Elements of Support for Capital Punishment: An Examination of Changing Attitudes," *Journal of Crime and Justice,* Vol. 21 (1998), pp.17–36.

chapter 8

Difference between Means
The *t*-Test

Statistical analysis frequently involves two forms of statistical inference: estimating population parameters and hypothesis testing. We demonstrate estimation when we determine confidence intervals (see chapter 7). Using sample statistics (the mean and standard deviation), we estimate the value of the population mean within a certain level of confidence (see chapter 5). Here, we introduce a method of parameter estimation for small samples using the *t* distribution.

This chapter also introduces the basic concepts behind hypothesis testing. Statistics provide a method of determining whether or not our research findings would hold true if we had population, instead of sample, data. Our first example of statistical testing is the *t*-test between sample means.

The *t* Distribution

Chapter 7 examined the use of the normal curve to estimate confidence intervals for the population mean (μ) given some sample. In the formula, we use the standard error of the mean (*s*/square root of *N*) as an estimate. The problem with this procedure is that it is inaccurate when you have a small sample of cases, say 30 or fewer. When the sample size is small, the variability in the standard error of the mean increases and the resulting figure is inaccurate. It also alters the assumption that the sampling distribution of the mean is normally distributed (the central limit theorem) because we have introduced another source of variability.

For these reasons, we cannot use *z* scores to estimate the confidence interval for small samples. William S. Gossett developed the distributions that are accurate in this case. Gossett wrote under the pseudonym "Student" to protect his work from his employer. This family of distributions became known as *t*. The shape of the *t* distribution varies by the size of the sample. The **degrees of freedom** determine the shape of the *t* distribution and are defined as the number of scores that are free to vary in a sample. Degrees of freedom are calculated by subtracting one from the sample size ($N - 1$). The *z* and *t* distributions are somewhat alike: they both have a mean of zero, are symmetrical, and are bell shaped. The areas under the t distribution, however, are spread farther out toward the tails of the distribution. As the sample size grows, the t distribution coincides with the normal curve.

When the sample size is small the t distribution is used instead of the normal curve. The formula for the 95 percent confidence interval is similar to that used with z scores:

$$95\% \text{ C.I.} = \bar{X} \pm (\text{the } t \text{ value})\left(s / \sqrt{N-1}\right)$$

The value of t at the 95 percent confidence level is dependent upon the degrees of freedom. Its value changes with the shape of the t distribution. Unlike the normal curve, the shape of the t distribution is not fixed.

Take the following example (see Table 8.1). We have a random sample of recently arrested sex offenders ($N = 10$) and their number of prior arrests on sex crime charges. The mean is 4 and the standard deviation is 1.7. The degree of freedom for this example is 9. The value of t associated with the 95 percent confidence level with 9 degrees of freedom is 2.26. Substitutions can be made in our formula:

$$95\% \text{ C.I.} = \text{the Sample Mean} \pm (\text{the } t \text{ value})\left(s / \sqrt{N-1}\right)$$

$$95\% \text{ C.I.} = 4 \pm (2.26)\left(1.7 / \sqrt{9}\right)$$

$$95\% \text{ C.I.} = 4 \pm (2.26)(1.7 / 3)$$

$$95\% \text{ C.I.} = 4 \pm (2.26)(0.57)$$

$$95\% \text{ C.I.} = 4 \pm (1.29)$$

$$95\% \text{ C.I.} = 2.71 \text{ to } 5.29$$

Table 8.1   Number of Prior Arrests for Sex Offenders

X (Number of Prior Arrests for Sex Crime Charges)	F (Number of Sex Offenders)	fX
6	3	18
5	2	10
4	1	4
3	2	6
2	1	2
1	1	1
	$N = 10$	$\Sigma fX = 41$

Therefore, using the t distribution, we are 95 percent certain that the population mean of prior sex-charge arrests for the population of sex offenders could be as low as 2.96 or as high as 5.04. Because of the small sample size ($N = 10$), this estimate using the t distribution is more appropriate and valid than using the normal curve to provide an estimate of the population mean.

Hypothesis Testing

To the uninitiated person, hypothesis testing may appear to be based upon a peculiar logic. Actually, it is an extension of what we did with confidence intervals (estimation): "Based upon our analysis of sample data, how certain can we be that the population parameter is a certain value?" In fact, this is what **statistical significance** means—there is a good chance that the statistical findings you made in your sample are also present in the population in question. Remember that researchers typically deal with a sample of data. Here, the statistical test gives you the probability that what you found in the sample is also present in the population from which it was drawn.

Attaining statistical significance does not mean that the finding is important. This hang-up comes from the term "significance." The importance of the finding actually comes from comparison to previous research and how it ties into theory. A small difference in crime rates may be statistically significant but rather unimportant.

Unfortunately, a lot of statistical jargon is also associated with the process. Falling into the trap of spouting jargon is a fatal error for students because it gets in the way of clarity. The rest of the world will not understand what you are talking about. A key to good statistical analysis is clarity of presentation. So your mission is to understand the jargon but to communicate what it means in the simplest manner possible.

Hypothesis testing uses statistical analysis to determine whether or not individual research (or sample) findings are the same as or different than the population, or whether the findings of a sample's pre- and post-test measurements are the same or different. A hypothesis is a statement of relationship between two variables. The "relationship" stated depends on whether the hypothesis is a null or research (alternative) hypothesis.

A **null hypothesis** (H_0) is a statement of no difference or no relationship between two variables. This is the hypothesis which is tested in hypothesis testing. A **research** or **alternative hypothesis** (H_a) states some relationship between two variables. Both the choice of variables and the "relationship" stated in an alternative hypothesis are grounded in theory or prior research.

Consider testing a research hypothesis that educational level is related to criminality. More specifically, after reviewing theory and prior research, the alternative hypothesis is: Individuals who have not earned a high school diploma are more likely to have been arrested for a violent crime. When one selects the sample and tests this hypothesis, he or she is essentially testing whether the finding in the sample is "significantly different" than the finding one would get if he or she was testing the entire population. Such a hypothesis test is interpreted much in the same way as confidence intervals; that is, we are 95% confident that the sample finding is the same as what we would find in the population, or we are confident in the alternative (that the findings are different or the findings are not related).

Stating Hypotheses

We also test hypotheses that compare two or more samples. For example, consider a study by Richard Tewksbury and Gennaro Vito.[1] They conducted an evaluation of a program designed to improve the educational performance of jail inmates. The hope was that if jail inmates could improve their reading and math skills, they would improve their ability to find employment. Employment could then reinforce their ties to the community. (According to Reckless's containment theory, the inmates would have a "stake in conformity" that would cause them to think twice about committing a crime.)

Therefore, the research hypothesis was as follows:

> The educational performance (as determined by reading and math scores) of the inmates would improve after they completed the program.

The research hypothesis emerges from theory or from the findings of previous research. This example comes from applied research—program evaluation. In evaluation research, the research hypothesis is usually stated in a fashion that is favorable to the program.

You should also note that this hypothesis is a **one-tailed** or **directional hypothesis** (see Figure 8.1). The researchers not only assert that differences in outcome will occur, they also state the direction that the differences will take. They predict that the educational performance of the inmates will improve following completion of the program. Typically, the reason for stating a one-tailed hypothesis comes from theory, previous research findings, or both. Here, the program would be judged a failure if the math and reading skills of the inmates did not improve. If we had no reason to expect a difference in outcome, we would state a **two-tailed** or **nondirectional hypothesis** (see Figure 8.2). This could occur when a new method of treatment was being tested or when the previous research findings about a program or policy were mixed or inconclusive.

It is important to note that in statistical analysis, you do not test the research hypothesis directly. Instead, you test the null hypothesis (H_0): the hypothesis of no difference or no relationship. In our example, one null hypothesis might be:

> There would be *no change in the educational performance* (as determined by reading and math scores) of the inmates after they completed the program.

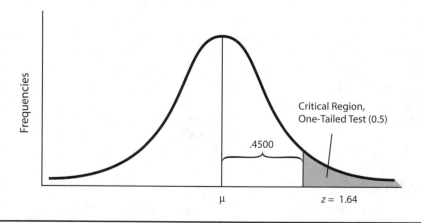

Figure 8.1   One-Tailed Test

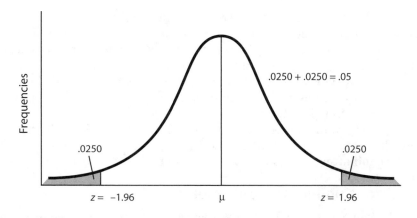

Figure 8.2   Two-Tailed Test

A second null hypothesis might be:

> There is no relationship between educational performance and completion of the program.

You can see that the null hypothesis is usually formed in the hope that it will ultimately be rejected. In other words, if the research results on this educational program fit the research hypothesis, the program will be considered a success. If the performance of the educational inmates improved, then the program was effective. In order for the null hypothesis to be "rejected," the test of significance findings would be "significant" or "significantly different."

If we retain the null hypothesis based upon the research results, the educational performance of the inmates would stay the same. If you found the null hypothesis to be true, you would be saying that the educational program had no effect. In any event, the null hypothesis is the hypothesis that you test statistically.

The reason we test the null hypothesis is that we cannot determine exactly whether or not the results of our sample (statistics) represent what the population value (parameter) is. This is why we never "prove" anything in social science research; rather, we determine if something is more or less likely to occur. Remember, we could only estimate and give a range that, within a certain probability (95 percent), contained the population mean (again, the confidence interval). The same logic is true in hypothesis testing. We can only state the probability that the results of our analysis of sample data actually represent what is going on in the population. Testing the null hypothesis is the heart of this process.

In addition, the research hypothesis in this case was not specific. Although it said that the inmates would improve their reading and math skills, it did not say by how much. The null hypothesis provided a clear-cut, specific statement: the difference between the groups would be zero. In other words, there would be no improvement in reading and math scores.

Another explanation is that testing the null hypothesis allows the researcher to consider all possible outcomes simultaneously. In our example, the research findings may support the program (i.e., the educational performance of the jail inmates improves after they complete the program) or find that inmate performance declines (they do not improve—their educational performance remains the same or deteriorates). Testing the null hypothesis would examine all of these possibilities.

In our example, a decision to reject the null hypothesis is the same as saying that there is a real difference between the reading and math test scores before and after the inmates took part in the instructional program.

Decisions under the Null Hypothesis

As you can see in Table 8.2, two types of errors can occur during the process. **Type I error** is committed when the researcher makes the decision to reject the null hypothesis when, in the population, H_0 is true. The chance of making a Type I error is known as the **level of significance** or the **alpha level (α).** The researcher sets it. The convention is to use the .05 level of significance as the probability of committing Type I error. If you make the decision to reject H_0, you are 95 percent certain that your decision accurately reflects what is true in the population, but there is a 5 percent chance that your decision is wrong. This concept is directly related to the confidence interval. Note that we are again talking about 95 percent certainty that we are correct or "confident." The only difference is that now we are focusing on the probability of being wrong (5 percent).

When using a statistical computer program such as SPSS, you must interpret the significance level to make a decision about the null hypothesis. The program will calculate the statistic that you have asked for and the actual probability of obtaining that value in the distribution in question. *Therefore, to reject the null hypothesis, the statistical value must have a significance level equal to or less than ($\geq$) .05.*

Table 8.2　Testing the Null Hypothesis

Decision	What Is True in the Population	
	H_0 is True	H_0 Is False
Reject H_0	Type I error	Correct
Accept H_0	Correct	Type II error

Type II error (β error) is committed when the researcher makes the decision to accept the null hypothesis when, in the population, H_0 is false. Your findings tell you that there is no statistical relationship in the population of cases when, in fact, there is a relationship. Type I and Type II errors are related in a seesaw manner. If the probability of Type I error decreases, the probability of Type II error increases. Unlike the probability of Type I error, the probability of Type II error cannot be computed. One source of Type II error is violating the assumptions of a statistical test. This would lead to the wrong conclusion about H_0.

Always remember that accepting or rejecting the null hypothesis is a decision, not a conclusion. You must discuss the findings and what happened in your analysis. In our example, we want to know if the inmate's educational performance improved. A conclusion of "I reject the null hypothesis" does not tell us what happened. Describe what happened in your sample first, and then make the decision about the null hypothesis.

To summarize, hypothesis testing involves

- Forming a research hypothesis (based upon a review of previous research findings on the subject and the relevant theories involved)
- Stating the null hypothesis
- Drawing a sample
- Collecting and analyzing the data
- Reaching a decision on the null hypothesis
- Interpreting the meaning of the results, including the policy implications of the findings to the criminal justice system

Let's return to our example and review this process.

t-Test for Related Samples

The *t*-test is a test of the difference between sample means. It is expressed as a ratio—the difference between the two means divided by the standard error of the difference.* There are two types of *t*-test. Their formulas are presented in the text box.

The **related (or paired) samples** *t*-test is used when you are comparing the same people over time. It is appropriate when your analysis is based upon two measurements of the same variable for the same individuals over time. With related *t*-tests, the difference between each pair of scores for each individual is computed. These differences are then used to estimate the standard error of the difference scores.

Our example fits the requirements for the related samples *t*-test. Tewksbury and Vito compared the mean math and reading scores of jail inmates before and after completion of the inmate literacy program. The higher the reading and math scores were on the CASAS (Comprehensive Adult Student Assessment System) scale, the better the performance was. They followed the math and reading performance of 20 jail inmates who completed the program.

Using SPSS, we analyzed the data to obtain a paired sample *t*-test. Our results (see Table 8.3) reveal that the mean score in math went up 10.4 points (from 216.2 to 226.6). The *t* value of 3.611 (10.4—the mean difference—divided by 2.88—the standard error of the mean—ignore the sign on a *t*-test) was statistically significant at the .002 level (two-tailed). This would make the one-tailed significance .001 (.002 divided by 2) much less than our alpha level of .05. So we would reject the null hypothesis that the scores remained the same. The difference in mean math scores was statistically significant. The chances

---

*The standard error of the difference between means $\left(\sigma = \bar{X}_1 - \bar{X}_2\right)$ is the standard deviation of the distribution of the difference between pairs of sample means. It is computed from the differences between the means of all possible pairs of samples that can be drawn from a given population.

Calculation Formula: *t*-Test for Related (or Paired) Samples

1. Estimate the population variance of the difference scores:

$$s_D^2 = N\Sigma D^2 - \left(\Sigma D^2\right)/N(N-1)$$

Where: $D = X_1 - X_2$ for each pair of scores

2. Estimate the population standard error of the mean difference score by taking the square root of step 1, divided by *N*:

$$\text{standard error of the difference} = \sqrt{s_D^2/N}$$

3. Calculate the *t*-test by taking the difference between the two means and dividing by the answer in step 2 (standard error of the difference).

$$t = \bar{X}_1 - \bar{X}_2 / \text{ standard error of the difference}$$

Where the degrees of freedom = the Number of Pairs of Scores − 1

---

are good that this program would benefit similarly situated jail inmates in other locations. The findings have some relevance beyond this population.

A similar pattern of improvement was recorded on the reading test. The mean score on the reading test improved by 12.75 points (from 221.85 to 234.6). The *t* value of 4.45 (12.75—the mean difference—divided by 2.87—the standard error of the mean) was statistically significant at the .000 level. This significance level is also less than .05, so the null hypothesis is rejected. The difference in mean reading scores was statistically significant. The reading scores of jail inmates elsewhere would likely improve if they took part in such an educational program.

Table 8.3 Paired Samples *t*-Test SPSS Results—Math and Reading Test Mean Scores*

	Math Results				
	Mean Score	**Mean Difference**	**Degrees of t-value**	**Sig. Level Freedom**	**(two-tailed)**
Pre-test	216.2	10.4	3.61	19	.002
Post-test	226.6				
	Reading Results				
	Mean Score	**Mean Difference**	**Degrees of t-value**	**Sig. Level Freedom**	**(two-tailed)**
Pre-test	221.85	12.75	4.45	19	.000
Post-test	234.6				

* The mean difference in Pair 1 (math pre-test – math post-test), the value is –10.4. This is because the mean of the math post-test (226.6) was subtracted from the mean on the math pre-test (216.2). So it is best to just ignore the sign of the figures on this entire table. The order of the tests determined the sign. The point is that both the math and reading scores of the jail inmates improved upon completion of the educational program.

Overall, we can say that this educational program improved the math and reading skills of the jail inmates who participated in it. This interpretation does not come from the statistical findings alone. It comes from the literature review—on the CASAS scale itself and what it represents. Under the CASAS scale, a score above 225 classifies a student as a "Level D Learner"—a person who is functioning at or above a high school entry level in basic reading or math. These students can profit from high school (or GED) level instruction; meet survival needs, routine work, and social demands; and perform work involving oral directions. Thus, the educational program readied the jail inmates for more educational work at the GED level and, it is hoped, improved their chance of obtaining employment upon release. Therefore, research findings are not simply interpreted in terms of statistical significance. The policy implications of the findings must be discussed.

None of the data sets on the CD that accompanies this text contain paired samples, but you should understand when to use the related samples t-test, how to calculate it, and what it represents.

t-Test for Independent Samples

Our previous example covered testing the difference between sample means when the two samples are related or paired. What if the two samples are independent? **Independent samples** are not related or paired in some fashion. If your samples have been assigned at random to experimental and control groups, they are independent samples. Another possibility is comparing segments of a sample that a variable divides into two different groups.

Now, we use our SPSS to calculate an independent samples t-test. We use the NCSD data set. In this example, we compare the mean scores on a police rating scale between Anglo and minority respondents. We constructed the police rating scale using three questions from the National Crime Survey. In the survey, respondents were asked to rate the police according to how quickly they responded to calls, their friendliness, and their fairness in dealing with the public. Each question was ranked in the following manner: (5)very high, (4) high, (3) average, (2) low, (1) very low. Therefore, the range in our police rating scale was 15 to 3. The higher the score, the higher the respondent's rating of the police. Traditionally, research findings indicate that race is one of the strongest predictors of attitudes toward the police. In terms of race, minority group members (especially African Americans) are distrustful of the police and believe that they are the victims of discriminatory treatment.[2]

Our research hypothesis is that Anglos will have higher mean police rating scores than their minority group counterparts. It is a one-tailed hypothesis. The null hypothesis is that there will be no difference in mean police rating scores between Anglo and minority respondents.

SPSS: t-Test for Independent Samples

To run the t-test for independent samples under SPSS, take the following steps.

1. Open the NCSD data set (Figure 8.3).

2. Click on "Analyze," then on "Compare Means," and then click on "Independent-Samples T Test" (Figure 8.4).

3. The next screen has the box "Independent-Samples T Test" (Figure 8.5). Find the variable "Police Rating Score," and click on the arrow to paste it into the "Test Variable(s)" window.

4. Find the variable, "Race Recode," click on it and then click on the arrow in the box to paste it into the "Grouping Variable" window. Then click on the box "Define Groups."

5. The next screen has the box "Define Groups" (Figure 8.6). Place a 1 in the blank for Group 1 and 2 in the blank for Group 2. Then click on the box labeled "Continue."

6. You will then return to the "Independent-Samples T Test" screen (Figure 8.7). and click on the box labeled "OK" to obtain your computer output and statistics (Table 8.4).

The first group of data in Table 8.4, Group Statistics, contains descriptive statistics concerning our two groups. The mean police rating score of Anglos (the first group) is 10.85. The mean police rating score of minorities (the second group) is 9.52. The Anglo survey respondents gave the police a higher

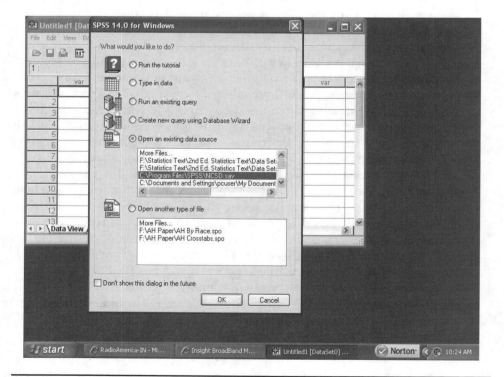

Figure 8.3

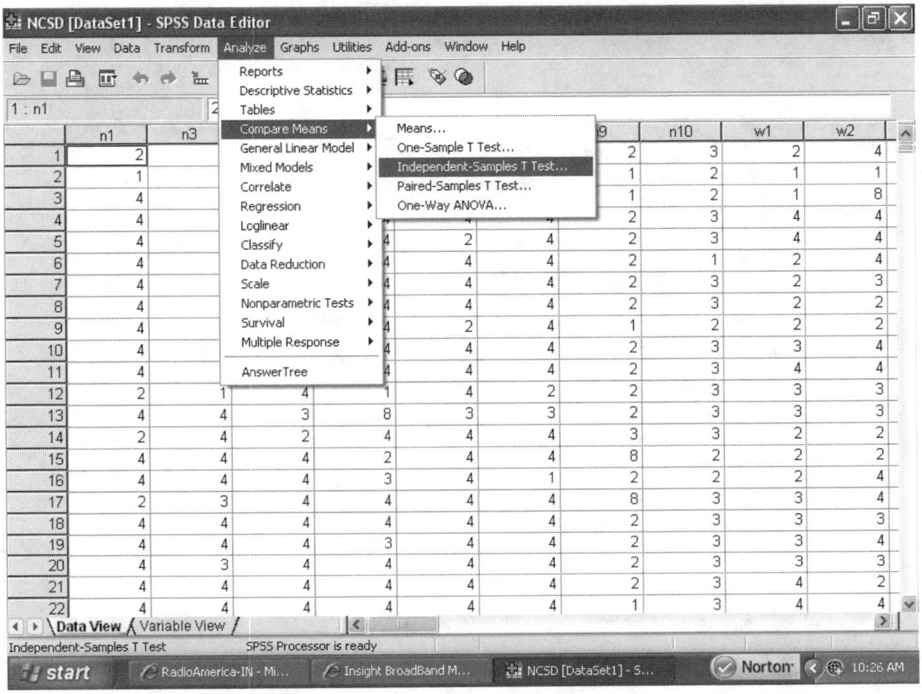

Figure 8.4

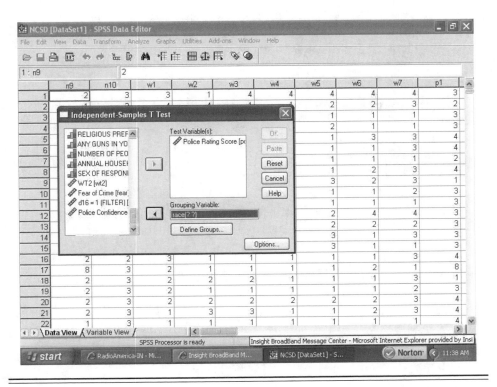

Figure 8.5

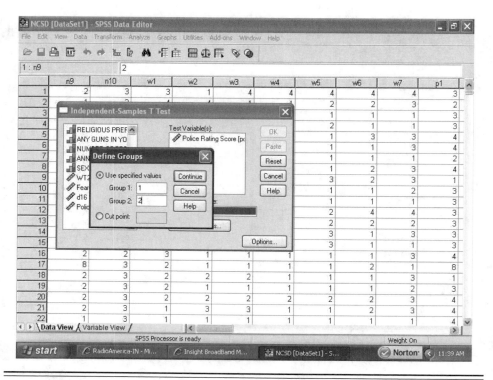

Figure 8.6

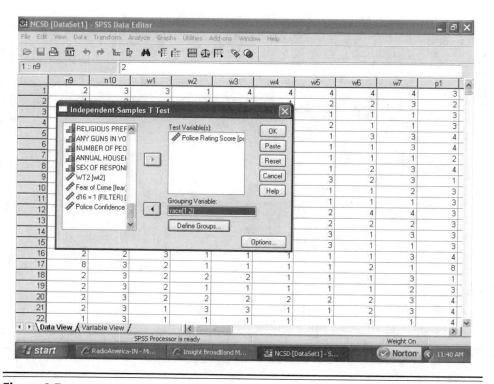

Figure 8.7

average rating than the minority respondents. This finding supports our research hypothesis. Anglos give the police higher ratings for service than minority group members do. This is our conclusion, and it is built on an interpretation of our research hypothesis. This conclusion, however, is an interpretation of the means between the groups in the survey. How do we know if this difference exists in the entire population (the nation) from which the sample was drawn?

This is exactly where inferential statistics come in. The t-test results will tell us if there is a substantial probability that the difference in the mean police rating scores between Anglos and minorities is true in the population. Remember that the t-test is a test of difference between means. It is this difference (if it does exist) that must be interpreted in terms of direction and amount.

The decision to accept or reject the null hypothesis is just that—a decision. It is not an interpretation of the results of the analysis. Once the conclusion is reached, however, the decision to reject or retain the null hypothesis will tell us whether or not we can assume that this finding would occur in the population and/or whether it was due to chance. You must remember this distinction between a conclusion and a decision. Otherwise, your analyses and reports will be filled with the worst type of statistical jargon that is difficult to comprehend. Avoid this mistake at all costs! Always interpret the data results first and then go on to make your decision about the null hypothesis. The formulas for t-test are presented in the text box.

The t-test formula is a ratio of the difference between sample means divided by the standard error (standard deviation) of the difference between sample means. In order to conduct this analysis, it is necessary to estimate the standard error of the difference.

Calculation Formula: t-test for Independent Samples

1. Estimate the pooled population variance for the data in the two samples.

$$s^2 = \sum x_1^2 + \sum x_2^2 / N_1 + N_2 - 2$$

Where:

$$\sum x_1^2 = \text{the sum of squares for the first sample}$$
$$\sum x_2^2 = \text{the sum of squares for the second sample}$$

2. Estimate the standard error of the difference between means. Take the answer from step 1, divide it by N_1 and then by N_2, add them together, and take the square root.

$$s\bar{X}_1 - \bar{X}_2 = \sqrt{s^2 / N_1 + s^2 / N_2}$$

3. Compute the t-test for independent samples by dividing the difference between the two sample means by the answer from step 2.

$$t = \bar{X}_1 - \bar{X}_2 / s\bar{X}_1 - \bar{X}_2$$

Degrees of Freedom $= N_1 + N_1 - 2$

First, we must determine whether the two sample variances are equal or not. In SPSS, Levine's Test for Equality of Variances (see Table 8.4) does this for us. Here, we must examine the significance value for the F test and the significance level associated with it. When we assume equal variances between samples, we are actually deciding whether to accept or reject the null hypothesis: there is no difference between the variance of samples one and two. To reject the null hypothesis, the significance of the statistical results must be *equal to or less than .05*. In this case, the significance level of F is .199. We cannot reject the null hypothesis, because .199 is greater than .05. We must assume that the variance in police rating scores is equal across the two groups.

Therefore, we can use the results labeled "Equal variances assumed" to interpret the t-test values. If we had rejected the null hypothesis using the Levine test results, we would use the t-test results listed under "Equal variances *not* assumed." This result is important because it affects the degrees of freedom used to calculate the t-test, the shape of the t distribution, and the region of rejection.

Turning to the Independent Samples Test (Table 8.4), the mean difference between the police rating scores of Anglos and minorities is 1.33. Anglos had a higher average police rating score.

This table also contains the results of our t-test. Under the t column, for the row labeled "Equal variances assumed," we see that the t value is 6.031 (Mean Difference/Std. Error of the Difference, with 876 degrees of freedom ($N_1 + N_2 - 2 = 878 - 2 = 876$).

Then, SPSS always computes the level of significance for a two-tailed test (under column labeled "Sig. (two-tailed)." If you have stated a nondirectional, two-tailed research hypothesis, then you can directly interpret the significance level in the standard way. If the significance is less than or equal to .05, you would reject the null hypothesis.

In this case, however, our research hypothesis is one-tailed. We would expect Anglos to have a higher average police rating score than minorities. When your research hypothesis is directional or one-tailed, simply divide the listed significance level in two and then make your decision regarding the null hypothesis. The significance level in our example would be .000 divided by two or .000. Because this significance level is lower than .05, we make the decision to reject the null hypothesis. This means that there is a 95 percent chance that the observed difference in police mean rating scores between the two samples (1.33) is a true difference that exists between the two samples and is not attributable to chance.

Here, the findings support previous research on citizens' attitudes toward the police. The findings are consistent with past research. Anglos have a higher opinion of the quality of police service than minority group members do.

Summary

The t-test helps us reach conclusions about the difference between sample means and whether the difference between sample means exists in the popu-

Table 8.4 SPSS Printout—t-Test for Independent Samples, Police Rating Score

Group Statistics

	Race Recode	N	Mean	Std. Deviation	Std. Error Mean
Police Rating Score	Anglo	696	10.85	2.57	9.76E-02
	Minorities	181	9.52	2.87	.21

Independent Samples Test

		Levine's Test for Equality of Variances		t-Test for Equality of Means						95% Confidence Interval of the Difference	
		F	Sig.	t	df	Sig. (two-tailed)	Mean Difference	Std. Error Difference		Lower	Upper
Police Rating Score	Equal variances assumed	1.652	.199	6.031	876	.000	1.33	.22		.89	1.76
	Equal variances not assumed			5.656	260.936	.000	1.33	.23		.86	1.79

lation. Here, we review the concept of significance testing and the null hypothesis. This process is followed throughout the remainder of this text.

The steps followed are:

1. The research and null hypotheses are developed and stated.

2. The means of two samples (or dividing one sample into two) are computed and compared.

3. Based upon this analysis, a conclusion is reached about

    a. Whether a difference between means exists

    b. The nature of this difference (whether it supports the research hypothesis or not)

4. The equality of variance between the two samples is calculated and determined.

5. The t ratio (the difference between the sample means divided by the standard error of the difference) is computed.

6. The probability of this ratio is determined.

7. A decision is made concerning the null hypothesis. If the probability of the t ratio is equal to or less than .05, the null hypothesis is rejected. If it is greater than .05, the null hypothesis is accepted. To reject the null hypothesis, the significance level on the printout must be less than or equal to .05.

The t-test is used when we are comparing the difference in means between two samples. There are two t-test—one for related and one for independent samples.

It is important to interpret the results of an analysis and reach a conclusion before making a decision about the null hypothesis. Otherwise, we lose sight of the purpose of the analysis that we are conducting and focus upon the jargon of statistics. This is a fatal flaw that must be avoided at all costs.

Key Terms

Degrees of Freedom: determine the shape of the t distribution; the number of scores that are free to vary in a distribution. Calculated by subtracting one from the sample size $(N - 1)$

Statistical Significance: a good chance (95 percent) that the statistical findings you made in your sample are also present in the population in question. Statistical significance changes based on the alpha level (amount of chance) one is willing to take in suggesting the sample size findings match those of the population. When we want to be 99 percent "sure" or 99.9 percent "sure," our statistical significance value comparisons will change from .05 to .01 to .001.

Hypothesis Testing: using statistical analysis to determine if there is a significant difference between variable or group scores. The null hypothesis is a statement of "no relationship" for a dependent variable between the groups. This hypothesis is "tested" to see if, in fact, the dependent variable is the same or "significantly" different for the groups.

Null Hypothesis (H_0): This is the statement of no difference or no relationship between two variables. In statistical analysis the null hypothesis is tested. You do not test the research hypothesis directly.

One-tailed (Directional) Hypothesis: This is a type of research or alternative hypothesis. It not only asserts that differences in outcome will occur, but it also states the direction that the differences will take. Typically, the reason for stating a one-tailed hypothesis comes from theory, previous research findings, or both.

Two-tailed (Nondirectional) Hypothesis: stated when you have no reason to expect a difference in outcome

Research hypothesis (H_a): The statement of some relationship (non-directional) or a specific relationship (one-tailed or directional) in analyzing the dependent variable.

Type I Error (or Level of Significance or Alpha Level (α)): is committed when the researcher makes the decision to reject the null hypothesis when, in the population, H_0 is true. The researcher sets the level of significance. The convention is to use the .05 level of significance as the probability of committing Type I error. If you make the decision to reject H_0, you are 95 percent certain that your decision accurately reflects what is true in the population, although there is a 5 percent chance that your decision is wrong. *To reject the null hypothesis, the statistical value must have a significance level equal to or less than ($\leq$) .05.*

Type II Error (β Error): is committed when the researcher makes the decision to accept the null hypothesis when, in the population, H_0 is false. Your statistical findings tell you that there is no relationship in the population of cases when, in fact, there is a relationship.

Related (or Paired) Samples: two samples that are linked in some way (e.g., the same people over time)

Independent Samples: two samples that are not related or paired in some fashion. If your samples have been assigned at random to experimental and control groups, they are independent samples. Another possibility is comparing segments of a sample that a variable divides into two different groups.

Data Analysis

1. Using the NCSD data set, compare the mean police confidence score between Anglo and minority survey respondents. Run and interpret the independent samples *t*-test results.

   a. State your research (is it one- or two-tailed?) and null hypotheses.

   b. Interpret the results of the analysis.

2. Using the NCSD data set, compare the mean fear of crime score between males and females. Run and interpret the independent samples *t*-test results.

   a. State your research (is it one- or two-tailed?) and null hypotheses.

   b. Interpret the results of the analysis.

3. Using State Data Set I, compare the mean homicide rate (Murder/ Non-Negligent Homicide per 100,000: 1997) in those states that have executed a prisoner since 1976 ("State has executed a prisoner since 1976") to those that have not (variable name: execute). Run and interpret the independent samples *t*-test results.

   a. State your research (is it one- or two-tailed?) and null hypotheses.

   b. Interpret the results of the analysis.

4. Using State Data Set II, compare the mean homicide rate (Murder/ Non-negligent Homicide per 100,000: 2003) in those states that have executed a prisoner since 1976 ("State has executed a prisoner since 1976") to those that have not (variable name: execute). Run and interpret the independent samples *t*-test results.

   a. State your research (is it one- or two-tailed?) and null hypotheses.

   b. Interpret the results of the analysis.

   c. Compare the results of your analyses in Questions 3 & 4. Has anything changed?

5. Using State Data Set I, compare the average prison population in those states that do and do not have a "Three Strikes Law." Run and interpret the independent samples *t*-test results.

   a. State your research (is it one- or two-tailed?) and null hypotheses.

   b. Interpret the results of the analysis.

6. Using State Data Set II, compare the average prison population in those states that do and do not have a "Three Strikes Law." Run and interpret the independent samples *t*-test results.

   a. State your research (is it one- or two-tailed?) and null hypotheses.

   b. Interpret the results of the analysis.

   c. Compare the results of your analyses in Questions 5 & 6. Has anything changed?

7. Using State Data Set I, compare the average number of gun-related homicides (Handgun Homicides per 100,000) between states with and without handgun waiting periods.

   a. State your research (is it one- or two-tailed?) and null hypotheses.

   b. Interpret the results of the analysis.

8. Using State Data Set II, compare the average number of gun-related homicides (Handgun Homicides per 100,000) between states with and without handgun waiting periods.

   a. State your research (is it one- or two-tailed?) and null hypotheses.

   b. Interpret the results of the analysis.

   c. Compare the results of your analyses in Questions 7 & 8. Has anything changed?

9. Using the 2004 Texas Crime Survey data, compare the mean score on the variable Concern for Crime (Rape) by Gender. Run and interpret the independent samples *t*-test results.

a. State your research (is it one- or two-tailed?) and null hypotheses.

b. Interpret the results of the analysis.

10. Using the 2004 Texas Crime Survey data, compare the mean score on the variable Concern for Crime (Rape) by Dichotomized Race. Run and interpret the independent samples *t*-test results.

a. State your research (is it one- or two-tailed?) and null hypotheses.

b. Interpret the results of the analysis.

11. Using the 2004 Texas Crime Survey data, compare the mean score on the variable Concern for Crime (Murder) by Dichotomized Race. Run and interpret the independent samples *t*-test results.

a. State your research (is it one- or two-tailed?) and null hypotheses.

b. Interpret the results of the analysis.

12. Using the 2004 Texas Crime Survey data, compare the mean score on the variable Concern for Crime (Aggravated Assault) by Dichotomized race. Run and interpret the independent samples *t*-test results.

a. State your research (is it one- or two-tailed?) and null hypotheses.

b. Interpret the results of the analysis.

13. Using the 2004 Texas Crime Survey data, compare the mean scores on the variables Concern for Crime (Burglary), (Aggravated Assault), (Auto Theft), and (Robbery) by Have PERSONALLY been a victim of a crime. Run and interpret the independent samples *t*-test results.

a. State your research (is it one- or two-tailed?) and null hypotheses.

b. Interpret the results of the analysis.

14. Using the 2004 Texas Crime Survey data, compare the mean scores on the variables Concern for Crime (Burglary), (Aggravated Assault), (Auto Theft), and (Robbery) by Have FAMILY MEMBER who has been a victim of a crime. Run and interpret the independent samples *t*-test results.

a. State your research (is it one- or two-tailed?) and null hypotheses.

b. Interpret the results of the analysis.

Notes

[1] Richard A. Tewksbury and Gennaro F. Vito, "Improving the Educational Skills of Jail Inmates: Preliminary Program Findings," *Federal Probation,* Vol. 58 (1994), pp. 55–59.

[2] W. S. Wilson Huang and Michael S. Vaughn, "Support and Confidence: Public Attitudes Toward the Police," in Timothy J. Flanagan and Dennis R. Longmire, eds., *Americans View Crime and Justice: A National Public Opinion Survey* (Thousand Oaks, CA: Sage Publications, 1996), pp. 32–33.

chapter 9

Analysis of Variance (One Way)

In chapter 8, we used the *t*-test to determine whether significant differences existed between two samples under study. The *t*-test is appropriate when you have a discrete or categorical independent variable (nominal or ordinal divided into two groups) and a continuous interval or ratio dependent variable that can be used to calculate a mean (average score). Oftentimes research designs consider analyses between more than two groups of subjects. **Analysis of variance (ANOVA)** is a statistical test that is designed to examine means across more than two groups by comparing variances. It is based upon the variability (variance from the mean) in each sample and in the combined samples. Ratios of the variances are used to determine if differences exist across the groups.[1]

Source of ANOVA

With ANOVA, there is no practical limit to the number of groups (or comparisons) that can be made. For example, you could examine the same group over three points in time. So, why not just use the *t*-test? When there are three or more levels for the nominal (grouping) variable, the number of comparisons increases with the number of groups. Multiple *t*-tests would be required (all possible comparisons, two groups at a time). At the end of this, the result would be very difficult, if not impossible, to interpret.

In one-way analysis of variance, the cases fall into three or more groups based upon their values for one independent variable. ANOVA reports the variance within the groups. This is how we have calculated the variance to this point. ANOVA then calculates how that variation would translate into differences between the groups while taking into account how many groups there are.

In State Data Set I, region is a grouping variable. States are classified as either eastern, southern, midwestern, or western. In our example, we use the number of prisoners executed between 1977 and 1995 as the independent variable. We compare the average number of prisoners executed across the four regions of the United States. Here, we see if different categories of states (region is measured at the nominal level) vary significantly in the mean number of prisoners executed (a ratio level variable) over this time period.

Under ANOVA, the null hypothesis is that the means for all of the groups are equal. In our example, the null hypothesis is that there is no difference in the average number of prisoners executed between 1977 and 1995 across the four regions of the country. The research hypothesis states that at least one of the sample means is different from the others, but it does not specify which one. Notice that the research hypothesis is non-directional. That is, it only states that one of the means is different, but not which one and which direction. One-way ANOVA tests the hypothesis that the single independent variable (here, region) is producing an effect—that at least one of the group means is different from the others.

When scores are divided into three or more groups, the variation among them can be divided into two parts:

1. The variation of scores **within the groups.** This is what we have examined in the past to calculate the variance and the standard deviation. We calculated how each score stood in relation to the mean of the distribution (deviation score: $x\left(X - \bar{X}\right)$). Then, we squared the deviation scores, multiplied them times f (the frequency of the score), and summed them to obtain the sum of squares (Σfx^2).

2. The variation of scores **between the groups.** There is variation from one group to the next. It accounts for the variability of the means between each sample.

ANOVA compares these two estimates of variability: the variance among the individual values in the groups and the variance among the means of the different groups. The heart of ANOVA involves whether the between-groups variance is significantly larger than the within-groups variance. Using the previous example, this means we are testing to see if variations across regions (e.g., between groups E, S, MW, and W) are greater than variations in one region (e.g., within S). If we show that the variance between the sample means is significantly larger than the within-groups variance, the null hypothesis will be rejected.

If the means of the groups are equal, then they also vary little around the total mean ($\bar{X}_T$) across the groups, even though there is some variation within each group. If the group means are really different, then they will vary considerably around $\bar{X}_T$ relatively more than they vary within their groups.

To test the null hypothesis (that all the group means are equal), ANOVA compares the variation between the groups to that within the groups. To compute ANOVA, you determine:

1. The total amount of variation among all scores combined (total sum of squares—SS_t)

2. The amount of variation between the groups (between-groups sum of squares—SS_b)

3. The amount of variation within the groups (within-groups sum of squares—SS_w)

ANOVA compares the last two estimates of the population variance to determine if the difference between them is due to sampling error.

The *F* Test (*F* Ratio)

The statistical procedure used in ANOVA—**the *F* test** (*F* ratio)—is a ratio of the two estimates of variability (between-groups mean square divided by the within-groups mean square variation). The within-groups mean square is based on how much the group means vary among themselves. If the null hypothesis is true (not rejected), the observed and estimated within-group and between-group variation should be about the same. Thus, the *F* test value equals one. If the null hypothesis is rejected (the scores are significant), the observed between-groups variation should exceed its estimate and the *F* ratio should be greater than one. One-way ANOVA determines whether or not the *F* ratio exceeds one by an amount too great to be explained by chance.

ANOVA always tests the null hypothesis that the group means are equal. In the example above, one might state the null as either "the means across regions are equal" or "there is no difference in means across regions." The research hypothesis is that there is a difference between the group means. The research hypothesis, however, does not specify where the difference between group means originates. It does not state which mean differs from the others in a specific way. Thus, the research hypothesis under ANOVA is always nondirectional and two-tailed.

If the *F* test value is statistically significant, you reject the null hypothesis. The group means are not equal. Of course, you can tell this by inspection of the group means. Inspection does not tell you, however, where the differences leading to the *F* value and the rejection of the null hypothesis originate. To pinpoint where the differences come from, you must use a multiple comparison procedure. These statistical tests protect you from concluding that too many of the differences between the group means are statistically significant. In our example, we have four group means and thus eight possible comparisons. In SPSS, the Bonferroni multiple comparison procedure (discussed later in the chapter) is recommended.

In sum, ANOVA is an extremely versatile tool. Its requirements are the following:

1. The data must be a random sample from a population.
2. The single dependent variable must be measured at the interval level (in order to compute a mean).
3. The independent variable need only to be measured categorically at either the nominal or ordinal level (to provide group means).

Calculating ANOVA by Hand

The calculation of ANOVA by hand is virtually impossible with large data sets. A "by hand" example, however, helps show where all these items actually come from. All of the formulas listed below are "whole score" formulas. In other words, to simplify calculations, the deviation scores are not used to calculate the variance estimates.

Calculation Formulas: ANOVA

Total Sum of Squares

Total sum of Squares $(SS_t) = SS_b + SS_w$
Where:
SS_b = between-groups sum of squares
SS_w = within-groups sum of squares

Sum of Squares

1. Total sum of squares: $SS_t = \sum X^2_t - \left(\sum X_t\right)^2 / N_t$
2. Sum of squares within groups: $SS_w = SS_1 + SS_2 + SS_3$
3. Sum of squares between groups (SS_b):

$$SS_b = N_1\left(\bar{X}_1 + \bar{X}_t\right)^2 + N_2\left(\bar{X}_2 - \bar{X}_t\right)^2 + N_3\left(\bar{X}_3 - \bar{X}_t\right)^2$$

ANOVA Degrees of Freedom

1. Total: $df_t = N - 1$
2. Between Groups: df_b = Number of Groups – 1
3. Within Groups: $df_w = df_t - df_b$

Mean Square

1. $MS_b = SS_b / df_b$
2. $MS_w = SS_w / df_w$

Suppose that nine people $(N = 9)$ with drug problems were randomly assigned to three different forms of treatment: inpatient (Group 1), outpatient (Group 2), and no treatment (Group 3). We then keep track of the number of positive drug test results after one month.

Group 1

X	X^2
2	4
1	1
3	9

$\sum X_1 = 6 \qquad \sum X^2_1 = 14$

$\bar{X}_1 = 2$

$N_1 = 3$

Group 2

X	X^2
4	16
3	9
6	36

$\sum X_2 = 13 \qquad \sum X^2_2 = 61$

$\bar{X}_2 = 4.3$

$N_2 = 3$

Group 3

X	X^2
7	49
9	81
9	81

$\sum X_3 = 25 \qquad \sum X_3^2 = 211$

$\bar{X}_3 = 8.3$

$N_3 = 3$

Group Total

X	X^2
9	81
9	81
7	49
6	36
4	16
3	9
3	9
2	4
1	1

$\sum X_t = 44 \qquad \sum X^2_t = 286$

$\bar{X}_t = 4.8$

$N_t = 9$

Using the formulas previously given, we calculate the total sum of squares and the sum of squares within each group.

Group Total: $SS_t = \sum X^2_t - \left(\sum X_t\right)^2 / N_t$

$$SS_t = 286 - (44)^2 / 9 = 286 - 1936/9$$

$$= 286 - 215.1 = 70.9$$

Group 1: $SS_1 = \sum X^2_1 - \left(\sum X_1\right)^2 / N_1$

$$SS_t = 14 - (6)^2 / 3 = 14 - 36/3$$

$$= 14 - 12 = 2$$

Group 2: $SS_2 = \sum X^2_2 - \left(\sum X_2\right)^2 / N_2$

$$SS_t = 61 - (13)^2 / 3 = 61 - 169/3$$

$$= 61 - 56.3 = 4.7$$

Group 3: $SS_3 = \sum X^2_3 - \left(\sum X_3\right)^2 / N_3$

$$SS_t = 211 - (25)^2 / 3 = 211 - 625/3$$

$$= 211 - 208.3 = 2.7$$

Next, compute the within-groups sum of squares.

$$SS_w = SS_1 + SS_2 + SS_3$$
$$SS_w = 2 + 4.7 + 2.7 = 9.4$$

Then, compute the between-groups sum of squares.

$$SS_b = N_1\left(\bar{X}_1 - \bar{X}_t\right)^2 + N_2\left(\bar{X}_2 - \bar{X}_t\right)^2 + N_3\left(\bar{X}_3 - \bar{X}_t\right)^2$$
$$SS_b = 3(2 - 4.8)^2 + 3(4.3 - 4.8)^2 + 3(8.3 - 4.8)^2$$
$$SS_b = 3(-2.8)^2 + 3(-0.5)^2 + 3(3.5)^2$$
$$SS_b = 3(7.84) + 3(0.25) + 3(12.25)$$
$$SS_b = 23.52 + 0.75 + 36.75$$
$$SS_b = 61.02$$

Next, calculate the degrees of freedom.

Total: $df_t = N - 1$
$$df_t = 9 - 1 = 8$$
Between Groups: $df_b = \text{Number of Groups} - 1$
$$df_b = 3 - 1 = 2$$
Within Groups: $df_w = df_t - df_b$
$$df_w = 8 - 2 = 6$$

Calculate the mean square variance estimates.

$$MS_b = SS_b / df_b$$
$$MS_b = 61.02 / 2 = 30.51$$
$$MS_w = SS_w / df_w$$
$$MS_w = 9.4 / 6 = 1.57$$

Calculation Formula: The F Ratio

$$F = MS_b / MS_w$$

Where: MS_b is the mean square (variance estimate) between groups
MS_w is the mean square (variance estimate) within groups

The final step is the determination of the F ratio—the key test in ANOVA.

$$F = MS_b / MS_w$$
$$F = 30.51 / 1.57 = 19.43$$

To clearly present these calculations, prepare an ANOVA table.

Source of Variation	Sum of Squares	Degrees of Freedom	Mean Square	F Ratio
Between groups	61.02	2	30.51	19.43
Within Groups	9.4	6	1.57	
Total	70.42			

If we consult a table of F, we see that (with the between-groups degrees of freedom equal to 2 and the within-groups degrees of freedom equal to 6) an F value of 5.14 or greater is required to reject the null hypothesis. Since our F value equals 19.43, we reject the null hypothesis. A difference exists between the three groups. The methods of drug treatment result in different rates of positive drug tests following treatment.

In this example, you see how difficult it is to calculate such statistics by hand. Mistakes in calculation are possible. Computers are much more capable and efficient to carry out the long calculations that are necessary to compute ANOVA. Plus, programs such as SPSS also determine the level of significance. Using tables to make this determination is unnecessary. Still, it is important to see where the sources of variation are and how the statistic is compiled. We also show how another test that accompanies ANOVA can help us reach a more thorough conclusion.

One-Way ANOVA Using SPSS

We use State Data Set I with region (eastern, southern, midwestern, western) as the grouping (independent) variable. Our dependent variable is the number of prisoners executed between 1977 and 1995. We compare the average number of inmates executed across the four regions of the United States to see if different categories of states (region is measured at the nominal level) vary significantly in the mean number of prisoners executed (a ratio level variable) over this time period.

To obtain your SPSS output, make the following choices from the menu:

1. Open "State Data Set I" (Figure 9.1).

2. Choose "Analyze," "Compare Means," and then "One-Way ANOVA" (Figure 9.2).

3. In the "One-Way ANOVA" window (Figure 9.3), select and enter the dependent variable—"Prisoners Executed Between 1977 and 1995"—in the "Dependent List" box. The program will calculate the mean and other statistics for this variable. Select and enter the independent variable—"Region"—in the "Factor" box. This variable divides the sample into groups.

4. Returning to the One-Way ANOVA window (Figure 9.4), click on the "Options" button to open the One-Way ANOVA: Options window.

Under Statistics, check "Descriptive." Click on "Continue" to return to the One-Way ANOVA window.

5. Click on "Post Hoc." Select the "Bonferroni" method (Figure 9.5). Click on "Continue" to return to the One-Way ANOVA window. Click on "OK" to generate your output.

In our example, we select "Prisoners Executed Between 1977 and 1995" as the dependent variable and "Region" as the independent variable. The null hypothesis is that there is no regional difference in the average number of prisoners executed between 1977 and 1995. Or, written another way, the null hypothesis could be that the average number of prisoners executed between 1977 and 1995 is equal for all regions. The research hypothesis is that the averages are different across regions.

In our "One-way" output (see Table 9.1 on pp. 169–170), the first table gives us our descriptive statistics on the number of prisoners executed between 1977 and 1995. Across the United States, the average number of prisoners executed during this period was 6.26. This figure is located in the row marked "Total" and in the column labeled "Mean." In the "Mean" column, we also find that the southern region had the highest mean number of prisoners executed (16.44) and the eastern region had the lowest mean number of executions (.22).

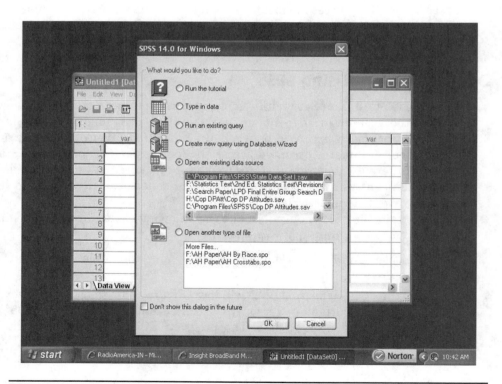

Figure 9.1

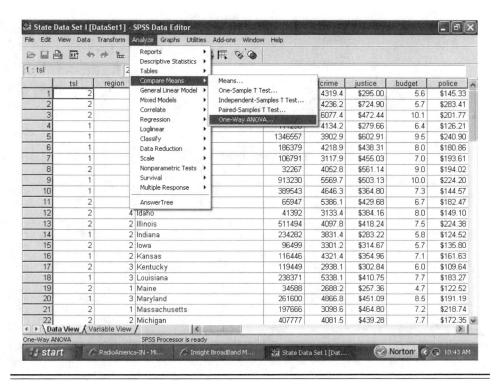

Figure 9.2

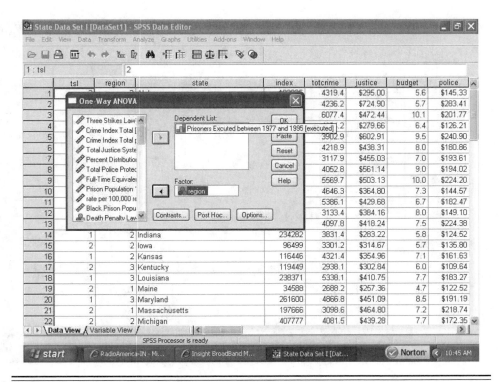

Figure 9.3

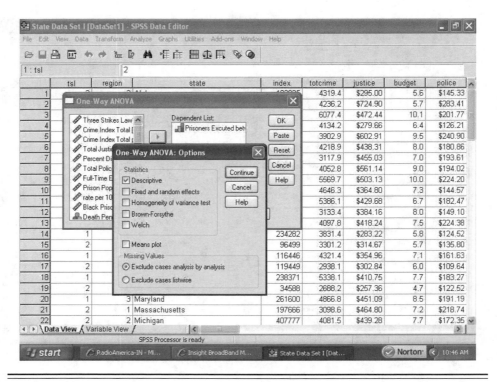

Figure 9.4

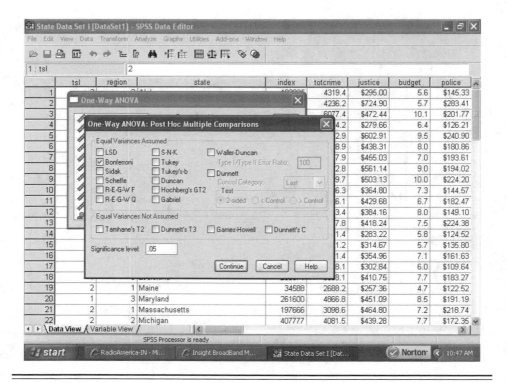

Figure 9.5

In the "Standard Deviation" column, we see that southern states had the greatest variation in executions (25.75) and eastern states had the lowest variability. The next column, "Standard Error," indicates how much the sample means vary in repeated samples from the same population. For each region, it represents the standard deviation divided by the square root of the sample size. The smallest standard error is for the eastern states (.22).

The last column lists the number of prisoners executed in each region during this time period. The South executed the highest number of inmates (104). The eastern states executed only two inmates between 1977 and 1995. Overall, the descriptive statistics reveal substantial variation between regions of the country and the number of prisoners executed during the time period.

The ANOVA table is the heart of the matter. Remember that we are testing the null hypothesis that there is no difference in the average number of executions across the regions during this time period. Now, we must make the decision to accept or reject the null hypothesis.

Table 9.1   SPSS ANOVA Output—Executions by Region

Descriptives
Prisoners Executed between 1977 and 1995

	N	Mean	Std. Deviation	Std. Error	95% Confidence Interval for Mean Lower Bound	Upper Bound	Minimum	Maximum
Eastern States	9	.22	.67	.22	–.29	.73	0	2
Midwestern States	10	2.80	5.47	1.73	–1.12	6.72	0	17
Southern States	16	16.44	25.75	6.44	2.72	30.16	0	104
Western States	15	1.33	1.72	.44	.38	2.28	0	5
Total	50	6.26	16.12	2.28	1.68	10.84	0	104

ANOVA
Prisoners Executed between 1977 and 1995

	Sum of Squares	*df*	Mean Square	*F*	Sig.
Between Groups	2469.194	3	823.065	3.690	.018
Within Groups	10260.426	46	223.053		
Total	12729.620	49			

(continued)

Table 9.1 *(continued)*

Multiple Comparisons
Dependent Variable: Prisoners Executed between 1977 and 1995
Bonferroni

(I) Region	(J) Region	Mean Difference (I – J)	Std. Error	Sig.	95% Confidence Interval Lower Bound	Upper Bound
Eastern States	Midwestern States	−2.58	6.86	1.000	−21.50	16.34
	Southern States	−16.22	6.22	.072	−33.37	.94
	Western States	−1.11	6.30	1.000	−18.47	16.25
Midwestern States	Eastern States	2.58	6.86	1.000	−16.34	21.50
	Southern States	−13.64	6.02	.170	−30.24	2.96
	Western States	1.47	6.10	1.000	−15.34	18.28
Southern States	Eastern States	16.22	6.22	.072	−.94	33.37
	Midwestern States	13.64	6.02	.170	−2.96	30.24
	Western States	15.10*	5.37	.043	.30	29.90
Western States	Eastern States	1.11	6.30	1.000	−16.25	18.47
	Midwestern States	−1.47	6.10	1.000	−18.28	15.34
	Southern States	−15.10*	5.37	.043	−29.90	−.30

*The mean difference is significant at the .05 level.

The first column of the ANOVA table gives us the sum of squares between and within groups and for the entire sample. The total sum of squares represents the entire variance on the dependent variable for the entire sample. It is obtained in the same manner that we calculate the sum of squares in chapter 5. First, the group mean of the dependent variable is determined (6.26). The group mean is then subtracted from the score of every case to obtain the deviation score (x). These deviation scores are then squared, multiplied by the number of cases, and added together. The same procedure is used to determine the between-groups and within-groups sum of squares.

In the second (df) column, the total degrees of freedom equals $N - 1$ cases ($50 - 1 = 49$). The degrees of freedom between groups equal the number of groups minus one ($4 - 1 = 3$). The within-groups degrees of freedom are equal to the total degrees of freedom minus the between-groups degrees of freedom ($49 - 3 = 46$).

The third (mean square) column contains the estimates of variability between and within groups. The mean square estimate is equal to the sum of squares divided by the degrees of freedom. The between-groups mean square is 823.065 (2469.194/3). The within-groups mean square is 223.053 (10260.426/46).

In the fourth column, the F ratio is calculated by dividing the mean square between groups by the mean square within groups. If the null hypothesis is true (not rejected), both mean square estimates should be equal and the F ratio should be one. The larger the value of the F ratio, the greater the likelihood that the difference between means does not result from chance. In our example, the F ratio is 3.69 (823.065/223.053).

The last column (Sig. or significance level) tells us that the value of our F ratio (3.69) is large enough to reject the null hypothesis. The significance level (.018) is less than .05. The mean numbers of executions in the different regions of the country between 1977 and 1995 were significantly different, and this difference is greater than we would expect by chance. We still cannot say where the differences lie, however, even though it looks as if the southern states have the largest mean number of executions.

This is where the **Bonferroni procedure** comes in (Post Hoc Tests). It adjusts the observed significance level divided by the number of comparisons being made. Because we are making eight possible comparisons of group means, the observed significance level must be 0.05/8 or 0.006 for the difference between group means to be significant at the .05 level. The multiple comparison procedures minimize the probability of claiming that differences are significant when they are not (Type II Error). The more comparisons you make, the larger the difference between pairs of means must be for a multiple comparison procedure to call it statistically significant. When you use a multiple comparison procedure, you can be more confident that you are finding true differences.[2]

The multiple comparisons table gives us all possible comparisons here. Each block represents one region compared to all the others by row. For example, the third block gives us the southern states compared to all the others. The mean difference column gives us the difference in the mean number of executions between the regions in question. An asterisk marks the pairs of mean differences that are statistically significant at .05 or less. The difference in the mean number of executions between the southern and western states is statistically significant. In fact, this is the only significant difference in the entire table. This is where the key difference lies. The southern states executed a statistically significant higher number of inmates than all the other regions but more than the western states in particular.

Summary

ANOVA is a statistical technique that compares the difference between sample means when you have more than two samples or groups. Basically, we are analyzing the variance within and between the samples to determine the significance of any differences.

The F ratio between the mean squares between groups (MS_b) and the mean squares within groups (MS_w) is the heart of ANOVA. On the basis of the analysis of the F test, a decision is made about the null hypothesis. If the null hypothesis is rejected, there is a statistically significant difference between the means of the groups. In order to determine exactly where the significant difference lies, however, the Bonferroni multiple comparison method must be used. This test tells you exactly which of the multiple comparisons between groups is statistically significant and accounts for the initial result from the F test.

Key Terms

Analysis of Variance (ANOVA): a statistical technique that compares the difference between sample means when you have more than two samples or groups.

Within-Groups Variance: how the scores in a distribution differ from themselves. This is what we have examined in the past to calculate the variance and the standard deviation. We calculated how each score stood in relation to the mean of the distribution. In ANOVA, it is designated as MS_b.

Between-Groups Variance: difference in scores from one group to the next. It accounts for the variability of the means between each sample. In ANOVA, it is designated as MS_w.

F Test (F Ratio): a statistical procedure used in ANOVA that is a ratio of the two estimates of variability (between-groups mean square divided by the within-groups mean square variation—MS_b/MS_w). The within-groups mean square is based on how much the group means vary among themselves. If the null hypothesis is true (not rejected), the observed and estimated within-group and between-group variation should be about the same. Thus, the F test value equals one. If the null hypothesis is false, the observed between-groups variation should exceed its estimate and the F ratio should be greater than one.

Bonferroni Procedure: a multiple classification technique that is used in conjunction with ANOVA. If the F test result is statistically significant, the Bonferroni procedure tells you just where the significant difference between the sample means lies.

Data Analysis

1. Using the State Data Set I, conduct an ANOVA analysis on the following crime rates. Be sure to use the Bonferroni procedure and to state your conclusions fully. Attempt to answer the following question: Which region of the country has the highest crime rate?

a. Crime Index Total by Region

b. Aggravated Assault by Region

c. Forcible Rape by Region

d. Handgun Homicides by Region

e. Murder/Nonnegligent Homicide by Region

f. Robbery by Region

2. Using the State Data Set II, conduct an ANOVA analysis on the following crime rates. Be sure to use the Bonferroni procedure and to state your conclusions fully. Attempt to answer the following question: Which region of the country has the highest crime rate?

a. Crime Index Total by Region

b. Aggravated Assault by Region

c. Forcible Rape by Region

d. Handgun Homicides by Region

e. Murder/Nonnegligent Homicide by Region

f. Robbery by Region

g. Compare your findings to those from Problem #1 above. Has anything changed over time?

3. Using the NCSD data set, conduct an ANOVA analysis on the fear of crime measure and the following grouping variables. Be sure to use the Bonferroni procedure and to state your conclusions fully. Attempt to answer the following question: Which groups have the greatest fear of crime?

a. Fear of Crime by Religion

b. Fear of Crime by Urbanization of the Community

c. Fear of Crime by Party Affiliation

4. Using the NCSD data set, conduct an ANOVA analysis on the police confidence score and the following grouping variables. Be sure to use the Bonferroni procedure and to state your conclusions fully. Attempt to answer the following question: Which groups have the highest level of confidence in police performance?

a. Police Confidence Score by Level of Education

b. Police Confidence Score by Marital Status

c. Police Confidence Score by Party Affiliation

d. Police Confidence Score by Urbanization of the Community

e. Police Confidence Score by Religion

f. Police Confidence Score by Income

5. Using the NCSD data set, conduct an ANOVA analysis on the police rating score and the following grouping variables. Be sure to use the

Bonferroni procedure and to state your conclusions fully. Attempt to answer the following question: Which groups give the police the highest rating?

a. Police Rating Score by Level of Education

b. Police Rating Score by Marital Status

c. Police Rating Score by Party Affiliation

d. Police Rating Score by Urbanization of the Community

e. Police Rating Score by Religion

f. Police Rating Score by Income

6. Using the 2004 Texas Crime Survey data set, conduct an ANOVA analysis on the following Concern for Crime questions (scaled 1 to 10 with 10 reflecting the highest concern) and the grouping variable "Age Group." Be sure to use the Bonferroni procedure and to state your conclusions fully. Attempt to answer the following question: Was there a pattern about concern for crime by age group among Texas residents in 2004? If so, describe this pattern fully.

a. Concern for Crime: Having someone break into your home while you are there

b. Concern for Crime: Being raped or sexually assaulted (Rape)

c. Concern for Crime: Being attacked by someone with a weapon (Aggravated Assault)

d. Concern for Crime: Having your car stolen (Auto Theft)

7. Using the 2004 Texas Crime Survey data set, conduct an ANOVA analysis on the following Concern for Crime questions (scaled 1 to 10 with 10 reflecting the highest concern) and the grouping variable "Annual Household Income." Be sure to use the Bonferroni procedure and to state your conclusions fully. Attempt to answer the following question: Was there a pattern about concern for crime by income among Texas residents in 2004? If so, describe this pattern fully.

a. Concern for Crime: Having any personal information about yourself accessed by computer

b. Concern for Crime: Having computer data stolen

8. Using the 2004 Texas Crime Survey data set, conduct an ANOVA analysis on the following Concern for Crime questions (scaled 1 to 10 with 10 reflecting the highest concern) and the grouping variable "Level of Education." Be sure to use the Bonferroni procedure and to state your conclusions fully. Attempt to answer the following question: Was there a pattern about concern for crime by education among Texas residents in 2004? If so, describe this pattern fully.

a. Concern for Crime: Being raped or sexually assaulted (Rape)

b. Concern for Crime: Being Murdered (Murder)

9. Using the 2004 Texas Crime Survey data set, conduct an ANOVA analysis on the following Job Satisfaction questions (scaled 1 to 5 with 5 reflecting excellence) and the grouping variable "Political Party." Be sure to use the Bonferroni procedure and to state your conclusions fully. Attempt to answer the following question: Was there a pattern about job satisfaction by political party among Texas residents in 2004? If so, describe this pattern fully.

a. Job done by Local Police

b. Job done by State Prison System

10. Using the 2004 Texas Crime Survey data set, conduct an ANOVA analysis on the following Job Satisfaction questions (scaled 1 to 5 with 5 reflecting excellence) and the grouping variable "Annual Household Income." Be sure to use the Bonferroni procedure and to state your conclusions fully. Attempt to answer the following question: Was there a pattern about job satisfaction by income among Texas residents in 2004? If so, describe this pattern fully.

a. Job done by Local Police

b. Job done by Local Judges

Notes

[1] Gudmund R. Iversen and Helmut Norpoth, *Analysis of Variance* (Beverly Hills, CA: Sage, 1976), p. 8.

[2] Marija J. Norusis, *SPSS Guide to Data Analysis* (Upper Saddle River, NJ: Prentice Hall, 1999), p. 271.

chapter 10 —————————————————————————

Correlation

One of the major quests in criminology is the etiology (causes) of crime. A goal of criminological research is to discover and to better understand factors that cause, or exist simultaneously with, crime in order to develop treatment programs and crime control policies. For this reason, many criminological studies are concerned with the relationship between two (or more) variables. Instead of looking for differences between groups (as we did with the t-test, contingency table analysis, and ANOVA), we want to determine to what extent two variables are related and whether the relationship is one that we expect to find in the population. Furthermore, if they are related, then we wish to see how strongly they are associated. One method of analysis that serves both of these purposes is correlation.

Defining Correlation

Correlation describes the relationship between two interval/ratio variables—the independent variable (X) and the dependent variable (Y). In hypothesis testing, we assume only a cause and effect relationship between these two variables, but a correlation shows the degree to which these variables vary (change) together—the extent to which the variation in X and the variation in Y are related to one another.

Several possible relationships exist with correlation. Consider the relationship between the size of the jail population (X) and the crime rate (Y).[1] In the first case, the size of the jail population may affect the crime rate by deterring and/or incapacitating criminals. If a deterrent or incapacitative effect were present, the crime rate would go down when the size of the jail population increased. We would assume that X and Y are **inversely (or negatively) related.** As the jail population (X) increases, the crime rate (Y) decreases. The values of the two variables change in opposite directions simultaneously.

A second possibility is that X and Y are **positively related.** As the size of the jail population increases, so does the crime rate. They vary together in the same direction. The other possibility for a positive correlation is that as the size of the jail population decreases, so does the crime rate. Both types are considered positive because X and Y change in the same direction. Either they increase or they decrease together.

A third possibility is that there is no relationship at all between the variables. The size of the jail population and the crime rate are unrelated. There is no correlation between them.

Thus, a **correlation coefficient** is a number between –1 and 1 that measures the degree to which two variables are linerally related; it indicates the strength and direction of a linear relationship between two random variables.

Finally, the relationship between X and Y may be **spurious**—the relationship is due to the fact that both X and Y are associated with a third variable. The size of the jail population (X^1) may be related to the unemployment rate (X^2), which may be strongly associated with the crime rate (Y).

To isolate the effect of X^1, it is necessary to examine the correlation coefficient between both X^1 and X^2 upon Y. It may be that the original correlation between the size of the jail population and the crime rate was due to their relationship with the unemployment rate. If, when the unemployment rate is held constant, the effect of the size of the jail population on the crime rate disappears, then the original correlation is spurious. That is, the relationship between the jail population and the crime rate has been "explained away"—instead, a perceived relationship only exists through a third variable (unemployment rate) being present. If the size of the jail population has an **independent effect** upon the crime rate, the unemployment rate should have little or no effect upon the crime rate.

Another possibility is that the unemployment rate has an **indirect effect** on the crime rate due to its relationship with the size of the jail population. Such a relationship could result when the unemployment rate (X^2) as well as the jail population (X^1) increases—a positive correlation. But the crime rate decreases as both X^1 and X^2 increase—a negative or inverse correlation.

Gary Sykes, Gennaro Vito, and Karen McElrath examined the relationship between the percent change in the size of the jail population between 1978 and 1982 and the crime rate between 1979 and 1983 for the largest 100 jails in the country. They reported statistically significant inverse correlations between the jail population and the burglary (–.31305), larceny-theft (–.27944), and motor vehicle theft (–.19837) rates.[2] The direction of the correlation (negative) supported the research hypothesis. As the change in the jail population increased, the rates for these crimes decreased.

Interpreting Correlation

With correlation, both the direction and magnitude of the relationship should be considered. The direction indicates the pattern of the relationship between X and Y. Direction could mean a positive or negative, or even no relationship between X and Y. The magnitude indicates the strength of the relationship between X and Y. The value of the magnitude is between negative 1 and positive 1, or a "perfect" negative or positive variation between the independent and dependent variables.

Direction of the Correlation Coefficient

To interpret the direction of the correlation coefficient, you would use a **scatter plot** (also known as scatter diagram and scattergram)—a graph that illustrates the pattern of the relationship between the two variables. The dots on the scatter plot are the paired values of X and Y. Figure 10.1 shows the pattern for a perfect negative correlation. The first dot is the paired value for $X =$ 1 and $Y = 10$. The pattern of the plot goes from the top left-hand corner to the lower right-hand corner. This is the pattern when, as the value of X increases, the value of Y decreases.

Figure 10.2 presents the scatter diagram for a perfect positive correlation. As the value of X increases, the value of Y also increases—they increase together. The plot ranges from the lower left-hand corner of the graph to the upper right-hand corner.

Figure 10.3 presents the pattern in a scatter diagram for a zero correlation—the indication of no relationship between the independent (X) and dependent (Y) variables. The points on the diagram follow no pattern. They are scattered throughout the graph.

Finally, Figure 10.4 presents a more realistic pattern of a strong, positive correlation. The patterns in Figures 10.1 and 10.2 followed a straight line because they were "perfect" correlations. The value of r in those cases would be -1 (Figure 10.1) and $+1$ (Figure 10.2)—the strongest possible value in a correlation. It is more likely that the pattern between X and Y will not follow a strong straight-line pattern. Typically, the pattern is inferred and is more general. In Figure 10.4, as X increases, Y increases, and the plot ranges from the lower left-hand corner to the upper right-hand corner but is not "perfect."

Thus, the scatter plot shows the direction of a relationship. Because there are two ways to have either a positive or a negative (or inverse) correlation, the scatter plot can show the exact manner in which X and Y are related. Of course, it can also demonstrate that X and Y are not related at all.

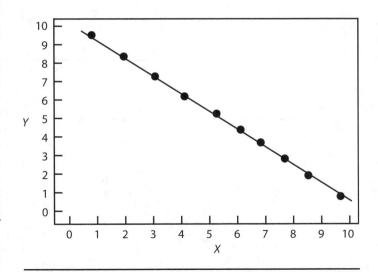

Figure 10.1 Perfect Negative Correlation

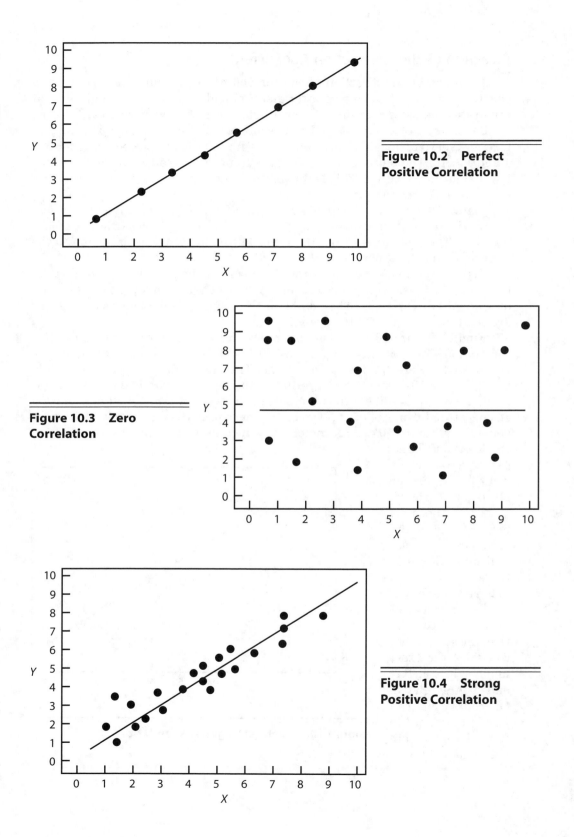

Figure 10.2   Perfect Positive Correlation

Figure 10.3   Zero Correlation

Figure 10.4   Strong Positive Correlation

Magnitude of the Correlation Coefficient

Another issue in the interpretation of the correlation coefficient is the strength of the relationship. Of course, the researcher must determine if the correlation coefficient is statistically significant. If the probability level of the correlation coefficient is less than or equal to .05, the value of r is statistically significant. Again, this means that the relationship that has been found between X and Y in the sample is likely to exist in the population from which the sample was drawn.

Correlation coefficients (r) range in value from –1 to +1. An r value of +1 or –1 is a perfect correlation. An r value of 0 indicates no relationship. The sign of the coefficient indicates the direction of the relationship and has nothing to do with its strength. Negative correlations are not weaker than positive correlations. In fact, correlations of .5 and –.5 are equal in strength. A negative sign is an indicator of an inverse relationship between X and Y. Naturally, the closer the r value is to 1, the stronger the relationship between X and Y. The closer the r value is to zero, the weaker the relationship between X and Y.

In our jail population and crime rate example, the reported, statistically significant correlations were not very strong. They ranged from –.31305 for burglary to –.27994 for larceny-theft and –.19837 for motor vehicle theft. Although the direction of the coefficients supported the deterrent or incapacitating effect of jail incarceration, the strength of the correlations was modest to weak in nature.

Percentage of Variance Explained

Correlation is actually a measure of the relationship between the variance in the independent variable (X) and the dependent variable (Y)—it determines to what extent they vary together. Recall that the variance is the average squared deviations from the mean for each score in a distribution. Here, r^2 is an important indicator of the relationship between X and Y; r^2 is also known as the **coefficient of determination**—the proportion of the total variation in the dependent variable (Y) that is explained by the variation in the independent variable (X). It measures the proportion of the total variation in the dependent variable that is explained or accounted for by the variation in the independent variable. Like any percentage, r^2 ranges from 0 to 100 percent. The higher the r^2, the greater the percentage of the variance in the dependent variable that is explained by the variance in the independent variable. Naturally, the higher the r^2, the stronger the nature of the relationship between X and Y.

In our jail population and crime rate example, the percentage of the variance explained by the change in the jail population in the crime rates was small and modest—9.8 percent for burglary, 7.8 percent for larceny-theft, and 3.9 percent for motor vehicle theft. This finding means that a great percentage of the variance (90 percent or more) in the dependent variable (crime rates) was due to some factor other than the change in the jail population.

Considering Causation

Because correlation is actually a measure of how the variance in the independent variable is related to that of the dependent variable, it is truly impossible to consider a causal relationship between X and Y. Causation can be assumed, however, if some measures are followed and practiced. The following criteria have been suggested as a way to approach causation.[3]

Five Criteria for a Causal Relationship

1. *Consistency of the association:* Have different studies resulted in the same findings? If so, then the present analysis can further confirm the findings by finding additional support for them. In our jail population and crime rates example, several studies had considered the relationship between prison populations and crime rates and reported "mixed and inconsistent" results between the two.[4] The jail population and crime rate results offered qualified support for the relationship.

2. *Strength of the association:* A weak association would offer little or no chance for a causal relationship. In our example, the strength of the correlations between changes in jail population and crime rates were modest and weak. Likewise, the r^2 values were low, indicating that other independent variables were accounting for the bulk of the variance in crime rates. Nevertheless, never assume that because the correlation is strong the relationship is causal. For example, a strong positive relationship exists between cigarette smoking and certain types of cancers, but we cannot state definitively that tobacco use causes the cancer because other influencing criteria also exist.

3. *Specificity and coherence of the association:* To what extent does one independent variable relate to one specific type of crime? In the jail example, the crime rates were broken down into specific types of crime rather than considering the entire crime rate or grouped rates for violent and property crime.

4. *Temporal relationship of the association:* **Causal time order** must be present: exposure to the independent variable (X) must precede the dependent variable (Y) in time. This is known as temporal precedence. In our example, the change in the jail population preceded the change in the crime rates in time. Conversely, is it possible that the crime rate influences the size of the jail population? As crime, or the fear of crime, increases, citizens may call for more punitive policies, including longer and increased use of incarceration. Thus, establishing the time order is somewhat problematic in criminal justice research.

5. *Consideration of "rival causal hypotheses":* Were other independent variables considered? The relationship between changes in the jail population and crime rates must be examined in conjunction with other independent variables. In other words, multivariate analysis is in order. Since rates were used in this analysis, the only other variable

that was considered was population size. So we know that population size did not affect the relationships. But the effects of other independent variables (such as the unemployment rate) were not considered and could account for the relationship and even make it spurious. Multivariate or advanced statistics are beyond the scope of this text. You will encounter it in your future study of statistical analysis. Meeting this criterion is the most difficult challenge in criminal justice research due to the complexity of crime and criminal behavior.

Samuel Gross notes that other potentially relevant factors (independent variables) must also meet some requirements.[5] First, the other independent variable must have a strong relationship with the dependent variable in question. In our example, if we wish to consider the unemployment rate as an independent variable, it must have a strong relationship (correlation) to the crime rates. Second, the new independent variable must also be strongly related to the other independent variable. In this case, the unemployment rate must be strongly related (correlated) to the change in the jail population. Finally, there must be no reasonable substitute for the new independent variable in the data that were examined. Here, there was no substitute for the unemployment rate in the analysis. Therefore, it seems logical that future studies of the relationship between the change in the jail population and the crime rate should consider the impact of the unemployment rate as a rival causal hypothesis.

Statistical methods alone cannot establish proof of a causal relationship in an association. After all, they are all based upon probability. Some chance always exists that you are wrong in rejecting the null hypothesis and stating that a relationship is statistically significant. As we have warned previously, the interpretation of correlation results must be conducted in a systematic manner. If a statistically significant and strong correlation is present, then check for bias or other methodological problems in the study. If the study is methodologically sound, apply the criteria listed earlier. If those criteria are satisfied, we are closer to a causal explanation.

Calculating Pearson's *r*

Calculation Formula: Pearson's *r* (correlation coefficient)

$$r = \frac{N\sum XY - (\sum X)(\sum Y)}{\sqrt{\left[N\sum X^2 - (\sum X)^2\right]\left[N\sum Y^2 - (\sum Y)^2\right]}}$$

Where: N = The number of pairs of scores

$df = N - 2$

In Table 10.1, we compute the Pearson's correlation coefficient (r) for the number of police killed as the result of criminal activity (X) and the number of civilians killed by the police (Y) for the years 1960 through 1974. The research hypothesis is that X and Y are positively related—as the number of police killed as the result of criminal activity (X) increases, the number of civilians killed by the police (Y) also increases. The null hypothesis is that there is no relationship between the number of police killed as the result of criminal activity and the number of civilians killed by the police.

Table 10.1 Data—Number of Police Killed as the Result of Criminal Activity (X) and the Number of Civilians Killed by the Police (Y), 1960–1974

Year	X	Y	XY	X^2	Y^2
1960	28	245	6860	784	60025
1961	37	237	8769	1369	56169
1962	48	187	8976	2304	34969
1963	55	246	13530	3025	60516
1964	57	278	15846	3249	77284
1965	53	271	14363	2809	73441
1966	57	298	16986	3249	88804
1967	76	387	29412	5776	149769
1968	64	350	22400	4096	122500
1969	86	354	30444	7396	125316
1970	100	333	33300	10000	110889
1971	129	412	53148	16641	169744
1972	116	300	34800	13456	90000
1973	134	376	50384	17956	141376
1974	132	375	49500	17424	140625
$N = 15$	$\Sigma X = 1172$	$\Sigma Y = 4649$	$\Sigma XY = 388718$	$\Sigma X^2 = 109534$	$\Sigma Y^2 = 1501427$

The table pairs the variables by year. Then, we multiply X times Y and sum the result. We square each X and Y value and sum those results. We now have the data to use in our formula that is presented above.

Using our formula, we begin with the numerator:

$$N \sum XY - (\sum X)(\sum Y) =$$
$$(15)(388,718) - (4649)(1172) =$$
$$5,830,770 - 5,448.628 = 382,142$$

Turning to the denominator of the formula:

$$\sqrt{\left[N\sum X^2 - (\sum X)^2\right]\left[N\sum Y^2 - (\sum Y)^2\right]}$$

$$N\sum X^2 = (15)(1,501,427) = 22,521,405$$

$$(\sum X)^2 = (4649)^2 = 21,613,201$$

$$\left[N\sum X^2 - (\sum X)^2\right] = 22,521,405 - 21,613,201 = 908,204$$

$$N\sum Y^2 = (15)(109,534) = 1,643,010$$

$$(\sum Y)^2 = (1172)^2 = 1,373,584$$

$$\left[N\sum Y^2 - (\sum Y)^2\right] = 1,643,010 - 1,373,584 = 269,426$$

$$\left[N\sum X^2 - (\sum X)^2\right]\left[N\sum Y^2 - (\sum Y)^2\right] = \left[(908,204)(269,426)\right] = 2.4469^{11}$$

$$\sqrt{2.4469^{11}} = 494,665.31$$

Now, we divide the numerator value by the denominator value (382,142/494,665.31 = .7725) to obtain our Person's r (correlation coefficient) value of .7725. Using a Pearson's r significance table, with 13 degrees of freedom ($df = N - 2$ or $15 - 2 = 13$), we determine that an r value of .514 or greater is required to reject the null hypothesis at the .05 level. Since our calculated value of .7725 is greater than .514, we can reject the null hypothesis.

We need to draw a scatter plot, however, to determine if X and Y are increasing or decreasing together. Using SPSS, we develop the scatter plot shown in Figure 10.5 (on p. 186). The figure indicates that as X (the number of police killed as the result of criminal activity) increases, so does Y (the number of civilians killed by the police).

The value of r (.7725) is high (close to 1). Another indicator is r^2. Here, r^2 is equal to .596. Therefore, during the period 1960 to 1974, close to 60 percent of the variance in the number of civilians killed by the police was explained by the number of police killed as a result of criminal activity. It is possible that police officers respond to danger in dangerous ways. The perception of the possibility of being killed on the job can lead to the use of deadly force on their part. Other independent variables, however, could also contribute to an explanation of the relationship between these two variables.

Once again, we can see how time consuming it is to calculate a statistic by hand. Now, we use SPSS to conduct a correlation analysis.

Bivariate Correlation Using SPSS

Here, we examine one method of computing a correlation coefficient, the **Pearson product-moment correlation coefficient.** Karl Pearson developed this measure by examining the functions of deviations from the "best-fitting" straight line between all the points of the values of X and Y. This

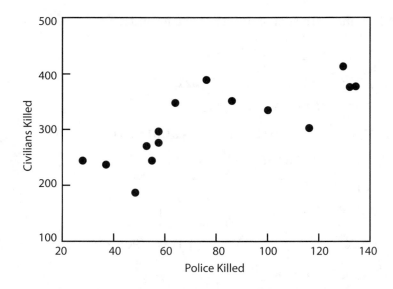

Figure 10.5   Number of Police Killed as the Result of Criminal Activity (X) and the Number of Civilians Killed by the Police (Y), 1960–1974

statistic (known as r) shows the degree of relationship between X and Y, providing that they are both measured at the interval or ratio level of measurement.[6] Other assumptions behind the use of r are that the two variables are linearly related (the plot of their values lies on a straight line) and that they come from normally distributed populations.

As with all statistical tests, it is important not to violate the assumptions. Some statistical tests are not very robust, meaning that they cannot withstand violations of assumptions very well, leading to a Type II error—failing to reject the null hypothesis when it is false. The consequences of committing a Type II error can be just as vexing as stating that a relationship does exist when the null hypothesis should have been retained (i.e., committing a Type I error).

Using State Data Set I, we examine the relationship between two ratio-level variables in each state: "Percentage of People in Poverty, Average 96–97 (X, the independent variable) and "Burglary per 100,000: 1997" (Y, the dependent variable). Our hypothesis is that the relationship between X and Y in this case is positive. As the average percentage of persons living in poverty increases (X), the burglary rate (Y) also increases. Note that virtually all of your hypotheses in correlation are one-tailed in nature because you are stating how the variables are related to each other. If your research hypothesis was one of a nondirectional relationship, then your test would be two-tailed.

To obtain your SPSS output, make the following choices from the menu:

1. Open State Data Set I (Figure 10.6).

2. Before you calculate r, you should examine the scatter plot between X and Y. On the toolbar, click on "Graphs" and then on "Scatter/Dot" (Fig-

ure 10.7). Choose "Simple Scatter" and then click on "Define" (Figure 10.8). You then must select your independent (*X*-axis) and dependent (*Y*-axis) variables. Choose "Percentage of People in Poverty, Average 96–97" as your independent (*X*-axis) variable and "Burglary per 100,000: 1997" as your dependent (*Y*-axis) variable (Figure 10.9). Click on "OK" and the graph you just constructed appears (Figure 10.10). Here, we see that the relationship between these two variables does follow a basic linear pattern.

3. To obtain *r* for these variables, stay with your graph and click on "Analyze" on the toolbar and then on "Correlate." Choose "Bivariate Correlation." The term "bivariate" means that you will calculate the correlation between two variables (Figure 10.11).

4. In the "Bivariate Correlations" window (Figure 10.12), select and paste the independent variable ("Percentage of People Living in Poverty, Average 96–97") first and then the dependent variable ("Burglary per 100,000: 1997"). Because our research hypothesis is directional, click on the dot in front of "One-tailed" on the "Test of Significance" line. Click on "OK" and the table (Table 10.2) is generated along with the graph.

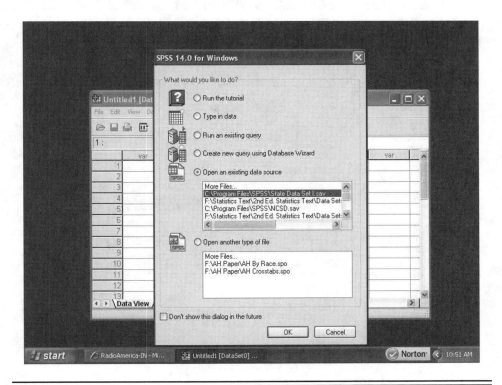

Figure 10.6

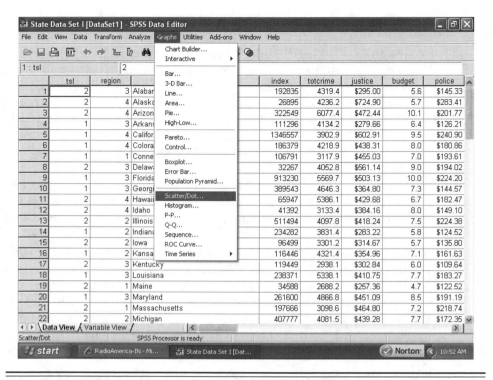

Figure 10.7

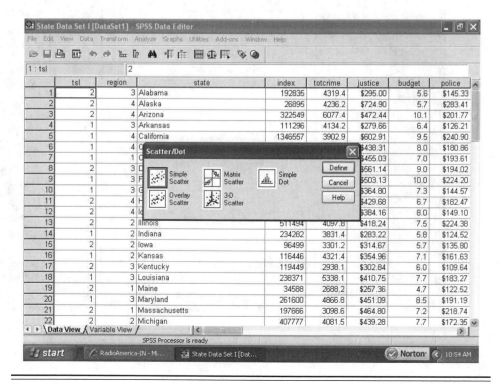

Figure 10.8

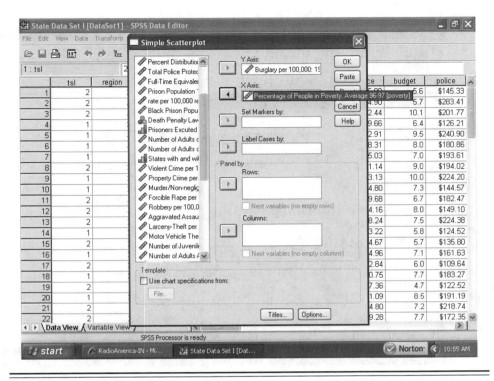

Figure 10.9

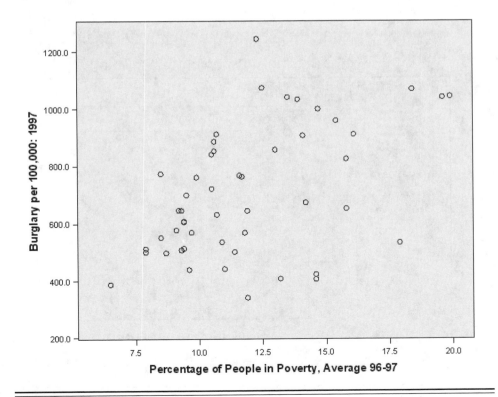

Figure 10.10

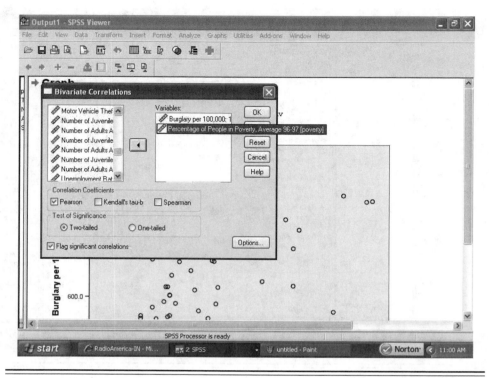

Figure 10.11

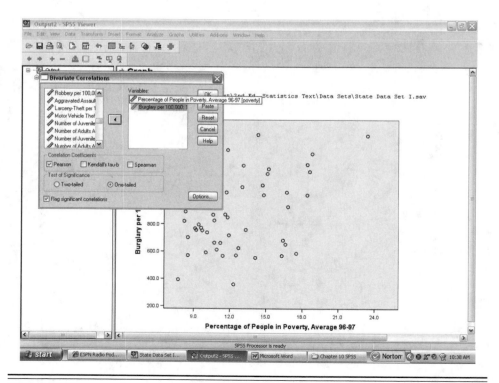

Figure 10.12

First, we examine the scatter plot in Figure 10.10. A general pattern indicates a positive relationship between X (Percentage of People Living in Poverty, Average 96–97) and Y (Burglary per 100,000: 1997). The variables appear to increase together with the spread of paired values ranging from the lower left-hand corner of the graph to the upper right-hand corner. As the percentage of people living in poverty increases, so too does the burglary rate.

The statistical analysis (Table 10.2) reveals that the correlation between X (Percentage of People Living in Poverty, Average 96–97) and Y (Burglary per 100,000: 1997) has a positive value of .425 and is statistically significant. The correlation is significant at the 0.01 level, so the null hypothesis is rejected. But, what is the probability of making a Type I error? If you guessed 42 percent, try again! If you answered less than 1 time out of 100, congratulations! In this case, we are 99% confident in our finding of a relationship between X and Y and that this same relationship exists in the population.

Table 10.2   SPSS Output—Correlation Matrix, Poverty and Burglary

		Percentage of People in Poverty, Average 96–97	Burglary per 100,000: 1997
Percentage of People in Poverty, Average 96–97	Pearson Correlation	1.000	.425*
	Sig. (one-tailed)		.001
	N	50	50
Burglary per 100,000: 1997	Pearson Correlation	.425*	1.000
	Sig. (one-tailed)	.001	
	N	50	50

*Correlation is significant at the 0.01 level (one-tailed).

Because r has a maximum value of 1 (perfect positive correlation) to 21 (perfect negative correlation), our r of .425 is moderate. Computing the coefficient of determination leads to another interpretation of the strength of a correlation. Simply square r to obtain r^2. In our example, .425 squared is .18; r^2 is interpreted as the percentage of the variance in Y that is explained by the variance in X. Therefore, 18 percent of the variation in the burglary rate per 100,000 (Y scores) is determined by the variance in the percentage of persons living in poverty (X scores). This interpretation also means that 82 percent of the variation in the burglary rate is determined by other factors, which could be the rate of alcohol consumption and the rate of illegal drug usage. Other independent variables such as these should be considered in the attempt to explain the forces behind the burglary rate.

Summary

This chapter reviews a measure of association between independent (X) and dependent (Y) variables—the correlation coefficient (r). It considers the degree of relationship between X and Y. It requires that both X and Y be measured at the interval or ratio level of measurement, that they are linearly related, and that they come from normally distributed populations.

To interpret a correlation coefficient, you must determine if it is statistically significant and then examine the direction and magnitude of r. The direction tells you if X and Y are positively or negatively (inversely) related. The best indication of the nature of the direction is the scatter diagram. The closer the value of r is to 1 or to -1, the stronger the relationship. The closer the value of r is to zero, the weaker the relationship. The value of r^2 tells you that the percentage of the variance in the dependent variable (Y) is explained by the variance in the independent variable (X).

Finally, consideration of the "five criteria" tells you the extent to which a causal relationship between X and Y can be approached. But remember that statistical results can never absolutely prove a cause and effect relationship between independent and dependent variables, rather, statistics tell us whether something is more or less likely to happen between the variables.

Key Terms

Correlation Coefficient: A number between -1 and 1 that indicates the strength and direction of a linear relationship between two random variables (X and Y).

Inverse (or Negative) Relationship between Variables: In the relationship between X (the independent variable) and Y (the dependent variable), a negative (or inverse) relationship can take two forms. As X increases, Y decreases, or as X decreases, Y increases. The two variables move in opposite directions. A negative correlation is indicated by a minus sign ($-$), but the sign does not indicate the strength of the relationship between X and Y. As noted, the negative sign indicates the direction of the relationship. It is necessary to create a scatter plot (see below) to determine which of the negative relationships is present.

Positive Relationship between Variables: In the relationship between X (the independent variable) and Y (the dependent variable), a positive relationship can take two forms. As X increases, Y increases, or as X decreases, Y decreases. The two variables move in the same direction together. Either they increase together or they decrease together. It is necessary to create a scatter plot to determine which of the positive relationships is present.

Spurious Relationship: This is a possibility when you have detected a relationship between X and Y that is actually false. Either X and Y influence each other or both X and Y are associated with a third variable (another independent variable). To find out if a relationship is spurious, you could control (hold constant) for the third variable or conduct a multivariate analysis.

Independent Effect: occurs when X directly affects Y and is independent of another relationship between variables.

Indirect Effect: Another possibility is that the second independent variable has an indirect effect on the dependent variable because it influences the first independent variable, which, in turn, is related to the dependent variable. For example, the unemployment rate (X^1) may have an indirect effect on the crime rate (Y) due to its relationship with the size of the jail population (X^2). Such a relationship could have the following pattern: as the unemployment rate increases (X^1), so does the jail population (X^2)—a positive correlation. But the crime rate decreases as both X^1 and X^2 increase— a negative or inverse correlation.

Scatter Plot: a graph that illustrates the pattern of the relationship between the two variables. The dots on the graph are the paired values of X and Y. The pattern reveals the type and direction of the relationship between X and Y.

r^2, the Coefficient of Determination: an important indicator of the relationship between X and Y. It represents the proportion of the total variation in the dependent variable (Y) that is explained by the variation in the independent variable (X). Like any percentage, r^2 ranges from 0 to 100 percent. The higher the r^2 is, the greater the percentage of the variance in the dependent variable that is explained by the variance in the independent variable. The higher the r^2 is, the stronger the nature of the relationship between X and Y.

Causal Time Order: exposure to the independent variable (X) must precede the dependent variable (Y) in time.

Pearson Product-Moment Correlation Coefficient: shows the degree of the relationship between X and Y. It requires that both variables be measured at the interval level and assumes that they are linearly related and that they come from normally distributed populations.

Data Analysis

Directions: Do a correlation analysis on the following topics and variables using State Data Set I. Be sure to run (and include in your analysis) the scatter plot (graph option) and the bivariate correlation matrix. Specify the independent and dependent variables and state your research hypothesis. State and interpret the direction of the correlation.

1. Number of Black Males Unemployed and the Black Prison Population (12/31/95)

2. Teen Unemployment Rate, 1995, and the Number of Juveniles Arrested Violent Crimes (Under 18), 1997

3. Rate per 100,000 residents of prisoners in 1995 and

   a. Crime Index Total per 100,000

   b. Property Crime per 100,000, 1997

   c. Violent Crime per 100,000, 1997

4. Number of All Employed Females and
   a. Number of Juveniles Arrested (Under 18), 1997
   b. Number of Juveniles Arrested Property Crimes (Under 18), 1997
   c. Number of Juveniles Arrested Violent Crimes (Under 18), 1997

5. Unemployment rate, January 1996 and
   a. Number of Adults Arrested Property Crimes, 1997
   b. Number of Adults Arrested Violent Crimes, 1997

6. The Percentage of People in Poverty, Average 96–97 and
   a. Violent Crime Rate per 100,000, 1997
   b. Murder/Non-negligent Homicide per 100,000, 1997
   c. Aggravated Assault per 100,000, 1997

Directions: Do a correlation analysis on the following topics and variables using State Data Set II. Be sure to run (and include in your analysis) the scatter plot (graph option) and the bivariate correlation matrix. Specify the independent and dependent variables and state your research hypothesis. State and interpret the direction of the correlation. Be sure to compare your results to the appropriate results in Questions 1—6 above. Has anything changed?

7. Number of Black Males Unemployed and the Black Prison Population (12/31/98)

8. Teen Unemployment Rate, 1995, and the Number of Juveniles Arrested Violent Crimes (Under 18), 2003

9. Rate per 100,000 residents of prisoners in 1995 and
   a. Crime Index Total per 100,000, 2003
   b. Property Crime per 100,000, 2003
   c. Violent Crime per 100,000, 2003

10. Number of All Employed Females and
    a. Number of Juveniles Arrested (Under 18), 2003
    b. Number of Juveniles Arrested Property Crimes (Under 18), 2003
    c. Number of Juveniles Arrested Violent Crimes (Under 18), 2003

11. Unemployment rate, January 1996 and
    a. Number of Adults Arrested Property Crimes, 2003
    b. Number of Adults Arrested Violent Crimes, 2003

12. The Percentage of People in Poverty, Average 96–97 and
    a. Violent Crime per 100,000, 2003
    b. Murder/Non-negligent Homicide per 100,000, 2003
    c. Aggravated Assault per 100,000, 2003

13. Using State Data Set II, conduct a bivariate correlation analysis (complete with graph—scatter plot) of the relationship between the Total Police Protection Per Capita Expenditures 1999 and:

a. Crime Index Total 2003

b. Number of Adults Arrested, 2003

c. Number of Juveniles Arrested, 2003

d. Prison Population 12/31/2003

Specify the independent and dependent variables and state your research hypothesis. State and interpret the direction of the correlation. What do these correlations say about the impact of police expenditures on the criminal justice system?

14. Using State Data Set II, examine the relationship between unemployment and incarceration by conducting a bivariate correlation analysis (complete with graph—scatter plot) between the variables: Unemployment Rate, Jan 1996, and rate per 100,000 residents of prisoners in 2003. Specify the independent and dependent variables and state your research hypothesis. State and interpret the direction of the correlation. What do the findings say about the impact of unemployment upon incarceration?

Notes

[1] Gary W. Sykes, Gennaro F. Vito, and Karen McElrath, "Jail Populations and Crime Rates: An Exploratory Analysis," *Journal of Police Science and Administration,* Vol. 15 (1987), pp. 72–77.

[2] Ibid, p. 75.

[3] Travis Hirschi and Hanan C. Selvin, *Delinquency Research: An Appraisal of Analytic Methods* (New York: Free Press, 1967), pp. 37–51. See also Richard F. Morton, J. Richard Hebel, and Robert J. McCarter, *A Study Guide to Epidemiology and Biostatistics* (Gaithersburg, MD: Aspen, 1996), pp. 156–157.

[4] Lee Bowker, "Crime and the Use of Prisons in the United States: A Time Series Analysis," *Crime and Delinquency,* Vol. 27 (1981), pp. 39–43.

[5] Samuel R. Gross, "Proof of Discrimination Under the Kentucky Racial Justice Act," in *The Racial Justice Act and the Politics of the Death Penalty: Proceedings of the Kentucky Bar Association Annual Convention in Louisville, Kentucky, June 16–18, 1999,* by the Kentucky Bar Association Criminal Law and Young Lawyers Sections, 1999, pp. 19–20.

[6] Pearson's r is called "product-moment" because it is calculated by multiplying the z scores of two variables to get their product and then calculating the average (mean value, which is called a "moment") of these products. W. Paul Vogt, *Dictionary of Statistics and Methodology* (Newbury Park, CA: Sage, 1993), p. 169.

chapter 11

Regression

In chapter 10, we explained that the correlation coefficient is an indication of the degree of association between two variables (X, independent; and Y, dependent). If two variables are correlated, we can estimate the values of the dependent variable based upon the values of the independent variable. We can do this through the use of regression analysis. The focus of regression analysis is prediction. We can predict the values of the dependent variable when we know the values of the independent variable. Actually, we are making projections about the values of the dependent variable, when the values of the independent variable are known.

The prediction is based upon linear regression, which is the "best fitting" straight line that can be plotted at the closest distance to all points on a scatter plot of the independent and dependent variables. In linear regression, this means that the independent and dependent variables must be linearly correlated. This line can be used to predict the value of Y through our knowledge of the scores on X.

Defining Regression

This chapter reviews the format known as simple linear regression, which features one independent variable and one dependent variable. As in correlation, the assumption is that the independent variable influences the variation in the dependent variable.

Simple linear regression takes the form of a mathematical equation:

$$\hat{Y} = a + bX$$

where: 1. a *is the Y intercept*. It is the point at which the regression line crosses the Y-axis. It equals $\hat{Y}$ (the predicted value of Y) when X is 0. The value of the Y intercept can be positive or negative.

2. b *represents the slope of the regression line*. It represents the change in Y per one unit change in X. As X increases by one, Y changes by the value of b. The slope shows how much and in which direction $\hat{Y}$ will vary per one unit change in the value of X. The value of b can be positive or negative. A positive value

for b indicates that a one unit increase in X leads to an increase in $\hat{Y}$ by the value of b. A negative b value indicates that a one unit increase in X leads to a decrease in $\hat{Y}$ by the value of b.

If you remember Algebra from high school, this equation should look familiar to you; it is the equation for a straight line! Just like when solving for "x" or "y" in Algebra, when we know the values of a and b, we can calculate an estimate of $\hat{Y}$ for every value of X. For example, consider the relationship between "number of prior convictions" (independent variable) and "length of time in prison in months" (dependent variable). We might suggest that as number of prior convictions (X) increases, so does the length of the sentence (Y). Let's suppose the relationship is captured with the equation $\hat{Y} = 36 + 13.3X$. This means that $\hat{Y}$ (length of prison sentence in months) equals 36 months + (13.3 months)(number of prior incarcerations). The equation provides a mathematical description of the relationship between the two variables. So, for an individual having only one prior conviction, the length of prison sentence predicted is 36 + 13.3(1) or 49.3 months. Meanwhile, an individual with 15 prior convictions has a predicted sentence of 36 + 13.3(15) = 235.5 months!

Regression analysis uses the **least squares technique** to establish the equation. It constructs the straight line that comes closest to all points in the scatter plot between X and Y. The least squares procedure provides the best fit in that it lies at the point where the squared deviations from all the points on the scatter plot are minimized, and thus the accuracy of the prediction is maximized.[1] The distance between the line and the points are actually errors in prediction called **residuals.** The residual is the difference between the actual and the predicted value of Y. Again, the regression line allows us to predict the values of Y when we have values for X.

Using Regression to Predict Prison Population Size

Prediction is especially useful in criminal justice planning. For example, decision makers (especially the legislature) typically desire information on the expected size of the prison population. Regression analysis can provide such information so that the costs of incarceration can be estimated and the budgetary needs of the state in terms of prison operations can be considered.

For example, the National Council on Crime and Delinquency (NCCD) developed prison population projections in 1995 to consider the effects of changes designed to increase length of stay for inmates—changes such as abolition of parole and enhancement of mandatory minimum and "truth in sentencing" measures. The council estimated that these changes would increase the U.S. prison population by 19 percent (1.4 million inmates) by the year 2000.[2]

Because time has passed, we can check the accuracy of this prediction. Table 11.1[3] contains data on the size of the prison population in 1995 and by the end of 1999. The actual 1999 prison population size exceeded the estimate made by the NCCD. The prison population was more than 1.8 million by the end of 1999—

greater than the 1.4 million NCCD estimate. The actual rate of change (+17.8 percent), however, was somewhat lower than the NCCD projection of a 19 percent increase. Overall, the NCCD estimates were remarkably accurate.[4]

Table 11.1 Size of the U.S. Prison Population, 1995 and 1999

	1995	1999	Change
Prison Population Size	1,585,586	1,869,169	+17.8%

Calculating Regression Coefficients by Hand

As we have stated, one of the major uses of regression is to attempt to anticipate future conditions. The assumption is that the future will be like the past. If present trends continue, the regression equation gives us information as to what can be expected. In this example, we conduct a regression analysis on the murder rate per 100,000 for the United States during the period 1976–1998 (Table 11.2). From this analysis we predict what the national homicide rate will be in the year 2005.

The formulas used to calculate regression coefficients are presented in the text box (on p. 200). To calculate regression coefficients by hand, you must first construct a table. Table 11.3 (on p. 200) consists of our murder rate data with one change. Instead of entering the year as X (the independent variable), you enter the number of the year in the data. For example, the first year, 1976, is entered as 1. This change will make our calculations less cumbersome. Y is still the murder rate per 100,000 population.

Table 11.2 Murder Rates per 100,000 in the United States, 1976–1998

Year	Murder Rate
1976	8.8
1977	8.8
1978	9.0
1979	9.7
1980	10.2
1981	9.8
1982	9.1
1983	8.3
1984	7.9
1985	7.9
1986	8.6
1987	8.3
1988	8.4
1989	8.7
1990	9.4
1991	9.8
1992	9.3
1993	9.5
1994	9.0
1995	8.2
1996	7.4
1997	6.8
1998	6.3

The calculations in the table were obtained in the following manner. Again, X is the number for each year beginning with 1976. These figures were added together to arrive at ΣX. The Y column is a list of the murder rates for each year. The Y column figures were totaled to derive ΣY.

Calculation Formulas: Regression Coefficients

1. $b \text{ (Slope)} = \dfrac{N\sum XY - (\sum X)(\sum Y)}{N\sum X^2 - (\sum X)^2}$

2. $a \text{ (}y \text{ intercept)} = \dfrac{\sum Y - b(\sum X)}{N}$

3. Regression equation: $\hat{Y} = a + bX$

For each line, XY represents the values of X times Y. The figures in this column were summed to arrive at $\sum X^2$. In the last column, each value of X was squared and then summed to total $\sum X^2$.

Table 11.3   Regression Calculation Table

X	Y	XY	X²
1	8.8	8.8	1
2	8.8	17.6	4
3	9.0	27.0	9
4	9.7	38.8	16
5	10.2	51.0	25
6	9.8	58.8	36
7	9.1	63.7	49
8	8.3	66.4	64
9	7.9	71.1	81
10	7.9	79.0	100
11	8.6	94.6	121
12	8.3	99.6	144
13	8.4	109.2	169
14	8.7	121.8	196
15	9.4	141.0	225
16	9.8	156.8	256
17	9.3	158.1	289
18	9.5	171.0	324
19	9.0	171.0	361
20	8.2	164.0	400
21	7.4	155.4	441
22	6.8	149.6	484
23	6.3	144.9	529
$\sum X = 276$	$\sum Y = 199.2$	$\sum XY = 2319.2$	$\sum X^2 = 4324$

Using our formula, calculate the value of b (the slope of the regression line):

$$b \text{ (Slope)} = \frac{N\sum XY - (\sum X)(\sum Y)}{N\sum X^2 - (\sum X)^2}$$

$$b \text{ (Slope)} = \frac{(23)(2319.2) - (276)(199.2)}{(23)(4324) - (276)^2}$$

$$b \text{ (Slope)} = \frac{(23)(2319.2) - (276)(199.2)}{(23)(4324) - (76,176)}$$

$$b \text{ (Slope)} = \frac{(53,341.6) - (54,979.2)}{(99,452) - (76,176)}$$

$$b \text{ (Slope)} = \frac{-1637.6}{23,276}$$

$$b \text{ (Slope)} = -0.07$$

In this example, b can be interpreted in the following way. As the value of X increases by 1, the value of predicted Y ($\hat{Y}$) decreases (because of the negative sign of b) by 0.07. In other words, with each passing year (X), the murder rate (Y) will decrease by 0.07.

Now, we can calculate the value of a—the y intercept. Again, a represents the value of predicted Y when X equals zero. It is the point where the regression line crosses the Y-axis of the scatter plot. Because we are using years as the independent variable (X), we cannot interpret it in words because "if X equals zero" would translate as "if there is no year (or time)." But it is still important as the y intercept—the "anchor" of the regression line of best fit.

$$a \text{ (}y\text{ intercept)} = \frac{\sum Y - b(\sum X)}{N}$$

$$a \text{ (}y\text{ intercept)} = \frac{(199.2) - (-0.07)(276)}{23}$$

$$a \text{ (}y\text{ intercept)} = \frac{(199.2) - (-19.32)}{23}$$

$$a \text{ (}y\text{ intercept)} = \frac{(199.2) + (19.32)}{23}$$

$$a \text{ (}y\text{ intercept)} = \frac{218.52}{23}$$

$$a \text{ (}y\text{ intercept)} = 9.5$$

Plugging in our computed values of a and b, our regression equation ($\hat{Y} = a + bX$) becomes $\hat{Y} = 9.5 + (-0.07)X$. Because we want to generate a prediction of the murder rate in the U.S. in the year 2005, we plug in 30 for X (2005 would be the 30th year in Table 11.2) and solve the equation.

$$\hat{Y} = 9.5 + (-0.07)\,X$$
$$\hat{Y} = 9.5 + (-0.07)\,(30)$$
$$\hat{Y} = 9.5 + (-2.1)$$
$$\hat{Y} = 7.4$$

Therefore, using the pattern of murder rates per 100,000 in the U.S. for 1976–1998, we would predict that the murder rate in the year 2005 will be 7.4/100,000. Again, this prediction is limited by the assumption that the past pattern will continue into the future.

Figure 11.1 is a scatter plot of the murder rates per 100,000 in the U.S. for the period 1976–1998. Here, we see a **curvilinear relationship.** The murder rate follows a curved line for this time period. It is also clear that the murder rate is decreasing over time.

In Figure 11.2, we see our regression line for these data. The plotted straight line is the line of best fit—it is the straight line that comes closest to all the points on the graph. Note that, if the upper left-hand end of the line was extended across the Y-axis, it would cross the line at 9.5—the value of our y intercept.

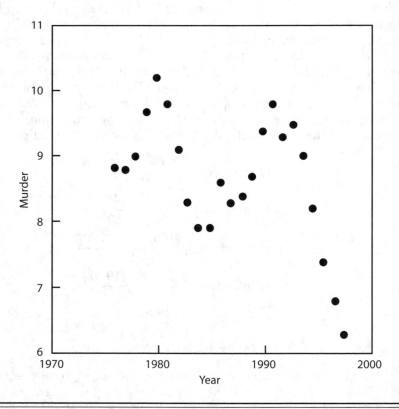

Figure 11.1 Scatter Plot of Murder Rates per 100,000 in the United States, 1976–1998

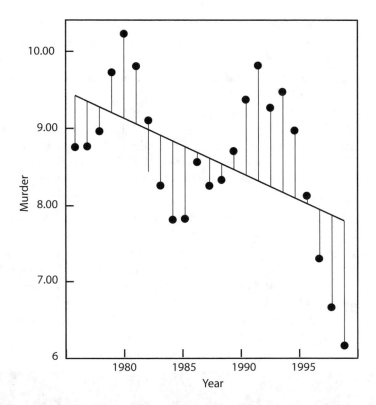

Figure 11.2   Regression Line and Equation: Murder Rates per 100,000 in the United States, 1976–1998

Linear Regression Using SPSS

In our example on correlation (chapter 10), we examined the relationship between the percentage of people in poverty, average 1996–1997 (*X*, the independent variable) and the rate of burglary per 100,000 for 1997 (*Y*, the dependent variable). We found a positive correlation between the two variables of .425 that was statistically significant. The scatter plot showed us that as the average level of poverty increased, so did the burglary rate. Because these two variables are correlated, we can now use regression analysis to try to predict how the burglary rate might be affected by the percentage of people living in poverty in the future.

Regression analysis uses a mathematical model to fit a straight line (the regression line) to the data. If the points cluster around a straight line, we can summarize the relationship by finding the equation for the line: ($\hat{Y} = a + bX$). Remember that our objective is to derive an equation based upon a straight line that will allow us to predict what the burglary rate will be for a given rate of poverty.

In SPSS, here are the steps you follow to conduct a linear regression analysis:

1. Open "State Data Set I" (Figure 11.3). Again, this data set contains crime and other data from the criminal justice system for all 50 states.

2. Go to the tool bar and click on "Analyze," then on "Regression" and then on "Linear" (Figure 11.4).

3. Highlight the variable "Percentage of People in Poverty, Average 96–97" (Figure 11.5). Click on the arrow in front of the "Independent" window to paste this variable, making it the independent variable (X) in our analysis. Highlight "Burglary per 100,000: 1997," click on the arrow in front of the "Dependent" window to make it the dependent variable (Y) in our analysis.

4. Click on "OK" to obtain your regression output.

5. After you obtain the regression output, click on "Graphs" on the toolbar, then on "Interactive" and finally on "Scatterplot" (Figure 11.6).

6. To create the scatter plot: click on "Burglary per 100,000, 1997" and drag it to the first box (Y-axis, the vertical line). Click on "Percentage of People in Poverty, Average 96–97" and drag it to the second box (X-axis, the horizontal line) (Figure 11.7).

7. Then, click on "OK" to add the graph (Figure 11.8) to your final output (Table 11.4, p. 208) and then print it out.

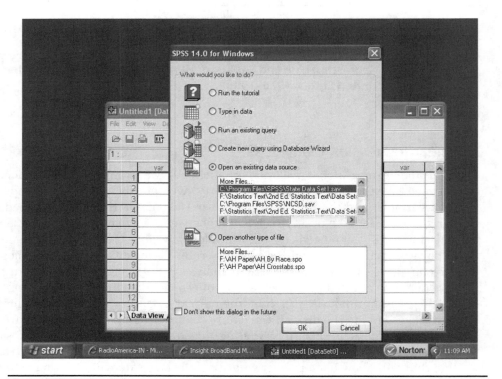

Figure 11.3

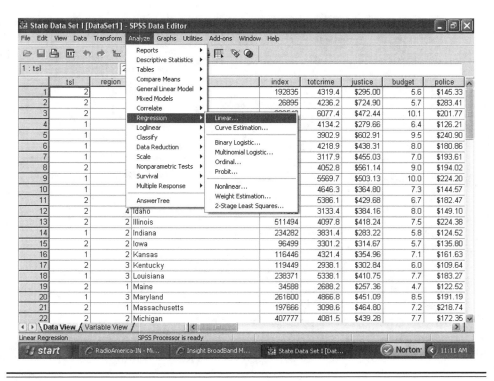

Figure 11.4

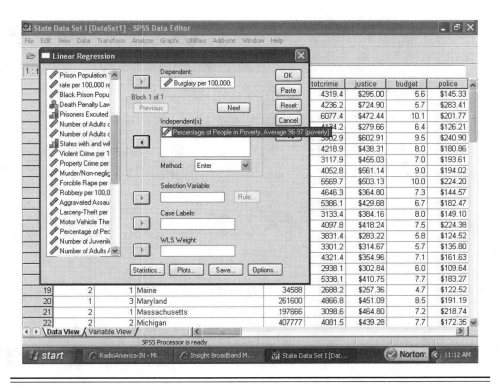

Figure 11.5

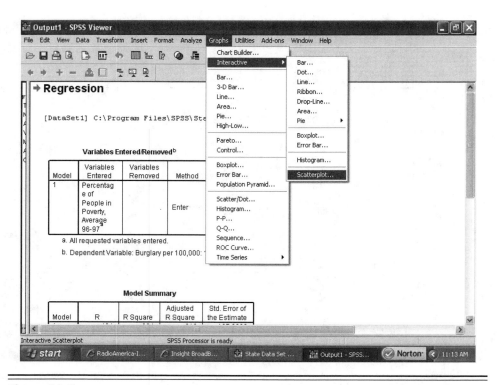

Figure 11.6

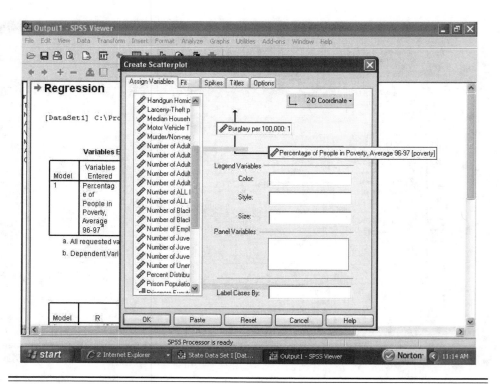

Figure 11.7

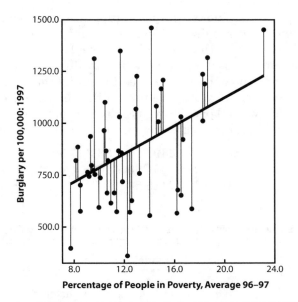

Figure 11.8

The "Model Summary" table in Table 11.4 contains the correlation between the average percentage of persons living in poverty and the burglary rate. As we determined in chapter 10, the r is .425 and is statistically significant at the .001 level. The table also contains the r^2 value (.181). The important reading from this table is the r^2 value or the coefficient of determination. An r^2 of .181 means that 18.1% of the variation in the dependent variable (burglary rate) is explained by the independent variable (average percentage of people living in poverty). The second table contains an ANOVA analysis. The ANOVA was covered in chapter 9. Recall the important reading from this table is the significance value of the F test and tests whether our model fit is significant.

Now, you have the regression equation. Where? In the third table labeled "Coefficients," look at the line labeled (Constant). In column B, 449.790 is the value of a. Remember, a is the y intercept or the value of predicted Y when $X = 0$. In our example, this means that the burglary rate would still be 449.790/100,000 even if the average percentage of persons living in poverty is zero. Even if poverty is eliminated, we would still have a rate of burglary equal to about 450/100,000.

The second line in this table is the "Percentage of People in Poverty, Average 96–97." In column B is the value of b—the slope of the regression line (33.335). In our example, this means that as the average percentage of people living in poverty increases by one percentage point, the violent crime rate increases by 33.335/100,000.

Therefore, our regression model is

$$\hat{Y} = 449.790 + 33.335X$$

When you examine the graph (Figure 11.8), you see the line of best fit. The vertical lines that are drawn from each point to the regression line represent the residuals. Again, the residuals represent errors in prediction—the difference between the observed and predicted values.

This equation could now be used to predict the expected burglary rate for a given level of poverty. For example, if the percentage of people living in poverty next year was 50 percent, you could determine the projected burglary rate by plugging 50 into the regression equation and solving for $\hat{Y}$.

$$\hat{Y} = 449.790 + 33.335(50)$$
$$\hat{Y} = 449.790 + 1666.75$$
$$\hat{Y} = 2116.54$$

Table 11.4 SPSS Regression Output—Poverty and Burglary Rates

Model Summary

Model	r	r^2	Adjusted r^2	Std. Error of the Estimate
1	.425[a]	.181	.164	250.590

[a] Predictors: (Constant), Percentage of People in Poverty, Average 96–97

ANOVA[b]

Model		Sum of Squares	df	Mean Square	F	Sig.
1	Regression	665588.020	1	665588.020	10.599	.002[c]
	Residual	3014169.247	48	62795.193		
	Total	3679757.267	49			

[b] Dependent Variable: Burglary per 100,000: 1997
[c] Predictors: (Constant), Percentage of People in Poverty, Average 96–97

Coefficients[d]

Model		Unstandardized Coefficients		Standardized Coefficients		
		B	Std. Error	Beta	t	Sig
1	(Constant)	449.790	134.859		3.335	.002
	Percentage of People in Poverty, Average 96–97	33.335	10.239	.425	3.256	.002

[d] Dependent Variable: Burglary per 100,000: 1997

If the percentage of people living in poverty is 50 percent, then the burglary rate should be 2116.54/100,000.

In terms of causation, we would still use the methods described in correlation to describe this relationship. The r^2 gives you the percentage of the variation in the dependent variable that is explained by the independent variable. Here, 18 percent of the variation in the burglary rate is explained by the variation in the percentage of people living in poverty (see Table 11.4, "Model Summary"—r^2). Therefore, 82 percent of the variation in the burglary rate is attributable to factors other than the percentage of persons living in poverty. This is why we need to conduct multivariate analysis—to see what other independent variables affect the burglary rate and thus further determine the strength of the association with the poverty rate.

Summary

In this chapter, we introduce linear regression—a statistical method based upon correlation that is used to make projections or predictions. The major assumptions are that the independent and dependent variables are correlated and that they share a linear relationship.

The mathematical equation for the line of "best fit" between all the points of X and Y in a scatter plot is ($\hat{Y} = a + bX$). The value of a tells you the value of $\hat{Y}$ when $X = 0$. The slope of b tells you how much $\hat{Y}$ increases (or decreases) for every one unit change in X.

Regression analyses are used to predict jail and prison populations. They can also be used to anticipate the demand for police services and courtroom space.

Key Terms

Simple Linear Regression: features one independent variable and one dependent variable. It takes the form of a mathematical equation:

$$\hat{Y} = a + bX$$

where: 1. a *is the Y intercept.* It is the point at which the regression line crosses the Y-axis. It equals $\hat{Y}$ (the predicted value of Y) when X is 0. The value of a can be positive or negative.

2. b *represents the slope of the regression line.* It represents the change in Y per one unit change in X. As X increases by one, Y changes by the value of b. The slope shows how much and in which direction $\hat{Y}$ will vary per one unit change in the value of X. The value of b can be positive or negative. A positive value for b indicates that a one-unit increase in X leads to an increase in $\hat{Y}$ by the value of i. A negative b value indicates that a one-unit increase in X leads to a decrease in $\hat{Y}$ by the value of b.

Least Squares Technique: constructs the straight line that comes closest to all points in the scatter plot between X and Y. The least squares procedure provides the best fit in that it lies at the point where the squared deviations from all the points on the scatter plot are minimized and thus the accuracy of the prediction is maximized.

Residuals: The distance between the regression line and the points are actually errors in prediction called residuals. The residual is the difference between the actual and the predicted value of Y.

Curvilinear Relationship: determined when the scatter plot between X and Y follows a curved line.

Data Analysis

1. Using SPSS, enter the data from Table 11.2 and conduct a regression analysis. To enter data take the following steps.

   a. Open the SPSS program. Click on "Type in Data" and then on "OK." The screen in Figure 11.9 will appear.

   b. At the bottom of the screen, click on the tab "Variable View." The screen in Figure 11.10 will appear.

   c. On this screen, click on the blank field under name and enter "year" and make the width for this variable 4 (Figure 11.11).

   d. Click on the second line under year and enter "murderrate" and make the width for this variable 2, with 1 as the decimal (Figure 11.11).

   e. Click on the tab "Data View." Click on the cell under year and enter 1976 and 8.8 under murderrate (Figure 11.12). Then continue to enter the data from Table 11.2.

   f. Don't forget to name and save this data set.

Directions: Using the same variables from the Data Analysis exercises in chapter 10, conduct a regression analysis on the following topics and variables from State Data Set I "Data Analysis." The aim is to predict values of your dependent variable from those of the independent variable. Interpret the a, b, and r^2 values fully. What predictions can you make using these equations?

2. Number of Black Males Unemployed and the Black Prison Population (12/31/95)

3. Teen Unemployment Rate, 1995, and the Number of Juveniles Arrested Violent Crimes (Under 18), 1997

4. Rate per 100,000 residents of prisoners in 1995 and

   a. Crime Index Total per 100,000

   b. Property Crime per 100,000, 1997

   c. Violent Crime per 100,000, 1997

5. Number of All Employed Females and

   a. Number of Juveniles Arrested (Under 18), 1997

   b. Number of Juveniles Arrested Property Crimes (Under 18), 1997

   c. Number of Juveniles Arrested Violent Crimes (Under 18), 1997

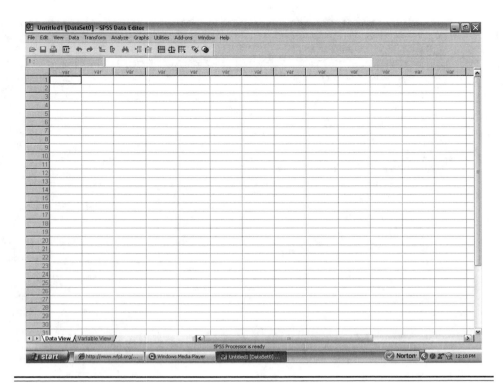

Figure 11.9

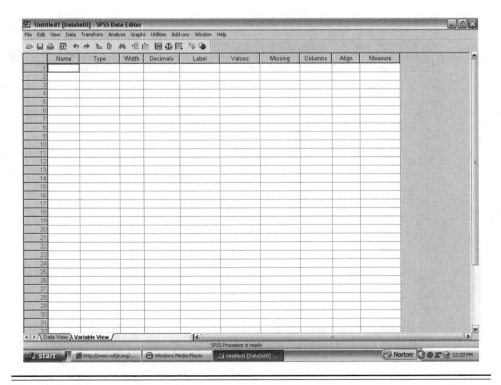

Figure 11.10

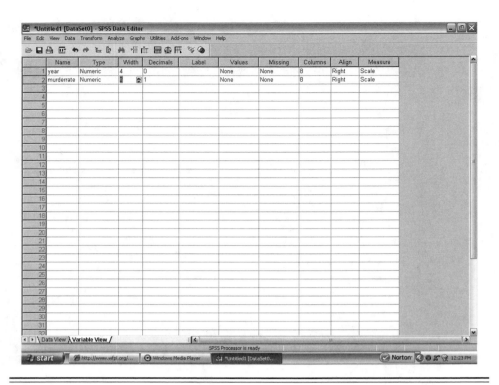

Figure 11.11

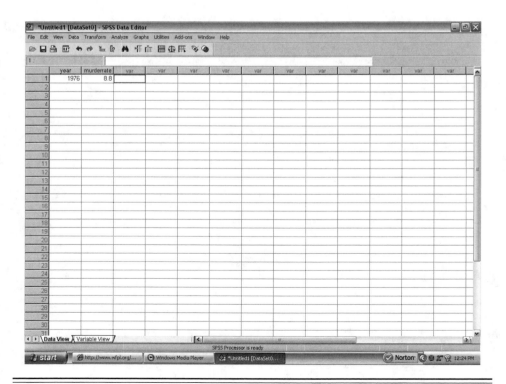

Figure 11.12

6. Unemployment rate, January 1996 and

a. Number of Adults Arrested Property Crimes, 1997

b. Number of Adults Arrested Violent Crimes, 1997

7. The Percentage of People in Poverty, Average 96–97 and

a. Violent Crime Rate per 100,000, 1997

b. Murder/Non-negligent Homicide per 100,000, 1997

c. Aggravated Assault per 100,000, 1997

Directions: Using the same variables from the Data Analysis exercises in chapter 10, conduct a regression analysis on the following topics and variables from State Data Set II. The aim is to predict values of your dependent variable from those of the independent variable. Interpret the a, b, and r^2 values fully. What predictions can you make using these equations?

8. Number of Black Males Unemployed and the Black Prison Population (12/31/98)

9. Teen Unemployment Rate, 1995, and the Number of Juveniles Arrested Violent Crimes (Under 18), 2003

10. Rate per 100,000 residents of prisoners in 1995 and

a. Crime Index Total per 100,000, 2003

b. Property Crime per 100,000, 2003

c. Violent Crime per 100,000, 2003

11. Number of All Employed Females and

a. Number of Juveniles Arrested (Under 18), 2003

b. Number of Juveniles Arrested Property Crimes (Under 18), 2003

c. Number of Juveniles Arrested Violent Crimes (Under 18), 2003

12. Unemployment rate, January 1996 and

a. Number of Adults Arrested Property Crimes, 2003

b. Number of Adults Arrested Violent Crimes, 2003

13. The Percentage of People in Poverty, Average 96–97 and

a. Violent Crime Rate per 100,000, 2003

b. Murder/Non-negligent Homicide per 100,000, 2003

c. Aggravated Assault per 100,000, 2003

14. Total Police Protection Per Capita Expenditures in 1999 and:

a. Crime Index Total 2003

b. Number of Adults Arrested 2003

c. Number of Juveniles Arrested 2003

d. Prison Population 12/31/2003

15. Unemployment Rate, Jan 1996 and rate per 100,000 residents of prisoners in 2003

Notes

[1] W. Paul Vogt, *Dictionary of Statistics and Methodology*, 3d ed. (Thousand Oaks, CA: Sage, 2005).

[2] M. A. Jones and J. Austin, *NCCD 1995 Prison Population Forecast: The Cost of Truth-in-Sentencing Laws* (Rockville, MD: National Criminal Justice Reference Service, 1995).

[3] Allen J. Beck, *Prisoners in 1999—Bureau of Justice Statistics Bulletin* (Washington, DC: U.S. Department of Justice), p. 2.

[4] Such projections, however, are typically made via multiple regression and other advanced multivariate statistical techniques that can take several independent variables into account. Of course, such methods are beyond the scope of this text. See Lin Bin Shan, Doris L. MacKenzie, and Thomas R. Gulledge Jr., "Using ARIMA Models to Predict Prison Populations," *Journal of Quantitative Criminology*, Vol. 2 (1986), pp. 251–264.

chapter 12

The Use of Statistics in Policy Analysis

When speculation has done its worst, two and two still make four.
—Samuel Johnson, *The Idler*

The skills that you have learned in this text were designed to generate information that can be put to many uses. It is difficult to imagine any area of criminal justice and criminology for which analysis of data is inappropriate. Unfortunately, the present reality is that crime control policies lag behind other social policies in terms of decisions made based on data and facts. This sad situation is because many crime control issues remain largely ideological and are thus resistant to change based on data that reveals what works and what does not. Furthermore, as it relates to policy analysis as a "pre-impact" evaluation, criminal justice policy is often legislated as a "reaction" to some event or particularly heinous crime. It remains for future generations of practitioners to bring a greater degree of rationality to bear on the management of crime and related issues, including the rational creation and evaluation of criminal justice policy. This goal is one of the major motivations behind this text and our research.

The Purpose of Research

Criminological research falls into two broad categories: basic and applied. Basic research includes developing theories and testing their validity through various methods. Applied research is oriented toward specific problems and may generate practical solutions to crime or may evaluate the effectiveness or efficiency of a program or policy. For example, J. P. Gibbs identified four major questions that criminologists traditionally attempt to answer:

1. Why does the crime rate vary?
2. Why are crimes committed by certain individuals and not others?
3. Why is there variation in reactions to alleged criminality?
4. What are the possible means of controlling criminality?[1]

Further, Gibbs asserts that research should have a clear purpose:

> No scientific enterprise will be supported indefinitely unless it benefits someone other than the scientists, and perhaps much of criminology's support stems from a concern with crime prevention. There is simply no justification for the indifference of theorists to attempts to prevent criminality, including delinquency.[2]

Research on the causes of crime and criminal behavior can provide information that can be used either to prevent crime from occurring or to lessen its impact on society. For example, research exists that tests routine activities theory and incapacitation theory. When considering tests of such theories, one might question, "What is considered a suitable guardian?" or "What is the optimal incarceration length for a violent offender?" The idea of an optimal sentence is one that we've not been terribly good at identifying as criminal justice administrators, but it's the idea of incapacitating an individual only as long as it takes for that individual not to commit another offense. This concept is important in terms of evaluating the cost-efficiency of incarceration. For example, if an individual is serving a 30-year sentence, but she will no longer offend after 5 years, then we've incarcerated her for 25 years more than what was needed, from a deterrence and/or rehabilitation perspective. This is a cost of incarceration, a cost of not having her as a potential wage-earner in the community, and a cost of taking up a bed that might otherwise be utilized by another (more violent) offender. Furthermore, applied research, such as program evaluation, can be incorporated into the decision making process regarding the efficacy of various criminal justice practices and policies: How do we know drug courts are an effective alternative to traditional prosecution? Is electronic monitoring a cost-effective alternative to incarceration for all types of offenders or only certain types?

The detailed information that is generated by criminal justice research can be a tool for management. It can guide daily operations throughout the criminal justice system as well as inform long-term crime control policies. For example, problem solving has become a key component of police operations— from the community and the street cop to the chief. Research and statistical analysis informs the problem-solving function. Police managers must be able to assess agency performance (both individually and collectively), analyze and solve community problems, and judge the competency of programs designed to address them. Criminal justice research can guide decision making in the following manner:

> Research can provide useful and exciting insights into community problems and how police agencies operate. It can reveal potentially useful programs and strategies for dealing with problems. It can show which programs are successful and which are not. It can suggest new strategies to deal with old issues. It can provide information needed to improve existing programs. And it can inform the public and elected officials. In short, research is a tool for police managers who want to make rational, informed decisions.[3]

Specifically, research can guide management decisions to allocate resources in the department and in the community. How should the department deal with calls for service, routine patrol, and crime investigation and prevention and engage in problem solving? Efficient allocation of resources requires information.[4] Joan Petersilia asserts that research can be an unimpeachable guide to policy. She argues that criminologists should strive for "research [that is] more likely to influence the way policy makers think about problems than to provide solutions 'off the shelf.'" Furthermore, she urges criminologists to make clear the policy implications of their research findings.[5] As noted throughout this text, this is not an easy task, but it is certainly essential if criminology is to stay relevant.

Examples of Successes and Failures

The history of crime control in this country is replete with examples of successes and failures. Space does not permit us to review this body of literature, but we include three examples that are illustrative of the point that policy formulation not based on research is problematic, to say the least.

Kansas City Preventive Patrol Experiment

Perhaps no other study is as frequently cited in the police literature as the Kansas City Preventive Patrol Experiment.[6] Since the inception of modern policing in 1829, police have been assigned to wander a geographic area during their work shift. In 1972, George Kelling and a group of researchers evaluated the effect of uniformed police patrol on a number of factors such as reported crime (via official reports and community surveys), citizens' fear of crime, and the relationship between police response time and the apprehension of offenders.

The results of this classic experiment suggested that, despite varying the level of uniform police patrol, the crime rate and citizens' fear of crime remained largely unchanged over the course of the study. Police response time was found to have no significant relationship to the apprehension of offenders because by the time the police were summoned the perpetrator had left the crime scene. The findings of these and other studies on police patrol were summarized by Carl Klockars: "It makes about as much sense to have police patrol routinely in police cars to fight crime as it does to have firemen patrol routinely in fire trucks to fight fire."[7]

The impact of the Kansas City Preventive Patrol Experiment has been mixed. On the one hand, a plethora of studies followed the 1972 study on how best to deploy police officers. This seminal study seems to have spurred interest in increasing the efficiency of police patrol in hopes of improving effectiveness in reducing crime and related concerns. On the other hand, while specialization has increased dramatically, the modal category of police delivery of service is still random uniform patrol.

Kansas City Gun Experiment

Despite the continued decrease in overall violent crimes during the last decade, gun violence has continued to escalate. Lawrence Sherman and his colleagues decided to test the proposition that decreasing the number of available guns would result in a decline in gun-related violence.[8]

The researchers selected an area for the experiment that had a homicide rate 20 times higher than the national average. Police officers used different techniques to detect and seize guns. At the conclusion of the study, the researchers observed that gun seizures in the target area increased 65 percent and that gun-related crimes declined by 49 percent. Thinking that perhaps the increased emphasis on seizing guns might have simply displaced gun-related crimes to other locations, the researchers examined gun crimes in areas surrounding the target area and found no changes. Using a quasi-experimental design, the researchers also discovered that neither gun seizures nor gun-related violence had changed in an area similar to the target area while the experiment was underway.

Despite this and other evidence, gun control remains a divisive public policy issue, even reaching the level of presidential campaigns. Handgun Control reports, "In one year, firearms killed no children in Japan, 19 in Great Britain, 57 in Germany, 109 in France, 153 in Canada, and 5,285 in the United States,"[9] while the National Rifle Association cites the following as part of its justification for unfettered gun ownership: "Handguns are used for protection against criminals nearly two million times per year, up to five times more often than to commit crimes."[10] Thus, while both sides of the issue use data to support their position, the issue is likely to remain immersed in political rhetoric and ideological gridlock.

Capital Punishment

If abortion was the political litmus test of the 1980s, we believe that the issue of capital punishment has replaced it (or at least rivaled it). For example, a Tennessee Supreme Court Justice was turned out of office while seeking re-election, based in part on the belief by a segment of voters that she was soft on crime, and especially on death penalty cases. Analysis of Justice White's voting record, however, suggested an opposite conclusion.

Capital punishment remains a popular prescription among politicians and the general population for controlling violent crime. Research has shown, however, that support for capital punishment declines among supporters when those surveyed are given alternatives beyond life or death sentencing. Moreover, research has shown the following:

- Race of the victim is an important predictor in who does and doesn't receive a capital sentence.
- The quality of one's lawyer is also a predictor of death sentencing outcomes.
- Jurors are confused over sentencing instructions used in capital cases.
- The meting out of death sentences also has a class and gender bias.
- Capital punishment is no more effective as a general deterrent to violent crime than are life sentences.
- Seeking and imposing death sentences is far more expensive than enforcing a life sentence.

- Each year, more and more *innocent* people have been removed from death row. Sentencing innocent people to death achieves none of the goals sought by proponents of capital punishment.

Despite the empirical evidence that capital punishment is not an effective crime control policy, the United States continues to embrace this practice, which is counter to the trend in the rest of the world. Thus, the lack of rationality makes capital punishment one of the most ideologically driven policies currently in use.

Closing Comments

By completing this course, you have taken steps to prepare yourself for career advancement and for lifelong learning. Statistical analysis allows those who master its techniques to create knowledge, and it also provides a means of inquiring about the validity of statements made by others, regardless of the subject. You have learned to speak a new language!

While you may never use all of the statistical tests in this text, you will probably encounter occasions where one or more will be useful to you. We hope, however, that you will practice the larger tenets that are part of the world of critical inquiry. In parting, please keep in mind some of these basic principles:

1. A degree of skepticism is healthy. When you encounter facts and statistics, ask yourself a few questions about the validity and reliability of the information.

2. Always keep in mind three questions:

   a. How large is the sample? Remember the problems associated with small sample sizes.

   b. Is it a random sample or an availability sample? You cannot infer from an availability sample to a population.

   c. Was the statistical test appropriate for the kind of data collected? What is the probability of making a Type I or Type II error?

3. Statistical analysis is a tool—it is the means to an end and not the end itself.

4. Always remember that crime control policies and related issues have a powerful political and ideological dimension. Even though you may have an answer to a problem, the intended audience may not be receptive. The research cited in the previous section is proof positive of this phenomenon.

5. Never give up the struggle to improve the quality of professional and social life through rigorous application of the scientific method.

Notes

[1] J.P. Gibbs, "The State of Criminological Theory," *Criminology,* Vol. 25 (1987), pp. 821–840.

[2] Ibid., p. 824.

[3] John E. Eck and Nancy G. La Vigne, *Using Research: A Primer for Law Enforcement Managers* (Washington, DC: Police Executive Research Forum, 1994), p. 2.

[4] William Spelman, *Beyond Bean Counting: New Approaches for Managing Crime Data* (Washington, DC: Police Executive Research Forum, 1988).

[5] Joan Petersilia, "Policy Relevance and the Future of Criminology," *Criminology*, Vol. 29 (1991), pp. 1–16.

[6] George Kelling et al., *The Kansas City Preventive Patrol Experiment* (Washington, DC: Police Foundation, 1974).

[7] Carl Klockars, *The Idea of Police,* (Beverly Hills, CA: Sage, 1985), p. 120.

[8] Lawrence W. Sherman, James W. Shaw, and Dennis P. Rogan, *The Kansas City Gun Experiment. National Institute of Justice Research in Brief* (Washington, DC: U.S. Department of Justice, 1995).

[9] www.bradycampaign.org/facts/issues/?page=kids (accessed 4/26/07).

[10] www.nraila.org/Armedcitizen/Default.aspx (accessed 4/26/07).

Appendix

Table A.1 Binomial Distribution

This table shows the probability of x successes in n independent trials, each with probability of success p.

						p				
n	x	.01	.05	.10	.15	.20	.25	.30	.35	.40
2	0	.980	.902	.810	.723	.640	.563	.490	.423	.360
	1	.020	.095	.180	.255	.320	.375	.420	.455	.480
	2	.000	.002	.010	.023	.040	.063	.090	.123	.160
3	0	.970	.857	.729	.614	.512	.422	.343	.275	.216
	1	.029	.135	.243	.325	.384	.422	.441	.444	.432
	2	.000	.007	.027	.057	.096	.141	.189	.239	.288
	3	.000	.000	.001	.003	.008	.016	.027	.043	.064
4	0	.961	.815	.656	.522	.410	.316	.240	.179	.130
	1	.039	.171	.292	.368	.410	.422	.412	.384	.346
	2	.001	.014	.049	.098	.154	.211	.265	.311	.346
	3	.000	.000	.004	.011	.026	.047	.076	.112	.154
	4	.000	.000	.000	.001	.002	.004	.008	.015	.026
5	0	.951	.774	.590	.444	.328	.237	.168	.116	.078
	1	.048	.204	.328	.392	.410	.396	.360	.312	.259
	2	.001	.021	.073	.138	.205	.264	.309	.336	.346
	3	.000	.001	.008	.024	.051	.088	.132	.181	.230
	4	.000	.000	.000	.002	.006	.015	.028	.049	.077
	5	.000	.000	.000	.000	.000	.001	.002	.005	.010
6	0	.941	.735	.531	.377	.262	.178	.118	.075	.047
	1	.057	.232	.354	.399	.393	.356	.303	.244	.187
	2	.001	.031	.098	.176	.246	.297	.324	.328	.311
	3	.000	.002	.015	.042	.082	.132	.185	.236	.276
	4	.000	.000	.001	.006	.015	.033	.060	.095	.138
	5	.000	.000	.000	.000	.002	.004	.010	.020	.037
	6	.000	.000	.000	.000	.000	.000	.001	.002	.004
7	0	.932	.698	.478	.321	.210	.133	.082	.049	.028
	1	.066	.257	.372	.396	.367	.311	.247	.185	.131
	2	.002	.041	.124	.210	.275	.311	.318	.299	.261
	3	.000	.004	.023	.062	.115	.173	.227	.268	.290
	4	.000	.000	.003	.011	.029	.058	.097	.144	.194
	5	.000	.000	.000	.001	.004	.012	.025	.047	.077
	6	.000	.000	.000	.000	.000	.001	.004	.008	.017
	7	.000	.000	.000	.000	.000	.000	.000	.001	.002

					p					
.45	**.50**	**.55**	**.60**	**.65**	**.70**	**.75**	**.80**	**.85**	**.90**	**.95**
.303	.250	.203	.160	.123	.090	.063	.040	.023	.010	.002
.495	.500	.495	.480	.455	.420	.375	.320	.255	.180	.095
.203	.250	.303	.360	.423	.490	.563	.640	.723	.810	.902
.166	.125	.091	.064	.043	.027	.016	.008	.003	.001	.000
.408	.375	.334	.288	.239	.189	.141	.096	.057	.027	.007
.334	.375	.408	.432	.444	.441	.422	.384	.325	.243	.135
.091	.125	.166	.216	.275	.343	.422	.512	.614	.729	.857
.092	.062	.041	.026	.015	.008	.004	.002	.001	.000	.000
.300	.250	.200	.154	.112	.076	.047	.026	.011	.004	.000
.368	.375	.368	.346	.311	.265	.211	.154	.098	.049	.014
.200	.250	.300	.346	.384	.412	.422	.410	.368	.292	.171
.041	.062	.092	.130	.179	.240	.316	.410	.522	.656	.815
.050	.031	.019	.010	.005	.002	.001	.000	.000	.000	.000
.206	.156	.113	.077	.049	.028	.015	.006	.002	.000	.000
.337	.312	.276	.230	.181	.132	.088	.051	.024	.008	.001
.276	.312	.337	.346	.336	.309	.264	.205	.138	.073	.021
.113	.156	.206	.259	.312	.360	.396	.410	.392	.328	.204
.019	.031	.050	.078	.116	.168	.237	.328	.444	.590	.774
.028	.016	.008	.004	.002	.001	.000	.000	.000	.000	.000
.136	.094	.061	.037	.020	.010	.004	.002	.000	.000	.000
.278	.234	.186	.138	.095	.060	.033	.015	.006	.001	.000
.303	.312	.303	.276	.236	.185	.132	.082	.042	.015	.002
.186	.234	.278	.311	.328	.324	.297	.246	.176	.098	.031
.061	.094	.136	.187	.244	.303	.356	.393	.399	.354	.232
.008	.016	.028	.047	.075	.118	.178	.262	.377	.531	.735
.015	.008	.004	.002	.001	.000	.000	.000	.000	.000	.000
.087	.055	.032	.017	.008	.004	.001	.000	.000	.000	.000
.214	.164	.117	.077	.047	.025	.012	.004	.001	.000	.000
.292	.273	.239	.194	.144	.097	.058	.029	.011	.003	.000
.239	.273	.292	.290	.268	.227	.173	.115	.062	.023	.004
.117	.164	.214	.261	.299	.318	.311	.275	.210	.124	.041
.032	.055	.087	.131	.185	.247	.311	.367	.396	.372	.257
.004	.008	.015	.028	.049	.082	.133	.210	.321	.478	.698

(continued)

Table A.1 *(continued)*

						p				
n	x	.01	.05	.10	.15	.20	.25	.30	.35	.40
8	0	.923	.663	.430	.272	.168	.100	.058	.032	.017
	1	.075	.279	.383	.385	.336	.267	.198	.137	.090
	2	.003	.051	.149	.238	.294	.311	.296	.259	.209
	3	.000	.005	.033	.084	.147	.208	.254	.279	.279
	4	.000	.000	.005	.018	.046	.087	.136	.188	.232
	5	.000	.000	.000	.003	.009	.023	.047	.081	.124
	6	.000	.000	.000	.000	.001	.004	.010	.022	.041
	7	.000	.000	.000	.000	.000	.000	.001	.003	.008
	8	.000	.000	.000	.000	.000	.000	.000	.000	.001
9	0	.914	.630	.387	.232	.134	.075	.040	.021	.010
	1	.083	.299	.387	.368	.302	.225	.156	.100	.060
	2	.003	.063	.172	.260	.302	.300	.267	.216	.161
	3	.000	.008	.045	.107	.176	.234	.267	.272	.251
	4	.000	.001	.007	.028	.066	.117	.172	.219	.251
	5	.000	.000	.001	.005	.017	.039	.074	.118	.167
	6	.000	.000	.000	.001	.003	.009	.021	.042	.074
	7	.000	.000	.000	.000	.000	.001	.004	.010	.021
	8	.000	.000	.000	.000	.000	.000	.000	.001	.004
	9	.000	.000	.000	.000	.000	.000	.000	.000	.000
10	0	.904	.599	.349	.197	.107	.056	.028	.014	.006
	1	.091	.315	.387	.347	.268	.188	.121	.072	.040
	2	.004	.075	.194	.276	.302	.282	.233	.176	.121
	3	.000	.010	.057	.130	.201	.250	.267	.252	.215
	4	.000	.001	.011	.040	.088	.146	.200	.238	.251
	5	.000	.000	.001	.008	.026	.058	.103	.154	.201
	6	.000	.000	.000	.001	.006	.016	.037	.069	.111
	7	.000	.000	.000	.000	.001	.003	.009	.021	.042
	8	.000	.000	.000	.000	.000	.000	.001	.004	.011
	9	.000	.000	.000	.000	.000	.000	.000	.000	.002
	10	.000	.000	.000	.000	.000	.000	.000	.000	.000
11	0	.895	.569	.314	.167	.086	.042	.020	.009	.004
	1	.099	.329	.384	.325	.236	.155	.093	.052	.027
	2	.005	.087	.213	.287	.295	.258	.200	.140	.089
	3	.000	.014	.071	.152	.221	.258	.257	.225	.177
	4	.000	.001	.016	.054	.111	.172	.220	.243	.236
	5	.000	.000	.002	.013	.039	.080	.132	.183	.221
	6	.000	.000	.000	.002	.010	.027	.057	.099	.147
	7	.000	.000	.000	.000	.002	.006	.017	.038	.070

					p					
.45	.50	.55	.60	.65	.70	.75	.80	.85	.90	.95
.008	.004	.002	.001	.000	.000	.000	.000	.000	.000	.000
.055	.031	.016	.008	.003	.001	.000	.000	.000	.000	.000
.157	.109	.070	.041	.022	.010	.004	.001	.000	.000	.000
.257	.219	.172	.124	.081	.047	.023	.009	.003	.000	.000
.263	.273	.263	.232	.188	.136	.087	.046	.018	.005	.000
.172	.219	.257	.279	.279	.254	.208	.147	.084	.033	.005
.070	.109	.157	.209	.259	.296	.311	.294	.238	.149	.051
.016	.031	.055	.090	.137	.198	.267	.336	.385	.383	.279
.002	.004	.008	.017	.032	.058	.100	.168	.272	.430	.663
.005	.002	.001	.000	.000	.000	.000	.000	.000	.000	.000
.034	.018	.008	.004	.001	.000	.000	.000	.000	.000	.000
.111	.070	.041	.021	.010	.004	.001	.000	.000	.000	.000
.212	.164	.116	.074	.042	.021	.009	.003	.001	.000	.000
.260	.246	.213	.167	.118	.074	.039	.017	.005	.001	.000
.213	.246	.260	.251	.219	.172	.117	.066	.028	.007	.001
.116	.164	.212	.251	.272	.267	.234	.176	.107	.045	.008
.041	.070	.111	.161	.216	.267	.300	.302	.260	.172	.063
.008	.018	.034	.060	.100	.156	.225	.302	.368	.387	.299
.001	.002	.005	.010	.021	.040	.075	.134	.232	.387	.630
.003	.001	.000	.000	.000	.000	.000	.000	.000	.000	.000
.021	.010	.004	.002	.000	.000	.000	.000	.000	.000	.000
.076	.044	.023	.011	.004	.001	.000	.000	.000	.000	.000
.166	.117	.075	.042	.021	.009	.003	.001	.000	.000	.000
.238	.205	.160	.111	.069	.037	.016	.006	.001	.000	.000
.234	.246	.234	.201	.154	.103	.058	.026	.008	.001	.000
.160	.205	.238	.251	.238	.200	.146	.088	.040	.011	.001
.075	.117	.166	.215	.252	.267	.250	.201	.130	.057	.010
.023	.044	.076	.121	.176	.233	.282	.302	.276	.194	.075
.004	.010	.021	.040	.072	.121	.188	.268	.347	.387	.315
.000	.001	.003	.006	.014	.028	.056	.107	.197	.349	.599
.001	.000	.000	.000	.000	.000	.000	.000	.000	.000	.000
.013	.005	.002	.001	.000	.000	.000	.000	.000	.000	.000
.051	.027	.013	.005	.002	.001	.000	.000	.000	.000	.000
.126	.081	.046	.023	.010	.004	.001	.000	.000	.000	.000
.206	.161	.113	.070	.038	.017	.006	.002	.000	.000	.000
.236	.226	.193	.147	.099	.057	.027	.010	.002	.000	.000
.193	.226	.236	.221	.183	.132	.080	.039	.013	.002	.000
.113	.161	.206	.236	.243	.220	.172	.111	.054	.016	.001

(continued)

Table A.1 *(continued)*

					p				
n	*x*	**.01**	**.05**	**.10**	**.15**	**.20**	**.25**	**.30**	**.35**	**.40**
	8	.000	.000	.000	.000	.000	.001	.004	.010	.023
	9	.000	.000	.000	.000	.000	.000	.001	.002	.005
	10	.000	.000	.000	.000	.000	.000	.000	.000	.001
	11	.000	.000	.000	.000	.000	.000	.000	.000	.000
12	0	.886	.540	.282	.142	.069	.032	.014	.006	.002
	1	.107	.341	.377	.301	.206	.127	.071	.037	.017
	2	.006	.099	.230	.292	.283	.232	.168	.109	.064
	3	.000	.017	.085	.172	.236	.258	.240	.195	.142
	4	.000	.002	.021	.068	.133	.194	.231	.237	.213
	5	.000	.000	.004	.019	.053	.103	.158	.204	.227
	6	.000	.000	.000	.004	.016	.040	.079	.128	.177
	7	.000	.000	.000	.001	.003	.011	.029	.059	.101
	8	.000	.000	.000	.000	.001	.002	.008	.020	.042
	9	.000	.000	.000	.000	.000	.000	.001	.005	.012
	10	.000	.000	.000	.000	.000	.000	.000	.001	.002
	11	.000	.000	.000	.000	.000	.000	.000	.000	.000
	12	.000	.000	.000	.000	.000	.000	.000	.000	.000
15	0	.860	.463	.206	.087	.035	.013	.005	.002	.000
	1	.130	.366	.343	.231	.132	.067	.031	.013	.005
	2	.009	.135	.267	.286	.231	.156	.092	.048	.022
	3	.000	.031	.129	.218	.250	.225	.170	.111	.063
	4	.000	.005	.043	.116	.188	.225	.219	.179	.127
	5	.000	.001	.010	.045	.103	.165	.206	.212	.186
	6	.000	.000	.002	.013	.043	.092	.147	.191	.207
	7	.000	.000	.000	.003	.014	.039	.081	.132	.177
	8	.000	.000	.000	.001	.003	.013	.035	.071	.118
	9	.000	.000	.000	.000	.001	.003	.012	.030	.061
	10	.000	.000	.000	.000	.000	.001	.003	.010	.024
	11	.000	.000	.000	.000	.000	.000	.001	.002	.007
	12	.000	.000	.000	.000	.000	.000	.000	.000	.002
	13	.000	.000	.000	.000	.000	.000	.000	.000	.000
	14	.000	.000	.000	.000	.000	.000	.000	.000	.000
	15	.000	.000	.000	.000	.000	.000	.000	.000	.000
16	0	.851	.440	.185	.074	.028	.010	.003	.001	.000
	1	.138	.371	.329	.210	.113	.053	.023	.009	.003
	2	.010	.146	.275	.277	.211	.134	.073	.035	.015
	3	.000	.036	.142	.229	.246	.208	.146	.089	.047
	4	.000	.006	.051	.131	.200	.225	.204	.155	.101

					p					
.45	**.50**	**.55**	**.60**	**.65**	**.70**	**.75**	**.80**	**.85**	**.90**	**.95**
.046	.081	.126	.177	.225	.257	.258	.221	.152	.071	.014
.013	.027	.051	.089	.140	.200	.258	.295	.287	.213	.087
.002	.005	.013	.027	.052	.093	.155	.236	.325	.384	.329
.000	.000	.001	.004	.009	.020	.042	.086	.167	.314	.569
.001	.000	.000	.000	.000	.000	.000	.000	.000	.000	.000
.008	.003	.001	.000	.000	.000	.000	.000	.000	.000	.000
.034	.016	.007	.002	.001	.000	.000	.000	.000	.000	.000
.092	.054	.028	.012	.005	.001	.000	.000	.000	.000	.000
.170	.121	.076	.042	.020	.008	.002	.001	.000	.000	.000
.223	.193	.149	.101	.059	.029	.011	.003	.001	.000	.000
.212	.226	.212	.177	.128	.079	.040	.016	.004	.000	.000
.149	.193	.223	.227	.204	.158	.103	.053	.019	.004	.000
.076	.121	.170	.213	.237	.231	.194	.133	.068	.021	.002
.028	.054	.092	.142	.195	.240	.258	.236	.172	.085	.017
.007	.016	.034	.064	.109	.168	.232	.283	.292	.230	.099
.001	.003	.008	.017	.037	.071	.127	.206	.301	.377	.341
.000	.000	.001	.002	.006	.014	.032	.069	.142	.282	.540
.000	.000	.000	.000	.000	.000	.000	.000	.000	.000	.000
.002	.000	.000	.000	.000	.000	.000	.000	.000	.000	.000
.009	.003	.001	.000	.000	.000	.000	.000	.000	.000	.000
.032	.014	.005	.002	.000	.000	.000	.000	.000	.000	.000
.078	.042	.019	.007	.002	.001	.000	.000	.000	.000	.000
.140	.092	.051	.024	.010	.003	.001	.000	.000	.000	.000
.191	.153	.105	.061	.030	.012	.003	.001	.000	.000	.000
.201	.196	.165	.118	.071	.035	.013	.003	.001	.000	.000
.165	.196	.201	.177	.132	.081	.039	.014	.003	.000	.000
.105	.153	.191	.207	.191	.147	.092	.043	.013	.002	.000
.051	.092	.140	.186	.212	.206	.165	.103	.045	.010	.001
.019	.042	.078	.127	.179	.219	.225	.188	.116	.043	.005
.005	.014	.032	.063	.111	.170	.225	.250	.218	.129	.031
.001	.003	.009	.022	.048	.092	.156	.231	.286	.267	.135
.000	.000	.002	.005	.013	.031	.067	.132	.231	.343	.366
.000	.000	.000	.000	.002	.005	.013	.035	.087	.206	.463
.000	.000	.000	.000	.000	.000	.000	.000	.000	.000	.000
.001	.000	.000	.000	.000	.000	.000	.000	.000	.000	.000
.006	.002	.001	.000	.000	.000	.000	.000	.000	.000	.000
.022	.009	.003	.001	.000	.000	.000	.000	.000	.000	.000
.057	.028	.011	.004	.001	.000	.000	.000	.000	.000	.000

(continued)

Table A.1 *(continued)*

n	x	.01	.05	.10	.15	.20	.25	.30	.35	.40
						p				
	5	.000	.001	.014	.056	.120	.180	.210	.201	.162
	6	.000	.000	.003	.018	.055	.110	.165	.198	.198
	7	.000	.000	.000	.005	.020	.052	.101	.152	.189
	8	.000	.000	.000	.001	.006	.020	.049	.092	.142
	9	.000	.000	.000	.000	.001	.006	.019	.044	.084
	10	.000	.000	.000	.000	.000	.001	.006	.017	.039
	11	.000	.000	.000	.000	.000	.000	.001	.005	.014
	12	.000	.000	.000	.000	.000	.000	.000	.001	.004
	13	.000	.000	.000	.000	.000	.000	.000	.000	.001
	14	.000	.000	.000	.000	.000	.000	.000	.000	.000
	15	.000	.000	.000	.000	.000	.000	.000	.000	.000
	16	.000	.000	.000	.000	.000	.000	.000	.000	.000
20	0	.818	.358	.122	.039	.012	.003	.001	.000	.000
	1	.165	.377	.270	.137	.058	.021	.007	.002	.000
	2	.016	.189	.285	.229	.137	.067	.028	.010	.003
	3	.001	.060	.190	.243	.205	.134	.072	.032	.012
	4	.000	.013	.090	.182	.218	.190	.130	.074	.035
	5	.000	.002	.032	.103	.175	.202	.179	.127	.075
	6	.000	.000	.009	.045	.109	.169	.192	.171	.124
	7	.000	.000	.002	.016	.055	.112	.164	.184	.166
	8	.000	.000	.000	.005	.022	.061	.114	.161	.180
	9	.000	.000	.000	.001	.007	.027	.065	.116	.160
	10	.000	.000	.000	.000	.002	.010	.031	.069	.117
	11	.000	.000	.000	.000	.000	.003	.012	.034	.071
	12	.000	.000	.000	.000	.000	.001	.004	.014	.035
	13	.000	.000	.000	.000	.000	.000	.001	.005	.015
	14	.000	.000	.000	.000	.000	.000	.000	.001	.005
	15	.000	.000	.000	.000	.000	.000	.000	.000	.001
	16	.000	.000	.000	.000	.000	.000	.000	.000	.000
	17	.000	.000	.000	.000	.000	.000	.000	.000	.000
	18	.000	.000	.000	.000	.000	.000	.000	.000	.000
	19	.000	.000	.000	.000	.000	.000	.000	.000	.000
	20	.000	.000	.000	.000	.000	.000	.000	.000	.000

					p					
.45	**.50**	**.55**	**.60**	**.65**	**.70**	**.75**	**.80**	**.85**	**.90**	**.95**
.112	.067	.034	.014	.005	.001	.000	.000	.000	.000	.000
.168	.122	.075	.039	.017	.006	.001	.000	.000	.000	.000
.197	.175	.132	.084	.044	.019	.006	.001	.000	.000	.000
.181	.196	.181	.142	.092	.049	.020	.006	.001	.000	.000
.132	.175	.197	.189	.152	.101	.052	.020	.005	.000	.000
.075	.122	.168	.198	.198	.165	.110	.055	.018	.003	.000
.034	.067	.112	.162	.201	.210	.180	.120	.056	.014	.001
.011	.028	.057	.101	.155	.204	.225	.200	.131	.051	.006
.003	.009	.022	.047	.089	.146	.208	.246	.229	.142	.036
.001	.002	.006	.015	.035	.073	.134	.211	.277	.275	.146
.000	.000	.001	.003	.009	.023	.053	.113	.210	.329	.371
.000	.000	.000	.000	.001	.003	.010	.028	.074	.185	.440
.000	.000	.000	.000	.000	.000	.000	.000	.000	.000	.000
.000	.000	.000	.000	.000	.000	.000	.000	.000	.000	.000
.001	.000	.000	.000	.000	.000	.000	.000	.000	.000	.000
.004	.001	.000	.000	.000	.000	.000	.000	.000	.000	.000
.014	.005	.001	.000	.000	.000	.000	.000	.000	.000	.000
.036	.015	.005	.001	.000	.000	.000	.000	.000	.000	.000
.075	.036	.015	.005	.001	.000	.000	.000	.000	.000	.000
.122	.074	.037	.015	.005	.001	.000	.000	.000	.000	.000
.162	.120	.073	.035	.014	.004	.001	.000	.000	.000	.000
.177	.160	.119	.071	.034	.012	.003	.000	.000	.000	.000
.159	.176	.159	.117	.069	.031	.010	.002	.000	.000	.000
.119	.160	.177	.160	.116	.065	.027	.007	.001	.000	.000
.073	.120	.162	.180	.161	.114	.061	.022	.005	.000	.000
.037	.074	.122	.166	.184	.164	.112	.055	.016	.002	.000
.015	.037	.075	.124	.171	.192	.169	.109	.045	.009	.000
.005	.015	.036	.075	.127	.179	.202	.175	.103	.032	.002
.001	.005	.014	.035	.074	.130	.190	.218	.182	.090	.013
.000	.001	.004	.012	.032	.072	.134	.205	.243	.190	.060
.000	.000	.001	.003	.010	.028	.067	.137	.229	.285	.189
.000	.000	.000	.000	.002	.007	.021	.058	.137	.270	.377
.000	.000	.000	.000	.000	.001	.003	.012	.039	.122	.358

Table A.2   Standard Normal Distribution

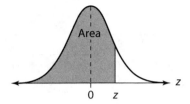

The value in the table represents the percentage of all scores to the left (or below) the score of the z-value.

z	.00	.01	.02	.03	.04	.05	.06	.07	.08	.09
−3.4	.0003	.0003	.0003	.0003	.0003	.0003	.0003	.0003	.0003	.0002
−3.3	.0005	.0005	.0005	.0004	.0004	.0004	.0004	.0004	.0004	.0003
−3.2	.0007	.0007	.0006	.0006	.0006	.0006	.0006	.0005	.0005	.0005
−3.1	.0010	.0009	.0009	.0009	.0008	.0008	.0008	.0008	.0007	.0007
−3.0	.0013	.0013	.0013	.0012	.0012	.0011	.0011	.0011	.0010	.0010
−2.9	.0019	.0018	.0017	.0017	.0016	.0016	.0015	.0015	.0014	.0014
−2.8	.0026	.0025	.0024	.0023	.0023	.0022	.0021	.0021	.0020	.0019
−2.7	.0035	.0034	.0033	.0032	.0031	.0030	.0029	.0028	.0027	.0026
−2.6	.0047	.0045	.0044	.0043	.0041	.0040	.0039	.0038	.0037	.0036
−2.5	.0062	.0060	.0059	.0057	.0055	.0054	.0052	.0051	.0049	.0048
−2.4	.0082	.0080	.0078	.0075	.0073	.0071	.0069	.0068	.0066	.0064
−2.3	.0107	.0104	.0102	.0099	.0096	.0094	.0091	.0089	.0087	.0084
−2.2	.0139	.0136	.0132	.0129	.0125	.0122	.0119	.0116	.0113	.0110
−2.1	.0179	.0174	.0170	.0166	.0162	.0158	.0154	.0150	.0146	.0143
−2.0	.0228	.0222	.0217	.0212	.0207	.0202	.0197	.0192	.0188	.0183
−1.9	.0287	.0281	.0274	.0268	.0262	.0256	.0250	.0244	.0239	.0233
−1.8	.0359	.0352	.0344	.0336	.0329	.0322	.0314	.0307	.0301	.0294
−1.7	.0446	.0436	.0427	.0418	.0409	.0401	.0392	.0384	.0375	.0367
−1.6	.0548	.0537	.0526	.0516	.0505	.0495	.0485	.0475	.0465	.0455
−1.5	.0668	.0655	.0643	.0630	.0618	.0606	.0594	.0582	.0571	.0559
−1.4	.0808	.0793	.0778	.0764	.0749	.0735	.0722	.0708	.0694	.0681
−1.3	.0968	.0951	.0934	.0918	.0901	.0885	.0869	.0853	.0838	.0823
−1.2	.1151	.1131	.1112	.1093	.1075	.1056	.1038	.1020	.1003	.0985
−1.1	.1357	.1335	.1314	.1292	.1271	.1251	.1230	.1210	.1190	.1170
−1.0	.1587	.1562	.1539	.1515	.1492	.1469	.1446	.1423	.1401	.1379
−0.9	.1841	.1814	.1788	.1762	.1736	.1711	.1685	.1660	.1635	.1611
−0.8	.2119	.2090	.2061	.2033	.2005	.1977	.1949	.1922	.1894	.1867
−0.7	.2420	.2389	.2358	.2327	.2296	.2266	.2236	.2206	.2177	.2148
−0.6	.2743	.2709	.2676	.2643	.2611	.2578	.2546	.2514	.2483	.2451
−0.5	.3085	.3050	.3015	.2981	.2946	.2912	.2877	.2843	.2810	.2776
−0.4	.3446	.3409	.3372	.3336	.3300	.3264	.3228	.3192	.3156	.3121
−0.3	.3821	.3783	.3745	.3707	.3669	.3632	.3594	.3557	.3520	.3483
−0.2	.4207	.4168	.4129	.4090	.4052	.4013	.3974	.3936	.3897	.3859
−0.1	.4602	.4562	.4522	.4483	.4443	.4404	.4364	.4325	.4286	.4247
−0.0	.5000	.4960	.4920	.4880	.4840	.4801	.4761	.4721	.4681	.4641

z	.00	.01	.02	.03	.04	.05	.06	.07	.08	.09
0.0	.5000	.5040	.5080	.5120	.5160	.5199	.5239	.5279	.5319	.5359
0.1	.5398	.5438	.5478	.5517	.5557	.5596	.5636	.5675	.5714	.5753
0.2	.5793	.5832	.5871	.5910	.5948	.5987	.6026	.6064	.6103	.6141
0.3	.6179	.6217	.6255	.6293	.6331	.6368	.6406	.6443	.6480	.6517
0.4	.6554	.6591	.6628	.6664	.6700	.6736	.6772	.6808	.6844	.6879
0.5	.6915	.6950	.6985	.7019	.7054	.7088	.7123	.7157	.7190	.7224
0.6	.7257	.7291	.7324	.7357	.7389	.7422	.7454	.7486	.7517	.7549
0.7	.7580	.7611	.7642	.7673	.7704	.7734	.7764	.7794	.7823	.7852
0.8	.7881	.7910	.7939	.7967	.7995	.8023	.8051	.8078	.8106	.8133
0.9	.8159	.8186	.8212	.8238	.8264	.8289	.8315	.8340	.8365	.8389
1.0	.8413	.8438	.8461	.8485	.8508	.8531	.8554	.8577	.8599	.8621
1.1	.8643	.8665	.8686	.8708	.8729	.8749	.8770	.8790	.8810	.8830
1.2	.8849	.8869	.8888	.8907	.8925	.8944	.8962	.8980	.8997	.9015
1.3	.9032	.9049	.9066	.9082	.9099	.9115	.9131	.9147	.9162	.9177
1.4	.9192	.9207	.9222	.9236	.9251	.9265	.9278	.9292	.9306	.9319
1.5	.9332	.9345	.9357	.9370	.9382	.9394	.9406	.9418	.9429	.9441
1.6	.9452	.9463	.9474	.9484	.9495	.9505	.9515	.9525	.9535	.9545
1.7	.9554	.9564	.9573	.9582	.9591	.9599	.9608	.9616	.9625	.9633
1.8	.9641	.9649	.9656	.9664	.9671	.9678	.9686	.9693	.9699	.9706
1.9	.9713	.9719	.9726	.9732	.9738	.9744	.9750	.9756	.9761	.9767
2.0	.9772	.9778	.9783	.9788	.9793	.9798	.9803	.9808	.9812	.9817
2.1	.9821	.9826	.9830	.9834	.9838	.9842	.9846	.9850	.9854	.9857
2.2	.9861	.9864	.9868	.9871	.9875	.9878	.9881	.9884	.9887	.9890
2.3	.9893	.9896	.9898	.9901	.9904	.9906	.9909	.9911	.9913	.9916
2.4	.9918	.9920	.9922	.9925	.9927	.9929	.9931	.9932	.9934	.9936
2.5	.9938	.9940	.9941	.9943	.9945	.9946	.9948	.9949	.9951	.9952
2.6	.9953	.9955	.9956	.9957	.9959	.9960	.9961	.9962	.9963	.9964
2.7	.9965	.9966	.9967	.9968	.9969	.9970	.9971	.9972	.9973	.9974
2.8	.9974	.9975	.9976	.9977	.9977	.9978	.9979	.9979	.9980	.9981
2.9	.9981	.9982	.9982	.9983	.9984	.9984	.9985	.9985	.9986	.9986
3.0	.9987	.9987	.9987	.9988	.9988	.9989	.9989	.9989	.9990	.9990
3.1	.9990	.9991	.9991	.9991	.9992	.9992	.9992	.9992	.9993	.9993
3.2	.9993	.9993	.9994	.9994	.9994	.9994	.9994	.9995	.9995	.9995
3.3	.9995	.9995	.9995	.9996	.9996	.9996	.9996	.9996	.9996	.9997
3.4	.9997	.9997	.9997	.9997	.9997	.9997	.9997	.9997	.9997	.9998

Table A.3 t-Distribution

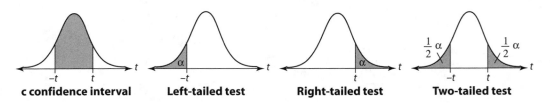

| c confidence interval | Left-tailed test | Right-tailed test | Two-tailed test |

	Level of confidence, c	0.50	0.80	0.90	0.95	0.98	0.99
	One tail, α	0.25	0.10	0.05	0.025	0.01	0.005
d.f.	Two tails, α	0.50	0.20	0.10	0.05	0.02	0.01
1		1.000	3.078	6.314	12.706	31.821	63.657
2		.816	1.886	2.920	4.303	6.965	9.925
3		.765	1.638	2.353	3.182	4.541	5.841
4		.741	1.533	2.132	2.776	3.747	4.604
5		.727	1.476	2.015	2.571	3.365	4.032
6		.718	1.440	1.943	2.447	3.143	3.707
7		.711	1.415	1.895	2.365	2.998	3.499
8		.706	1.397	1.860	2.306	2.896	3.355
9		.703	1.383	1.833	2.262	2.821	3.250
10		.700	1.372	1.812	2.228	2.764	3.169
11		.697	1.363	1.796	2.201	2.718	3.106
12		.695	1.356	1.782	2.179	2.681	3.055
13		.694	1.350	1.771	2.160	2.650	3.012
14		.692	1.345	1.761	2.145	2.624	2.977
15		.691	1.341	1.753	2.131	2.602	2.947
16		.690	1.337	1.746	2.120	2.583	2.921
17		.689	1.333	1.740	2.110	2.567	2.898
18		.688	1.330	1.734	2.101	2.552	2.878
19		.688	1.328	1.729	2.093	2.539	2.861
20		.687	1.325	1.725	2.086	2.528	2.845
21		.686	1.323	1.721	2.080	2.518	2.831
22		.686	1.321	1.717	2.074	2.508	2.819
23		.685	1.319	1.714	2.069	2.500	2.807
24		.685	1.318	1.711	2.064	2.492	2.797
25		.684	1.316	1.708	2.060	2.485	2.787
26		.684	1.315	1.706	2.056	2.479	2.779
27		.684	1.314	1.703	2.052	2.473	2.771
28		.683	1.313	1.701	2.048	2.467	2.763
29		.683	1.311	1.699	2.045	2.462	2.756
∞		.674	1.282	1.645	1.960	2.326	2.576

Table A.4   Chi-Square Distribution

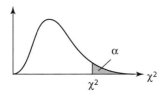

Right-tail

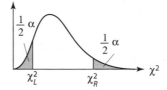

Two-tails

Degrees of freedom	α									
	0.995	**0.99**	**0.975**	**0.95**	**0.90**	**0.10**	**0.05**	**0.025**	**0.01**	**0.005**
1	—	—	0.001	0.004	0.016	2.706	3.841	5.024	6.635	7.879
2	0.010	0.020	0.051	0.103	0.211	4.605	5.991	7.378	9.210	10.597
3	0.072	0.115	0.216	0.352	0.584	6.251	7.815	9.348	11.345	12.838
4	0.207	0.297	0.484	0.711	1.064	7.779	9.488	11.143	13.277	14.860
5	0.412	0.554	0.831	1.145	1.610	9.236	11.071	12.833	15.086	16.750
6	0.676	0.872	1.237	1.635	2.204	10.645	12.592	14.449	16.812	18.548
7	0.989	1.239	1.690	2.167	2.833	12.017	14.067	16.013	18.475	20.278
8	1.344	1.646	2.180	2.733	3.490	13.362	15.507	17.535	20.090	21.955
9	1.735	2.088	2.700	3.325	4.168	14.684	16.919	19.023	21.666	23.589
10	2.156	2.558	3.247	3.940	4.865	15.987	18.307	20.483	23.209	25.188
11	2.603	3.053	3.816	4.575	5.578	17.275	19.675	21.920	24.725	26.757
12	3.074	3.571	4.404	5.226	6.304	18.549	21.026	23.337	26.217	28.299
13	3.565	4.107	5.009	5.892	7.042	19.812	22.362	24.736	27.688	29.819
14	4.075	4.660	5.629	6.571	7.790	21.064	23.685	26.119	29.141	31.319
15	4.601	5.229	6.262	7.261	8.547	22.307	24.996	27.488	30.578	32.801
16	5.142	5.812	6.908	7.962	9.312	23.542	26.296	28.845	32.000	34.267
17	5.697	6.408	7.564	8.672	10.085	24.769	27.587	30.191	33.409	35.718
18	6.265	7.015	8.231	9.390	10.865	25.989	28.869	31.526	34.805	37.156
19	6.844	7.633	8.907	10.117	11.651	27.204	30.144	32.852	36.191	38.582
20	7.434	8.260	9.591	10.851	12.443	28.412	31.410	34.170	37.566	39.997
21	8.034	8.897	10.283	11.591	13.240	29.615	32.671	35.479	38.932	41.401
22	8.643	9.542	10.982	12.338	14.042	30.813	33.924	36.781	40.289	42.796
23	9.262	10.196	11.689	13.091	14.848	32.007	35.172	38.076	41.638	44.181
24	9.886	10.856	12.401	13.848	15.659	33.196	36.415	39.364	42.980	45.559
25	10.520	11.524	13.120	14.611	16.473	34.382	37.652	40.646	44.314	46.928
26	11.160	12.198	13.844	15.379	17.292	35.563	38.885	41.923	45.642	48.290
27	11.808	12.879	14.573	16.151	18.114	36.741	40.113	43.194	46.963	49.645
28	12.461	13.565	15.308	16.928	18.939	37.916	41.337	44.461	48.278	50.993
29	13.121	14.257	16.047	17.708	19.768	39.087	42.557	45.722	49.588	52.336
30	13.787	14.954	16.791	18.493	20.599	40.256	43.773	46.979	50.892	53.672
40	20.707	22.164	24.433	26.509	29.051	51.805	55.758	59.342	63.691	66.766
50	27.991	29.707	32.357	34.764	37.689	63.167	67.505	71.420	76.154	79.490
60	35.534	37.485	40.482	43.188	46.459	74.397	79.082	83.298	88.379	91.952
70	43.275	45.442	48.758	51.739	55.329	85.527	90.531	95.023	100.425	104.215
80	51.172	53.540	57.153	60.391	64.278	96.578	101.879	106.629	112.329	116.321
90	59.196	61.754	65.647	69.126	73.291	107.565	113.145	118.136	124.116	128.299
100	67.328	70.065	74.222	77.929	82.358	118.498	124.342	129.561	135.807	140.169

Table A.5 *F*-Distribution

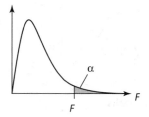

d.f.D: Degrees of freedom, denominator	α = 0.005								
	d.f.N: Degrees of freedom, numerator								
	1	**2**	**3**	**4**	**5**	**6**	**7**	**8**	**9**
1	16211	20000	21615	22500	23056	23437	23715	23925	24091
2	198.5	199.0	199.2	199.2	199.3	199.3	199.4	199.4	199.4
3	55.55	49.80	47.47	46.19	45.39	44.84	44.43	44.13	43.88
4	31.33	26.28	24.26	23.15	22.46	21.97	21.62	21.35	21.14
5	22.78	18.31	16.53	15.56	14.94	14.51	14.20	13.96	13.77
6	18.63	14.54	12.92	12.03	11.46	11.07	10.79	10.57	10.39
7	16.24	12.40	10.88	10.05	9.52	9.16	8.89	8.68	8.51
8	14.69	11.04	9.60	8.81	8.30	7.95	7.69	7.50	7.34
9	13.61	10.11	8.72	7.96	7.47	7.13	6.88	6.69	6.54
10	12.83	9.43	8.08	7.34	6.87	6.54	6.30	6.12	5.97
11	12.73	8.91	7.60	6.88	6.42	6.10	5.86	5.68	5.54
12	11.75	8.51	7.23	6.52	6.07	5.76	5.52	5.35	5.20
13	11.37	8.19	6.93	6.23	5.79	5.48	5.25	5.08	4.94
14	11.06	7.92	6.68	6.00	5.56	5.26	5.03	4.86	4.72
15	10.80	7.70	6.48	5.80	5.37	5.07	4.85	4.67	4.54
16	10.58	7.51	6.30	5.64	5.21	4.91	4.69	4.52	4.38
17	10.38	7.35	6.16	5.50	5.07	4.78	4.56	4.39	4.25
18	10.22	7.21	6.03	5.37	4.96	4.66	4.44	4.28	4.14
19	10.07	7.09	5.92	5.27	4.85	4.56	4.34	4.18	4.04
20	9.94	6.99	5.82	5.17	4.76	4.47	4.26	4.09	3.96
21	9.83	6.89	5.73	5.09	4.68	4.39	4.18	4.01	3.88
22	9.73	6.81	5.65	5.02	4.61	4.32	4.11	3.94	3.81
23	9.63	6.73	5.58	4.95	4.54	4.26	4.05	3.88	3.75
24	9.55	6.66	5.52	4.89	4.49	4.20	3.99	3.83	3.69
25	9.48	6.60	5.46	4.84	4.43	4.15	3.94	3.78	3.64
26	9.41	6.54	5.41	4.79	4.38	4.10	3.89	3.73	3.60
27	9.34	6.49	5.36	4.74	4.34	4.06	3.85	3.69	3.56
28	9.28	6.44	5.32	4.70	4.30	4.02	3.81	3.65	3.52
29	9.23	6.40	5.28	4.66	4.26	3.98	3.77	3.61	3.48
30	9.18	6.35	5.24	4.62	4.23	3.95	3.74	3.58	3.45
40	8.83	6.07	4.98	4.37	3.99	3.71	3.51	3.35	3.22
60	8.49	5.79	4.73	4.14	3.76	3.49	3.29	3.13	3.01
120	8.18	5.54	4.50	3.92	3.55	3.28	3.09	2.93	2.81
∞	7.88	5.30	4.28	3.72	3.35	3.09	2.90	2.74	2.62

			$\alpha = \mathbf{0.005}$						
			d.f.$_N$: Degrees of freedom, numerator						
10	**12**	**15**	**20**	**24**	**30**	**40**	**60**	**120**	∞
24224	24426	24630	24836	24940	25044	25148	25253	25359	25465
199.4	199.4	199.4	199.4	199.5	199.5	199.5	199.5	199.5	199.5
43.69	43.39	43.08	42.78	42.62	42.47	42.31	42.15	41.99	41.83
20.97	20.70	20.44	20.17	20.03	19.89	19.75	19.61	19.47	19.32
13.62	13.38	13.15	12.90	12.78	12.66	12.53	12.40	12.27	12.14
10.25	10.03	9.81	9.59	9.47	9.36	9.24	9.12	9.00	8.88
8.38	8.18	7.97	7.75	7.65	7.53	7.42	7.31	7.19	7.08
7.21	7.01	6.81	6.61	6.50	6.40	6.29	6.18	6.06	5.95
6.42	6.23	6.03	5.83	5.73	5.62	5.52	5.41	5.30	5.19
5.85	5.66	5.47	5.27	5.17	5.07	4.97	4.86	4.75	4.64
5.42	5.24	5.05	4.86	4.76	4.65	4.55	4.44	4.34	4.23
5.09	4.91	4.72	4.53	4.43	4.33	4.23	4.12	4.01	3.90
4.82	4.64	4.46	4.27	4.17	4.07	3.97	3.87	3.76	3.65
4.60	4.43	4.25	4.06	3.96	3.86	3.76	3.66	3.55	3.44
4.42	4.25	4.07	3.88	3.79	3.69	3.58	3.48	3.37	3.26
4.27	4.10	3.92	3.73	3.64	3.54	3.44	3.33	3.22	3.11
4.14	3.97	3.79	3.61	3.51	3.41	3.31	3.21	3.10	2.98
4.03	3.86	3.68	3.50	3.40	3.30	3.20	3.10	2.99	2.87
3.93	3.76	3.59	3.40	3.31	3.21	3.11	3.00	2.89	2.78
3.85	3.68	3.50	3.32	3.22	3.12	3.02	2.92	2.81	2.69
3.77	3.60	3.43	3.24	3.15	3.05	2.95	2.84	2.73	2.61
3.70	3.54	3.36	3.18	3.08	2.98	2.88	2.77	2.66	2.55
3.64	3.47	3.30	3.12	3.02	2.92	2.82	2.71	2.60	2.48
3.59	3.42	3.25	3.06	2.97	2.87	2.77	2.66	2.55	2.43
3.54	3.37	3.20	3.01	2.92	2.82	2.72	2.61	2.50	2.38
3.49	3.33	3.15	2.97	2.87	2.77	2.67	2.56	2.45	2.33
3.45	3.28	3.11	2.93	2.83	2.73	2.63	2.52	2.41	2.25
3.41	3.25	3.07	2.89	2.79	2.69	2.59	2.48	2.37	2.29
3.38	3.21	3.04	2.86	2.76	2.66	2.56	2.45	2.33	2.24
3.34	3.18	3.01	2.82	2.73	2.63	2.52	2.42	2.30	2.18
3.12	2.95	2.78	2.60	2.50	2.40	2.30	2.18	2.06	1.93
2.90	2.74	2.57	2.39	2.29	2.19	2.08	1.96	1.83	1.69
2.71	2.54	2.37	2.19	2.09	1.98	1.87	1.75	1.61	1.43
2.52	2.36	2.19	2.00	1.90	1.79	1.67	1.53	1.36	1.00

(continued)

Table A.5 *(continued)*

d.f._D: Degrees of freedom, denominator	$\alpha = 0.01$								
	d.f._N: Degrees of freedom, numerator								
	1	2	3	4	5	6	7	8	9
1	4052	4999.5	5403	5625	5764	5859	5928	5982	6022
2	98.50	99.00	99.17	99.25	99.30	99.33	99.36	99.37	99.39
3	34.12	30.82	29.46	28.71	28.24	27.91	27.67	27.49	27.35
4	21.20	18.00	16.69	15.98	15.52	15.21	14.98	14.80	14.66
5	16.26	13.27	12.06	11.39	10.97	10.67	10.46	10.29	10.16
6	13.75	10.92	9.78	9.15	8.75	8.47	8.26	8.10	7.98
7	12.25	9.55	8.45	7.85	7.46	7.19	6.99	6.84	6.72
8	11.26	8.65	7.59	7.01	6.63	6.37	6.18	6.03	5.91
9	10.56	8.02	6.99	6.42	6.06	5.80	5.61	5.47	5.35
10	10.04	7.56	6.55	5.99	5.64	5.39	5.20	5.06	4.94
11	9.65	7.21	6.22	5.67	5.32	5.07	4.89	4.74	4.63
12	9.33	6.93	5.95	5.41	5.06	4.82	4.64	4.50	4.39
13	9.07	6.70	5.74	5.21	4.86	4.62	4.44	4.30	4.19
14	8.86	6.51	5.56	5.04	4.69	4.46	4.28	4.14	4.03
15	8.68	6.36	5.42	4.89	4.56	4.32	4.14	4.00	3.89
16	8.53	6.23	5.29	4.77	4.44	4.20	4.03	3.89	3.78
17	8.40	6.11	5.18	4.67	4.34	4.10	3.93	3.79	3.68
18	8.29	6.01	5.09	4.58	4.25	4.01	3.84	3.71	3.60
19	8.18	5.93	5.01	4.50	4.17	3.94	3.77	3.63	3.52
20	8.10	5.85	4.94	4.43	4.10	3.87	3.70	3.56	3.46
21	8.02	5.78	4.87	4.37	4.04	3.81	3.64	3.51	3.40
22	7.95	5.72	4.82	4.31	3.99	3.76	3.59	3.45	3.35
23	7.88	5.66	4.76	4.26	3.94	3.71	3.54	3.41	3.30
24	7.82	5.61	4.72	4.22	3.90	3.67	3.50	3.36	3.26
25	7.77	5.57	4.68	4.18	3.85	3.63	3.46	3.32	3.22
26	7.72	5.53	4.64	4.14	3.82	3.59	3.42	3.29	3.18
27	7.68	5.49	4.60	4.11	3.78	3.56	3.39	3.26	3.15
28	7.64	5.45	4.57	4.07	3.75	3.53	3.36	3.23	3.12
29	7.60	5.42	4.54	4.04	3.73	3.50	3.33	3.20	3.09
30	7.56	5.39	4.51	4.02	3.70	3.47	3.30	3.17	3.07
40	7.31	5.18	4.31	3.83	3.51	3.29	3.12	2.99	2.89
60	7.08	4.98	4.13	3.65	3.34	3.12	2.95	2.82	2.72
120	6.85	4.79	3.95	3.48	3.17	2.96	2.79	2.66	2.56
∞	6.63	4.61	3.78	3.32	3.02	2.80	2.64	2.51	2.41

			$\alpha = 0.01$						
			d.f.$_N$: Degrees of freedom, numerator						
10	12	15	20	24	30	40	60	120	∞
6056	6106	6157	6209	6235	6261	6287	6313	6339	6366
99.40	99.42	99.43	99.45	99.46	99.47	99.47	99.48	99.49	99.50
27.23	27.05	26.87	26.69	26.60	26.50	26.41	26.32	26.22	26.13
14.55	4.37	14.20	14.02	13.93	13.84	13.75	13.65	13.56	13.46
10.05	9.89	9.72	9.55	9.47	9.38	9.29	9.20	9.11	9.02
7.87	7.72	7.56	7.40	7.31	7.23	7.14	7.06	6.97	6.88
6.62	6.47	6.31	6.16	6.07	5.99	5.91	5.82	5.74	5.65
5.81	5.67	5.52	5.36	5.28	5.20	5.12	5.03	4.95	4.86
5.26	5.11	4.96	4.81	4.73	4.65	4.57	4.48	4.40	4.31
4.85	4.71	4.56	4.41	4.33	4.25	4.17	4.08	4.00	3.91
4.54	4.40	4.25	4.10	4.02	3.94	3.86	3.78	3.69	3.60
4.30	4.16	4.01	3.86	3.78	3.70	3.62	3.54	3.45	3.36
4.10	3.96	3.82	3.66	3.59	3.51	3.43	3.34	3.25	3.17
3.94	3.80	3.66	3.51	3.43	3.35	3.27	3.18	3.09	3.00
3.80	3.67	3.52	3.37	3.29	3.21	3.13	3.05	2.96	2.87
3.69	3.55	3.41	3.26	3.18	3.10	3.02	2.93	2.84	2.75
3.59	3.46	3.31	3.16	3.08	3.00	2.92	2.83	2.75	2.65
3.51	3.37	3.23	3.08	3.00	2.92	2.84	2.75	2.66	2.57
3.43	3.30	3.15	3.00	2.92	2.84	2.76	2.67	2.58	2.49
3.37	3.23	3.09	2.94	2.86	2.78	2.69	2.61	2.52	2.42
3.31	3.17	3.03	2.88	2.80	2.72	2.64	2.55	2.46	2.36
3.26	3.12	2.98	2.83	2.75	2.67	2.58	2.50	2.40	2.31
3.21	3.07	2.93	2.78	2.70	2.62	2.54	2.45	2.35	2.26
3.17	3.03	2.89	2.74	2.66	2.58	2.49	2.40	2.31	2.21
3.13	2.99	2.85	2.70	2.62	2.54	2.45	2.36	2.27	2.17
3.09	2.96	2.81	2.66	2.58	2.50	2.42	2.33	2.23	2.13
3.06	2.93	2.78	2.63	2.55	2.47	2.38	2.29	2.20	2.10
3.03	2.90	2.75	2.60	2.52	2.44	2.35	2.26	2.17	2.06
3.00	2.87	2.73	2.57	2.49	2.41	2.33	2.23	2.14	2.03
2.98	2.84	2.70	2.55	2.47	2.39	2.30	2.21	2.11	2.01
2.80	2.66	2.52	2.37	2.29	2.20	2.11	2.02	1.92	1.80
2.63	2.50	2.35	2.20	2.12	2.03	1.94	1.84	1.73	1.60
2.47	2.34	2.19	2.03	1.95	1.86	1.76	1.66	1.53	1.38
2.32	2.18	2.04	1.88	1.79	1.70	1.59	1.47	1.32	1.00

(continued)

Table A.5 *(continued)*

d.f.$_D$: Degrees of freedom, denominator	$\alpha = 0.025$								
	d.f.$_N$: Degrees of freedom, numerator								
	1	2	3	4	5	6	7	8	9
1	647.8	799.5	864.2	899.6	921.8	937.1	948.2	956.7	963.3
2	38.51	39.00	39.17	39.25	39.30	39.33	39.36	39.37	39.39
3	17.44	16.04	15.44	15.10	14.88	14.73	14.62	14.54	14.47
4	12.22	10.65	9.98	9.60	9.36	9.20	9.07	8.98	8.90
5	10.01	8.43	7.76	7.39	7.15	6.98	6.85	6.76	6.68
6	8.81	7.26	6.60	6.23	5.99	5.82	5.70	5.60	5.52
7	8.07	6.54	5.89	5.52	5.29	5.12	4.99	4.90	4.82
8	7.57	6.06	5.42	5.05	4.82	4.65	4.53	4.43	4.36
9	7.21	5.71	5.08	4.72	4.48	4.32	4.20	4.10	4.03
10	6.94	5.46	4.83	4.47	4.24	4.07	3.95	3.85	3.78
11	6.72	5.26	4.63	4.28	4.04	3.88	3.76	3.66	3.59
12	6.55	5.10	4.47	4.12	3.89	3.73	3.61	3.51	3.44
13	6.41	4.97	4.35	4.00	3.77	3.60	3.48	3.39	3.31
14	6.30	4.86	4.24	3.89	3.66	3.50	3.38	3.29	3.21
15	6.20	4.77	4.15	3.80	3.58	3.41	3.29	3.20	3.12
16	6.12	4.69	4.08	3.73	3.50	3.34	3.22	3.12	3.05
17	6.04	4.62	4.01	3.66	3.44	3.28	3.16	3.06	2.98
18	5.98	4.56	3.95	3.61	3.38	3.22	3.10	3.01	2.93
19	5.92	4.51	3.90	3.56	3.33	3.17	3.05	2.96	2.88
20	5.87	4.46	3.86	3.51	3.29	3.13	3.01	2.91	2.84
21	5.83	4.42	3.82	3.48	3.25	3.09	2.97	2.87	2.80
22	5.79	4.38	3.78	3.44	3.22	3.05	2.93	2.84	2.76
23	5.75	4.35	3.75	3.41	3.18	3.02	2.90	2.81	2.73
24	5.72	4.32	3.72	3.38	3.15	2.99	2.87	2.78	2.70
25	5.69	4.29	3.69	3.35	3.13	2.97	2.85	2.75	2.68
26	5.66	4.27	3.67	3.33	3.10	2.94	2.82	2.73	2.65
27	5.63	4.24	3.65	3.31	3.08	2.92	2.80	2.71	2.63
28	5.61	4.22	3.63	3.29	3.06	2.90	2.78	2.69	2.61
29	5.59	4.20	3.61	3.27	3.04	2.88	2.76	2.67	2.59
30	5.57	4.18	3.59	3.25	3.03	2.87	2.75	2.65	2.57
40	5.42	4.05	3.46	3.13	2.90	2.74	2.62	2.53	2.45
60	5.29	3.93	3.34	3.01	2.79	2.63	2.51	2.41	2.33
120	5.15	3.80	3.23	2.89	2.67	2.52	2.39	2.30	2.22
∞	5.02	3.69	3.12	2.79	2.57	2.41	2.29	2.19	2.11

$\alpha = 0.025$

d.f.$_N$: Degrees of freedom, numerator

10	12	15	20	24	30	40	60	120	∞
968.6	976.7	984.9	993.1	997.2	1001	1006	1010	1014	1018
39.40	39.41	39.43	39.45	39.46	39.46	39.47	39.48	39.49	39.50
14.42	14.34	14.25	14.17	14.12	14.08	14.04	13.99	13.95	13.90
8.84	8.75	8.66	8.56	8.51	8.46	8.41	8.36	8.31	8.26
6.62	6.52	6.43	6.33	6.28	6.23	6.18	6.12	6.07	6.02
5.46	5.37	5.27	5.17	5.12	5.07	5.01	4.96	4.90	4.85
4.76	4.67	4.57	4.47	4.42	4.36	4.31	4.25	4.20	4.14
4.30	4.20	4.10	4.00	3.95	3.89	3.84	3.78	3.73	3.67
3.96	3.87	3.77	3.67	3.61	3.56	3.51	3.45	3.39	3.33
3.72	3.62	3.52	3.42	3.37	3.31	3.26	3.20	3.14	3.08
3.53	3.43	3.33	3.23	3.17	3.12	3.06	3.00	2.94	2.88
3.37	3.28	3.18	3.07	3.02	2.96	2.91	2.85	2.79	2.72
3.25	3.15	3.05	2.95	2.89	2.84	2.78	2.72	2.66	2.60
3.15	3.05	2.95	2.84	2.79	2.73	2.67	2.61	2.55	2.49
3.06	2.98	2.86	2.76	2.70	2.64	2.59	2.52	2.46	2.40
2.99	2.89	2.79	2.68	2.63	2.57	2.51	2.45	2.38	2.32
2.92	2.82	2.72	2.62	2.56	2.50	2.44	2.38	2.32	2.25
2.87	2.77	2.67	2.56	2.50	2.44	2.38	2.32	2.26	2.19
2.82	2.72	2.62	2.51	2.45	2.39	2.33	2.27	2.20	2.13
2.77	2.68	2.57	2.46	2.41	2.35	2.29	2.22	2.16	2.09
2.73	2.64	2.53	2.42	2.37	2.31	2.25	2.18	2.11	2.04
2.70	2.60	2.50	2.39	2.33	2.27	2.21	2.14	2.08	2.00
2.67	2.57	2.47	2.36	2.30	2.24	2.18	2.11	2.04	1.97
2.64	2.54	2.44	2.33	2.27	2.21	2.15	2.08	2.01	1.94
2.61	2.51	2.41	2.30	2.24	2.18	2.12	2.05	1.98	1.91
2.59	2.49	2.39	2.25	2.22	2.16	2.09	2.03	1.95	1.88
2.57	2.47	2.36	2.25	2.19	2.13	2.07	2.00	1.93	1.85
2.55	2.45	2.34	2.23	2.17	2.11	2.05	1.98	1.91	1.83
2.53	2.43	2.32	2.21	2.15	2.09	2.03	1.96	1.89	1.81
2.51	2.41	2.31	2.20	2.14	2.07	2.01	1.94	1.87	1.79
2.39	2.29	2.18	2.07	2.01	1.94	1.88	1.80	1.72	1.64
2.27	2.17	2.06	1.94	1.88	1.82	1.74	1.67	1.58	1.48
2.16	2.05	1.94	1.82	1.76	1.69	1.61	1.53	1.43	1.31
2.05	1.94	1.83	1.71	1.64	1.57	1.48	1.39	1.27	1.00

(continued)

Table A.5 *(continued)*

d.f._D: Degrees of freedom, denominator	$\alpha = 0.05$								
	d.f._N: Degrees of freedom, numerator								
	1	2	3	4	5	6	7	8	9
1	161.4	199.5	215.7	224.6	230.2	234.0	236.8	238.9	240.5
2	18.51	19.00	19.16	19.25	19.30	19.33	19.35	19.37	19.38
3	10.13	9.55	9.28	9.12	9.01	8.94	8.89	8.85	8.81
4	7.71	6.94	6.59	6.39	6.26	6.16	6.09	6.04	6.00
5	6.61	5.79	5.41	5.19	5.05	4.95	4.88	4.82	4.77
6	5.99	5.14	4.76	4.53	4.39	4.28	4.21	4.15	4.10
7	5.59	4.74	4.35	4.12	3.97	3.87	3.79	3.73	3.68
8	5.32	4.46	4.07	3.84	3.69	3.58	3.50	3.44	3.39
9	5.12	4.26	3.86	3.63	3.48	3.37	3.29	3.23	3.18
10	4.96	4.10	3.71	3.48	3.33	3.22	3.14	3.07	3.02
11	4.84	3.98	3.59	3.36	3.20	3.09	3.01	2.95	2.90
12	4.75	3.89	3.49	3.26	3.11	3.00	2.91	2.85	2.80
13	4.67	3.81	3.41	3.18	3.03	2.92	2.83	2.77	2.71
14	4.60	3.74	3.34	3.11	2.96	2.85	2.76	2.70	2.65
15	4.54	3.68	3.29	3.06	2.90	2.79	2.71	2.64	2.59
16	4.49	3.63	3.24	3.01	2.85	2.74	2.66	2.59	2.54
17	4.45	3.59	3.20	2.96	2.81	2.70	2.61	2.55	2.49
18	4.41	3.55	3.16	2.93	2.77	2.66	2.58	2.51	2.46
19	4.38	3.52	3.13	2.90	2.74	2.63	2.54	2.48	2.42
20	4.35	3.49	3.10	2.87	2.71	2.60	2.51	2.45	2.39
21	4.32	3.47	3.07	2.84	2.68	2.57	2.49	2.42	2.37
22	4.30	3.44	3.05	2.82	2.66	2.55	2.46	2.40	2.34
23	4.28	3.42	3.03	2.80	2.64	2.53	2.44	2.37	2.32
24	4.26	3.40	3.01	2.78	2.62	2.51	2.42	2.36	2.30
25	4.24	3.39	2.99	2.76	2.60	2.49	2.40	2.34	2.28
26	4.23	3.37	2.98	2.74	2.59	2.47	2.39	2.32	2.27
27	4.21	3.35	2.96	2.73	2.57	2.46	2.37	2.31	2.25
28	4.20	3.34	2.95	2.71	2.56	2.45	2.36	2.29	2.24
29	4.18	3.33	2.93	2.70	2.55	2.43	2.35	2.28	2.22
30	4.17	3.32	2.92	2.69	2.53	2.42	2.33	2.27	2.21
40	4.08	3.23	2.84	2.61	2.45	2.34	2.25	2.18	2.12
60	4.00	3.15	2.76	2.53	2.37	2.25	2.17	2.10	2.04
120	3.92	3.07	2.68	2.45	2.29	2.17	2.09	2.02	1.96
∞	3.84	3.00	2.60	2.37	2.21	2.10	2.01	1.94	1.88

				$\alpha = 0.05$						
			d.f.$_N$: Degrees of freedom, numerator							
10	**12**	**15**	**20**	**24**	**30**	**40**	**60**	**120**	**∞**
241.9	243.9	245.9	248.0	249.1	250.1	251.1	252.2	253.3	254.3
19.40	19.41	19.43	19.45	19.45	19.46	19.47	19.48	19.49	19.50
8.79	8.74	8.70	8.66	8.64	8.62	8.59	8.57	8.55	8.53
5.96	5.91	5.86	5.80	5.77	5.75	5.72	5.69	5.66	5.63
4.74	4.68	4.62	4.56	4.53	4.50	4.46	4.43	4.40	4.36
4.06	4.00	3.94	3.87	3.84	3.81	3.77	3.74	3.70	3.67
3.64	3.57	3.51	3.44	3.41	3.38	3.34	3.30	3.27	3.23
3.35	3.28	3.22	3.15	3.12	3.08	3.04	3.01	2.97	2.93
3.14	3.07	3.01	2.94	2.90	2.86	2.83	2.79	2.75	2.71
2.98	2.91	2.85	2.77	2.74	2.70	2.66	2.62	2.58	2.54
2.85	2.79	2.72	2.65	2.61	2.57	2.53	2.49	2.45	2.40
2.75	2.69	2.62	2.54	2.51	2.47	2.43	2.38	2.34	2.30
2.67	2.60	2.53	2.46	2.42	2.38	2.34	2.30	2.25	2.21
2.60	2.53	2.46	2.39	2.35	2.31	2.27	2.22	2.18	2.13
2.54	2.48	2.40	2.33	2.29	2.25	2.20	2.16	2.11	2.07
2.49	2.42	2.35	2.28	2.24	2.19	2.15	2.11	2.06	2.01
2.45	2.38	2.31	2.23	2.19	2.15	2.10	2.06	2.01	1.96
2.41	2.34	2.27	2.19	2.15	2.11	2.06	2.02	1.97	1.92
2.38	2.31	2.23	2.16	2.11	2.07	2.03	1.98	1.93	1.88
2.35	2.28	2.20	2.12	2.08	2.04	1.99	1.95	1.90	1.84
2.32	2.25	2.18	2.10	2.05	2.01	1.96	1.92	1.87	1.81
2.30	2.23	2.15	2.07	2.03	1.98	1.94	1.89	1.84	1.78
2.27	2.20	2.13	2.05	2.01	1.96	1.91	1.86	1.81	1.76
2.25	2.18	2.11	2.03	1.98	1.94	1.89	1.84	1.79	1.73
2.24	2.16	2.09	2.01	1.96	1.92	1.87	1.82	1.77	1.71
2.22	2.15	2.07	1.99	1.95	1.90	1.85	1.80	1.75	1.69
2.20	2.13	2.06	1.97	1.93	1.88	1.84	1.79	1.73	1.67
2.19	2.12	2.04	1.96	1.91	1.87	1.82	1.77	1.71	1.65
2.18	2.10	2.03	1.94	1.90	1.85	1.81	1.75	1.70	1.64
2.16	2.09	2.01	1.93	1.89	1.84	1.79	1.74	1.68	1.62
2.08	2.00	1.92	1.84	1.79	1.74	1.69	1.64	1.58	1.51
1.99	1.92	1.84	1.75	1.70	1.65	1.59	1.53	1.47	1.39
1.91	1.83	1.75	1.66	1.61	1.55	1.50	1.43	1.35	1.25
1.83	1.75	1.67	1.57	1.52	1.46	1.39	1.32	1.22	1.00

(continued)

Table A.5 *(continued)*

d.f._D: Degrees of freedom, denominator	α = 0.10								
	d.f._N: Degrees of freedom, numerator								
	1	2	3	4	5	6	7	8	9
1	39.86	49.50	53.59	55.83	57.24	58.20	58.91	59.44	59.86
2	8.53	9.00	9.16	9.24	9.29	9.33	9.35	9.37	9.38
3	5.54	5.46	5.39	5.34	5.31	5.28	5.27	5.25	5.24
4	4.54	4.32	4.19	4.11	4.05	4.01	3.98	3.95	3.94
5	4.06	3.78	3.62	3.52	3.45	3.40	3.37	3.34	3.32
6	3.78	3.46	3.29	3.18	3.11	3.05	3.01	2.98	2.96
7	3.59	3.26	3.07	2.96	2.88	2.83	2.78	2.75	2.72
8	3.46	3.11	2.92	2.81	2.73	2.67	2.62	2.59	2.56
9	3.36	3.01	2.81	2.69	2.61	2.55	2.51	2.47	2.44
10	3.29	2.92	2.73	2.61	2.52	2.46	2.41	2.38	2.35
11	3.23	2.86	2.66	2.54	2.45	2.39	2.34	2.30	2.27
12	3.18	2.81	2.61	2.48	2.39	2.33	2.28	2.24	2.21
13	3.14	2.76	2.56	2.43	2.35	2.28	2.23	2.20	2.16
14	3.10	2.73	2.52	2.39	2.31	2.24	2.19	2.15	2.12
15	3.07	2.70	2.49	2.36	2.27	2.21	2.16	2.12	2.09
16	3.05	2.67	2.46	2.33	2.24	2.18	2.13	2.09	2.06
17	3.03	2.64	2.44	2.31	2.22	2.15	2.10	2.06	2.03
18	3.01	2.62	2.42	2.29	2.20	2.13	2.08	2.04	2.00
19	2.99	2.61	2.40	2.27	2.18	2.11	2.06	2.02	1.98
20	2.97	2.59	2.38	2.25	2.16	2.09	2.04	2.00	1.96
21	2.96	2.57	2.36	2.23	2.14	2.08	2.02	1.98	1.95
22	2.95	2.56	2.35	2.22	2.13	2.06	2.01	1.97	1.93
23	2.94	2.55	2.34	2.21	2.11	2.05	1.99	1.95	1.92
24	2.93	2.54	2.33	2.19	2.10	2.04	1.98	1.94	1.91
25	2.92	2.53	2.32	2.18	2.09	2.02	1.97	1.93	1.89
26	2.91	2.52	2.31	2.17	2.08	2.01	1.96	1.92	1.88
27	2.90	2.51	2.30	2.17	2.07	2.00	1.95	1.91	1.87
28	2.89	2.50	2.29	2.16	2.06	2.00	1.94	1.90	1.87
29	2.89	2.50	2.28	2.15	2.06	1.99	1.93	1.89	1.86
30	2.88	2.49	2.28	2.14	2.05	1.98	1.93	1.88	1.85
40	2.84	2.44	2.23	2.09	2.00	1.93	1.87	1.83	1.79
60	2.79	2.39	2.18	2.04	1.95	1.87	1.82	1.77	1.74
120	2.75	2.35	2.13	1.99	1.90	1.82	1.77	1.72	1.68
∞	2.71	2.30	2.08	1.94	1.85	1.77	1.72	1.67	1.63

$\alpha = 0.10$									
d.f.$_N$: Degrees of freedom, numerator									
10	12	15	20	24	30	40	60	120	∞
60.19	60.71	61.22	61.74	62.00	62.26	62.53	62.79	63.06	63.33
9.39	9.41	9.42	9.44	9.45	9.46	9.47	9.47	9.48	9.49
5.23	5.22	5.20	5.18	5.18	5.17	5.16	5.15	5.14	5.13
3.92	3.90	3.87	3.84	3.83	3.82	3.80	3.79	3.78	3.76
3.30	3.27	3.24	3.21	3.19	3.17	3.16	3.14	3.12	3.10
2.94	2.90	2.87	2.84	2.82	2.80	2.78	2.76	2.74	2.72
2.70	2.67	2.63	2.59	2.58	2.56	2.54	2.51	2.49	2.47
2.54	2.50	2.46	2.42	2.40	2.38	2.36	2.34	2.32	2.29
2.42	2.38	2.34	2.30	2.28	2.25	2.23	2.21	2.18	2.16
2.32	2.28	2.24	2.20	2.18	2.16	2.13	2.11	2.08	2.06
2.25	2.21	2.17	2.12	2.10	2.08	2.05	2.03	2.00	1.97
2.19	2.15	2.10	2.06	2.04	2.01	1.99	1.96	1.93	1.90
2.14	2.10	2.05	2.01	1.98	1.96	1.93	1.90	1.88	1.85
2.10	2.05	2.01	1.96	1.94	1.91	1.89	1.86	1.83	1.80
2.06	2.02	1.97	1.92	1.90	1.87	1.85	1.82	1.79	1.76
2.03	1.99	1.94	1.89	1.87	1.84	1.81	1.78	1.75	1.72
2.00	1.96	1.91	1.86	1.84	1.81	1.78	1.75	1.72	1.69
1.98	1.93	1.89	1.84	1.81	1.78	1.75	1.72	1.69	1.66
1.96	1.91	1.86	1.81	1.79	1.76	1.73	1.70	1.67	1.63
1.94	1.89	1.84	1.79	1.77	1.74	1.71	1.68	1.64	1.61
1.92	1.87	1.83	1.78	1.75	1.72	1.69	1.66	1.62	1.59
1.90	1.86	1.81	1.76	1.73	1.70	1.67	1.64	1.60	1.57
1.89	1.84	1.80	1.74	1.72	1.69	1.66	1.62	1.59	1.55
1.88	1.83	1.78	1.73	1.70	1.67	1.64	1.61	1.57	1.53
1.87	1.82	1.77	1.72	1.69	1.66	1.63	1.59	1.56	1.52
1.86	1.81	1.76	1.71	1.68	1.65	1.61	1.58	1.54	1.50
1.85	1.80	1.75	1.70	1.67	1.64	1.60	1.57	1.53	1.49
1.84	1.79	1.74	1.69	1.66	1.63	1.59	1.56	1.52	1.48
1.83	1.78	1.73	1.68	1.65	1.62	1.58	1.55	1.51	1.47
1.82	1.77	1.72	1.67	1.64	1.61	1.57	1.54	1.50	1.46
1.76	1.71	1.66	1.61	1.57	1.54	1.51	1.47	1.42	1.38
1.71	1.66	1.60	1.54	1.51	1.48	1.44	1.40	1.35	1.29
1.65	1.60	1.55	1.48	1.45	1.41	1.37	1.32	1.26	1.19
1.60	1.55	1.49	1.42	1.38	1.34	1.30	1.24	1.17	1.00

Index

Accuracy
  of calls for service (CFS)
    data, 14
  lack of quality control in
    official statistics, 19
  of National Crime Vic-
    timization Survey, 11
  of police arrest statistics,
    14
Addition rule, 120
Adrian, R., 126
Alpha level, 144–145
Alternative hypothesis, 92,
  141, *See also* One-
  tailed hypothesis;
  Directional Hypothesis
Analysis of variance
  (ANOVA), 159–172
  calculating by hand,
    161–165
  computerized calculation
    of, 165–171
  definition of, 159
  F test/F ratio, 161
  one-way, 165–171
  source of, 159–160
Arrests, number of, vs. CFS
  data, 14
Association, measuring with
  chi-square, 102–104
Averages and percentages,
  calculation of, 18

Bar charts, 54–55
Bernoulli process. *See* Binomial distribution

Bernoulli, J., 126
Binomial distribution,
  129–130, 222–229
Bivariate correlation,
  185–191
Bonferroni multiple com-
  parison method (Post
  Hoc Tests), 170–171
Bratton, W., 16
Buerger, M., 15
Bursik, R., 14

Calculation formulas
  ANOVA, 162
  averages and percent-
    ages, 18
  chi-square statistic, 96
  contingency coefficient,
    103
  Cramer's V, 103
  F ratio/F test, 164
  mode, median, and
    mean, 67
  nonparametric measures
    of association for use
    with chi-square with
    nominal data, 103
  Pearson's r (correlation
    coefficient), 183
  Phi coefficient, 103, 113,
    115
  regression coefficients,
    200
  standard score, 127
  t-test for independent
    samples, 151

t-test for related (or
  paired) samples, 146
variance and standard
  deviation, 83
Calls for service (CFS) data
  number of arrests vs., 14
  purpose of, 3
  strengths and weak-
    nesses of, 13–14
  using with UCR data, 14
Capital punishment
  criminological research
    on, 218–219
  Kentuckian's attitudes
    toward, 131–134
  ordinal measurement of
    opinions on, 39
  policy analysis and,
    219-220
  race and, 92–98,
    101–108
Category size/limits/num-
  ber, 53
Causal time order, 182, 193
Causation, criteria for,
  182–183
Cavan, R. S., 126–127
Central limit theorem,
  130–131
Central tendency, mea-
  sures of, 41, 63–79, 85
CFS. *See* Calls for service
Charts
  bar charts, 54–55
  histograms, 56–58
  line charts, 59

pie charts, 56–57
scatter plots/scatter-
grams, 179–180
Chi-square
calculations by hand,
96–97
computerized calcula-
tions, 97–102
distribution table, 233
measures of association
with, 102–104
test for independent
samples, 94–95
Classical experiments,
32–33
Coefficient of determina-
tion, 181, 207–208
Compstat program, 16–18
Computer Aided Dispatch-
ing (CAD) system, 13
Computerized statistical
analysis/research. *See*
Statistical Package for
Social Science program
Concepts, definition of, 30
Confidence intervals,
131–134
Contingency coefficient,
103
Contingency tables
analysis of, 91–109
construction of, 92–94
Continuous variables, 42
Control variables, 104
Correlation
bivariate, 185–191
defining, 177–178
interpreting, 178–181
Correlation coefficient
calculating, 183–185
definition of, 178
direction of, 179–180
magnitude of, 181
Couzens, M., 19
Cramer's *V*, 102–104, 108
Craps, probability in,
120–121
Crime
incidence of, 2
index, 3

patterns, political pres-
sure to alter, 19
unreported/undiscov-
ered, 2–3
Crime in the United States
(FBI). *See* Uniform
Crime Report (UCR)
Crime reporting
impact of economic sta-
tus on, 12
impact of victims' wishes
on, 6
Crime statistics, validity
and reliability of, 2–3
Crime waves, preventing
misinterpretation of
statistics for, 19–20
Criminological research
purpose of, 215–217
successes and failures
in, 217–219
Crosstabulation, 92–93, 109
Curves, skewed/symmetri-
cal, 67–69
Curvilinear relationships,
202

Data set(s)
computerized analysis
of, 69–75
definition of, 1
summarization of, 51–58
de Moivre, A., 126
Degrees of freedom, 96–97,
102, 139, 233, 236–243
Dependent variables, 31
Descriptive statistics, 51
Deterrence, concept of, 31
Dice, probability in, 120–121
Directional hypothesis, 31,
142
Discrete variables, 41
Dispersion, measures of,
79–89
computerized calculation
of, 84–88
index of dispersion, 80
range, 80–81
variance and standard
deviation, 81–84

Distribution
chi-square, 233
F-distribution, 234–243
negatively skewed,
68–69
positively skewed, 67–68
shape of, 67–69
standard normal,
230–231
symmetrical, 67
t-distribution, 232
See also Frequency dis-
tribution

Economic status, impact on
crime reporting, 12
Empirical probability, 118,
121–125
Equal-sized categories, 53
Evaluation research, 36–38
Expected frequencies,
95–96

F ratio/*F* test, 161–164, 171
F-Distribution, 234–243
Fox, J. A., 8
Frequencies
marginal, 93
observed/expected, 95
Frequency distribution
computerized graphic
display of, 53–58
construction of, 63–66
contingency tables,
92–94
definition of, 38
measures of central ten-
dency in, 63–75
summarizing data with,
51–54
See also Distribution

Galvin, J., 19
Gambler's Fallacy, 118–121
Gartin, P., 15
Gauss, C. F., 126
Geerken, M., 5
General deterrence, theory
of, 31
Generalizability, 35

Gibbs, J. P., 215–216
Gossett, W. S., 139
Gove, W., 5
Grasmick, H., 14
Gross, S., 183
Gun control, research on, 217–218

Haack, D. G., 123
Histograms, 56–58
"Hot spots" for crime, explained by routine activities theory, 15
Household crime, reasons for reporting/not reporting to police, 13
Hughes, M., 5
Hypotheses
   one-tailed/directional, 142
   rival causal, 182–183
   testing, 141–144
   two-tailed/nondirectional, 142–142
Hypothesis testing, 140–141
Hypothesis, definition of, 31

Incident-based reporting, 2
Independence of categories, 95
Independent effect, 178
Independent samples
   chi-square test for, 94–95
   t-test for, 147–153
Independent variables, 31
Index of dispersion, 80
Index offenses, 3
Indirect effect, 178
Intelligence policing, 29
Interval level of measurement, 39–40

Kansas City Gun Experiment, 217–218
Kansas City Preventive Patrol Experiment, 217
Keil, T., 131
Kelling, G., 217
Klockars, C., 217

Laplace, P. S. de, 126
Law of probability, 118–119
Least squares technique, 198
Level of measurement, definition of, 38
Level of significance, 144, 152
Levine's Test for Equality of Variances, 152–153
Lind, D. A., 53
Line charts, 59
Line graphs, 57–58
Linear regression, using SPSS, 203–209

Maier, P. A., 15
Marchal, W. G., 53
Marginals, definition of, 93
Mason, R. D., 53
Matching, in quasi-experimental design, 34
Mathematical probability, 118
McElrath, K., 178
Mean(s)
   calculation formula for, 67
   definition of, 66
   difference between, testing, 139–154
   measures of dispersion and, 79
   sampling distribution of, 130–131
   standard error of, 131, 139
Measurement
   interval, 39–40
   nominal, 38–39
   ordinal, 39
   ratio, 40–41
   types of variables and, 41–42
Median, 65–67
Mode, 64–65, 67
Multiplication rule, 121
Multivariate analysis, 104–108
Mutual exclusion rule, 120–121

National Crime Victimization Survey (NCVS)
   as data source, 9–13
   distinction between UCR and, 10
   factors influencing crime reporting, 12–13
   improvements over UCR, 10
   limitations of, 11–12
   personal/property crime victimization rates, 10–11
   Web site for, 10
National Incident-Based Reporting System (NIBRS), 7–9
   categories of crime in, 6–7
   data elements for, 8
   as data source, 6–9
   differences between UCR and, 6
   distinction between UCR and, 7
   purpose/practical use of statistics from, 9
   Web site for, 9
Negatively skewed distribution, 68–69
Nixon, R., 19
Nominal level of measurement, 38–39
Nondirectional hypotheses, 142–143
Nonparametric statistics, 91–92
Normal curve
   binomial distribution of, 129–130
   sampling, distribution of the mean, 130–131
   standard error of the mean, 131, 139
   standard/z score on, 127–129
Null hypothesis
   decisions under, 144–145, 151
   definition of, 141

power of a statistic and, 91

testing, 31–32, 142–144, 169

Observed frequencies, 95
Odds vs. probability, 122
One-tailed hypothesis, 142
Open-ended/overlapping categories, 53
Operational definition, 30
Ordinal measurement, 39

Parametric statistics, definition of, 91
Pearson
  chi-square value, 102
  correlation coefficient (*r*), 184–185
  product-moment correlation coefficient, 185–191
Percentage change analysis, 17–18
Percentage trend analysis, 24–25
Petersilia, J., 217
Phi coefficient, 103, 113, 115
Pie charts, 56–57
Plots. *See* Charts
Polk, K., 19
Positively skewed distribution, 67–68
Post Hoc Tests, 166, 171
Power of a statistic, 91–92
PowerPoint presentations, 59–60
Pre-test/post-test outcomes, 33–34
Probability
  bounding rule of, 119
  complement of an event and, 119
  distributions, 125–126
  empirical, 121–125
  Gambler's Fallacy, 118–121
  law of, 118–119
  normal curve of, 126–129
  odds vs., 122

sampling, 34–35
theory, introduction to, 117–118
types of, 118
Program evaluation research, 36–38
Property crime rates, 4

Qualitative analysis, 30
Quantitative analysis, 19, 30
Quasi-experimental design, 34–35

Random sampling, 35
Random selection, 32–33
Range, computation of, 80–81
Ratio level of measurement, 40–41
Reaves, B. A., 7–8
Regression
  calculating coefficients by hand, 199–202
  defining, 197
  least squares technique, 198
  linear, computerized, 203–209
  predicting prison population size using, 198–199
Related (paired) samples, *t*-test for, 145–147
Reliability, 2–5
Research
  classical, 32–33
  criminological, 215–219
  data collection and analysis, 36
  fraudulent, 19
  on humans, 35–36
  interpretation/presentation of results, 36
  levels of measurement in, 38
  presenting results of, 58–60
  problem identification in, 30–31

program evaluation, 36–38
quasi-experimental, 34–35
scientific language of, 31–32
Statistical Package for Social Science, 42–45
Research hypothesis, 141
Residuals, 198
Robust parametric statistics, 92
Roncek, D. W., 15
Routine activities theory, explaining crime "hot spots" through, 15

Samples/sampling
  independent, 94–95, 147–152
  probability, 34–35
  random, 35, 95
  related (paired), 145–147
  See also t-Test
Sampling distribution of the mean, 130–131
Scatter plots/scattergrams, 179–180
Seidman, D., 19
Sex offenders, prior arrests of, 140
Shape, measure of, 67–69
Sherman, L., 15, 217
Simple linear regression, defined, 197
Skogan, W., 13
Slide presentations, 59–60
SPSS, *See* Statistical Package for Social Science program
Stamp, J., 19
Standard deviation, 81–83
Standard error of the mean, 131, 139
Standard normal distribution, 230–231
Standard score, calculation of, 127
Statistic, power of, 91–92

Statistical analysis, purpose of, 1–27

Statistical Package for Social Science program (SPSS)

  bar charts created with, 54–55

  bivariate correlation analysis using, 185–191

  chi-square calculation using, 97–102

  Cramer's *V* calculated with, 102–104

  data set analysis by, 69–75

  decision about the null hypothesis in, 144

  frequency distributions created in, 51–52

  frequency distributions graphically displayed with, 53–58

  histograms created with, 56–58

  introduction to, 42–45

  line charts created with, 59

  line graphs created with, 57–58

  linear regression using, 203–209

  measures of dispersion calculated with, 84–88

  one-way ANOVA calculation in, 165–171

  pie charts created with, 56–57

  t-test for independent samples, 147–15

  t-test for paired samples, 146

Statistical significance, 141

Statistics

  examination of percentage changes in the crime rate with, 17–18

  lying with, 11, 19–20

nonparametric/parametric, 91–92

planning and evaluating police operations with, 15–17

policy analysis and, 215–219

Subjective probability, 118

Sykes, G., 178

Symmetrical distribution, 67

t-Distribution, 139–140, 232

Tewksbury, R., 141, 145

Theft, reasons for reporting/not reporting to police, 13

Theory of general deterrence, 31

Theory, definition of, 30

Transitivity, definition of, 39

t-test

  computerized, 147–151, 153

  for independent samples, 147–153

  nonparametric vs. parametric measures and, 92

  for related (paired) samples, 145–147

Two-tailed hypothesis, 142–143

Type I errors, 144

Type II errors, 92, 144

Uniform Crime Report (UCR)

  as data source, 3–6

  factors influencing crime reporting, 6

  incidence of crime measured by, 2

  index offenses of, 3

  limitations of, 5

  measuring incidence of crime with, 4

  strengths of, 5–6

using NCVS data with, 10

Web site for, 3

Validity

  definition of, 2

  of National Crime Victimization Survey, 11–12

  of UCR data, 4–6

Variability, measures of. *See* Dispersion, measures of

Variable(s)

  contingency tables and, 92–93

  definition of, 30independent/control, 104

  inversely/negatively related, 177

  positively related, 177

  spurious relationships between, 178

  third, 104–106

  types of, 41–42

Variance

  analysis of. *See* Analysis of variance (ANOVA)

  definition of, 81

  Levine's test for equality of, 152

  percentage of, 181

  and standard deviation, calculation formulas for, 83

  within/between groups, 160

Victim(s)/victimization

  estimating risk of, 10

  predictors of, 124–125

  wishes of, impact on crime reporting, 6

  See also National Crime Victimization Survey (NCVS)

Violent crime, reasons for reporting/not reporting to police, 12–13

Vito, G., 131, 141, 145, 178

Washington, R. O., 36
Web sites
  for National Crime Vic-
    timization Survey, 10

for National Incident-
  Based Reporting Sys-
  tem, 9
for Uniform Crime
  Report, 3

Wilson, J. Q., 14

Z score formula, 127–129
Z value, 230
Zawitz, M. W., 8, 12